American Sports History Series

edited by
David B. Biesel

1. *Effa Manley and the Newark Eagles* by James Overmyer, 1993
2. *The United States and World Cup Competition: An Encyclopedic History of the United States in International Competition* by Colin Jose, 1994
3. *Slide, Kelly, Slide: The Wild Life and Times of Mike "King" Kelly, Baseball's First Superstar* by Marty Appel, 1995

Related title:

Can You Name That Team? A Guide to Professional Baseball, Football, Soccer, Hockey, and Basketball Teams and Leagues by David B. Biesel, 1991

Slide, Kelly, Slide

The Wild Life and Times of Mike "King" Kelly, Baseball's First Superstar

by
Marty Appel

American Sports History Series, No. 3

The Scarecrow Press, Inc.
Lanham, Md., & London

SCARECROW PRESS, INC.

Published in the United States of America
by Scarecrow Press, Inc.
4720 Boston Way
Lanham, Maryland 20706

4 Pleydell Gardens, Folkestone
Kent CT20 2DN, England

British Cataloguing-in-Publication Information Available

Library of Congress Cataloging-in-Publication Data

Appel, Martin.
Slide, Kelly, slide : the wild life and times of Mike "King" Kelly,
baseball's first superstar / by Marty Appel ; foreword by Lawrence
S. Ritter.
    p.   cm.— (American sports series : no. 3)
Includes bibliographical references and index.
1. King, Mike, 1857–1894. 2. Baseball players—United States—
Biography. 3. Baseball—United States—History—19th century.
I. Title. II. Series.
GV865.K52A67   1996   796.357'092—dc20   [B]   94–49546

ISBN 0–8108–2997–5 (cloth : alk. paper)

♾™ The paper used in this publication meets the minimum requirements of
American National Standard for Information Sciences—Permanence of
Paper for Printed Library Materials, ANSI Z39.48–1984.
Manufactured in the United States of America.

Dedication

Celia M. Appel
1925-1994

Table of Contents

Foreword by Lawrence S. Ritter   vii

Acknowledgments   ix

Introduction   xi

Troy   1
Washington, D.C.   9
Paterson   12
Columbus   19
Cincinnati   22
Chicago   31
Chicago II   47
Chicago III   73
The Sale   98
Boston   110
Boston II   129
Players League   146
Cincinnati II   156
Boston III   163
New York   170
Allentown and Yonkers   176
The Passing   182

The Record   197

Bibliography   201

Index   207

Foreword

Only a few scholars of the game know much about baseball in the 1800s. Many fans are aware that the first game resembling baseball as we now know it was played in Hoboken, New Jersey, in 1846, and that the first professional baseball team was the Cincinnati Red Stockings, who toured the country in 1869 and didn't lose a game all year. It is also widely known that the National League was organized in 1876, the American League in 1901, and that the first world series was played in 1903.

As far as most fans are concerned, that is just about the extent of the knowledge of "ancient history." Some have vaguely heard of Cap Anson, Dan Brouthers, Ed Delahanty, Amos Rusie, and John Montgomery Ward, although whether they were pitchers, outfielders, or Civil War generals is often unclear.

The most celebrated of the early baseball heroes was actually none of the above: he was Michael Joseph Kelly, better known as "King" Kelly, the King of Baseball, and it is a shame that his name and exploits have virtually disappeared from modern memory. With his era long past, with the image of underhand pitching and fingerless gloves making it seem as though they were playing a different game, in retrospect Michael Joseph Kelly seems more like fiction than reality.

But in fact King Kelly was real enough—the game's first full-blown superstar, an exciting and charismatic athlete whose daring and showmanship brought the game to the attention of all America, not just the core of "cranks" who sat on the wooden bleachers of Lake Front Park in Chicago and the South End Grounds in Boston. Kelly's personal magnetism managed to overwhelm an era in which personalities went unreported, an era when unsmiling portraits of baseball players effectively concealed their thoughts and feelings.

Marty Appel has done us all a favor; King Kelly has been out of circulation for far too long. Making the King's acquaintance is a pleasure because he is extraordinarily good company. His life was often tough but at the same time it was one long celebration. He drank too much and occasionally cheated on the basepaths, and once in a while failed to show up for a big game. Nevertheless, not only does he define the raw game of baseball in the 1880s and 1890s, but so too does he exemplify what it took to be a celebrity in America at that time.

With a few qualifications, I've often thought that the last quarter of the nineteenth century would have been a great time to be alive in the United States of America. Getting to know King Kelly makes me sure of it.

—Lawrence S. Ritter

Acknowledgments

A special thanks to the research facilities of the public libraries in Chicago, Boston, New York and Larchmont, New York; to the historical societies of Boston, Chicago, Passaic County, Dutchess County and Rensselaer County; the New England Sports Museum; Dave Biesel; numerous members of the Society for American Baseball Research, particularly Bill Gladstone, Ken Felden, Bill Haber, Mike Sowell, John Thorn, Mark Rucker, Dan Schlossberg, and Frank Phelps; Warner Fusselle, Allen Koeningsberg, Irving Appel, Ceil Appel, Stan Day, Tom Louden, Andrea Axelrod, Brian Appel, Debbie Appel, Barry Halper, Bill Madden, Charles Hamilton, Jimmy Bank, the research staff at *Billboard,* Jane Hamilton, Bill Guilfoile, Gayle Skluzacek, Joyce Quandt; the modern knights of the monthly roundable: Larry Ritter, Ray Robinson, Mike Gershman, Lee Lowenfish, Bob Creamer, Jonathan Segal, Rev. Darrell Berger, and David Falkner; and all of the gifted baseball scribes and journalists of the last century who contributed to the weaving of the tale.

Cover illustration: Lithograph by Frank O. Small of Mike Kelly sliding into second, which was featured in most Irish saloons of Boston after Kelly's arrival in 1887.

Introduction

Mike Kelly, perhaps better remembered as "King" Kelly or perhaps best recalled as the subject of "Slide, Kelly, Slide" (a poem? a song?), is in fact little remembered at all. Even the most astute of baseball fans, the card-carrying members of the Society for American Baseball Research, will nod knowingly, for he is, after all, in the Hall of Fame. But in truth, few know him as more than the subject of the song. (It was, indeed, a song.)

Yet in Kelly we have not only the game's first true "matinee idol" hero, but in fact, we have one of America's first true heroes who came not from fiction (as Horatio Alger did in the late 1860s), nor from political history (see George Washington or Abraham Lincoln). At a time when mass media meant word-of-mouth or small-type newspapers, it is in Kelly that we can take the measure of just what it meant to be a celebrity in post-Civil War America.

It is not an exaggeration to say that he enjoyed a celebrity comparable to Babe Ruth, relative to his era. In fact, today, one might more comfortably equate his celebrity with Michael Jordan's. Jordan, one of the very few athletic heroes of our time who might well appear on a *People* magazine cover, be the subject of a *60 Minutes* profile, sit for a Barbara Walters interview, endorse nonsports products on prime time, nonsports television, might well be the modern prototype. Had these forms of "celebrity" been around in Kelly's time, he—and not Spalding, Anson, Ward, or others among the game's early leaders—would have been the beneficiary. Note how he transcended baseball and made news in finance, literature, art, theater, music, and pop culture:

> When Kelly was sold from Chicago to Boston for $10,000, the event rocked baseball, and was more than comparable to the drama of Catfish Hunter's signing with the Yankees in 1974. (An event, which, coincidentally, took place on the 118th anniversary of Kelly's birth.)

> How many of today's athletes have been immortalized in song? "Slide, Kelly, Slide" not only accomplished that, but was, history tells us, the nation's first "pop hit record." It came not long after Edison patented his phonograph, at a time when people were looking for a vinyl cylinder containing other than classical music and patriotic tunes.

> His autobiography, published in 1888, was surely ghostwritten, but unmistakably contains his input. It was the first autobiography of a baseball player, and as one of the few sources for his inner thoughts and the "sound" of his voice, we turn to it often in weaving this tale.

> A lithograph of Kelly sliding into second replaced one of Custer's Last Stand in most Irish saloons in Boston.

> His fame permitted him to take his extroverted personality onto the stage, as a singer-dancer-actor on the vaudeville circuit, making him the first ballplayer to cross over into the theatrical world.

> And such was his endearing persona, that when young boys ran after him with pencils and scraps of paper, hopeful for some remembrance of a personal encounter, the cultural phenomenon of autographing was born.

Kelly was no scholar, but neither was he illiterate. He was no churchgoer, yet he enjoyed a warm relationship with evangelist Billy Sunday (the former baseball player and teammate). He was neither a politician nor an organizer within the confines of baseball, yet he played a key role in the development of the first player's union, and was clearly influenced by the rising voices of America's labor movement.

He was hardly an advertisement for temperance, but he knew his place as a role model and was ever appropriate with his young fans, reminding them of their manners and what society expected of them.

And when it came time to lay him to his rest at the young age of 36, the public spectacle of his funeral drew larger crowds in Boston than Reggie Lewis of the Celtics' would draw in 1993. And that, in a city whose population was a fraction of what it is today.

Kelly died before the 20th century, so that even the game's pioneer historians could barely claim a personal relationship with this devil-may-care good fellow, whose feats of derring-do on the field of play, his bantering with the fans, and his repeated championship seasons, made him a major force in the professional game's early years.

The other side of the equation of course, is whether a Kelly playing in this era would have been as beloved. Certainly, a hard-drinking athlete is less respected in this society. Would Kelly have kept his drinking hidden? Would he have sought reform in the Betty Ford Clinic as Mickey Mantle eventually did? Would he have given it a "damn the torpedoes" approach and gone on with his life?

His drinking must have contributed to an early diminutization of his talents, if not an early end to his life. Surely, under today's standards, we would not tend to look upon him lovingly. But it is important to keep in mind the era in which he lived. Roguish, buccaneer behavior was more hailed in his time; many wrote of his "manly" demeanor. Ever mindful of the press, we can probably assume that Mike Kelly in today's world would have modified his public image, if not his personal behavior, to conform to the standards expected of a celebrity. Armed with the greater understanding that we have today of alcoholism as a treatable illness, he might have even become an advertisement for moderation. He enjoyed being a hero, a role model. He might well have gone to great lengths to preserve it.

King Kelly certainly deserves his due for bringing hero worship onto the baseball diamonds. His contributions were many and his overall impact was mighty. Without doubt, it can be

argued that he won over countless young fans who would stay
with the game as the 20th century emerged and baseball matured.

What follows is the most thorough recounting to date of a life
that deserves greater renown today.

For he was in fact, "The Only Kel," America's first great
baseball star, whose celebrity today would have had him enjoying wealth and fame beyond anything he or his contemporaries
might ever have imagined.

He never took his final bow at the Palace Theater in Boston
on that fateful and blustery week in November, 1894. Had he
done so, the master of ceremonies would have simply waited for
the hush in the room, and the spotlight on the curtain to say
"Ladies and gentlemen, the greatest baseball player of our day,
the most beloved figure of our great city, please welcome the
King himself, Mr. Michael Joseph Kelly!"

Troy

The United States of December 1857 was a nation of thirty-one states, still populated by a few aged veterans of the Revolutionary War, still six years away from the Emancipation Proclamation, and still a curiosity to much of the world. It was seemingly successful with its democratic form of government, but fighting to remain one nation in the face of rising feelings for states' rights and the loud rhetoric from impatient secessionists.

Transportation, particularly in the form of a maze of interconnecting railroad tracks, was moving the nation into a new era of commercial trade. The ability to go from city to city within a day or two would be an important step towards the creation of such cultural milestones as the first professional baseball league within the next dozen years.

Until that time, the small act of striking a thrown ball with a rounded piece of wood would take shape through various rules depending on which town or hamlet one was visiting. The Massachusetts game was not necessarily the New York game, nor the New Jersey game, and there was little communication beyond county lines to share new rule modifications or successful experiments, such as the placement of a shortstop between second and third, or the concept of retiring a batter with a thrown ball at his person, rather than to a waiting fielder.

There were no players who earned cash for their play, to say the least, and the formation of a National Association, and then a National League, was distant. No one had yet heard of any great baseball players, let alone great athletes. John L. Sullivan, the great bare-knuckles boxing champion, did not achieve fame until crowned heavyweight champion in 1882. The first modern Olympic Games would not come until 1896.

Children born in the late 1850s would read no tales of great sports heroes. There were no Honus Wagners or Napoleon Lajoies to emulate. Christy Mathewson and Ty Cobb were not yet born, and a fellow named George Herman Ruth did not enter the world until 1895.

The 1850s boom in railroad travel was a setback of sorts for Troy, New York, a city on the banks of the Hudson River that had thrived since 1825 as an eastern port of the breakthrough Erie Canal. The canal, while enjoying its status as a principal route of trade prior to the railroad constructions, made Troy a major commercial center in what is known as the state's "capital district." Albany, the capital, lay eight miles southwest, and with some 50,000 inhabitants by the late '50s, it was about twice the size of Troy. Schenectady, to the west, was the third of the three cities that anchored the capital district.

As with any burgeoning industrial city in 19th century America, Troy attracted a large number of immigrant workers, anxious to find employment in the iron trades or in textile manufacturing. Troy, in fact, had its own cottage industry within the textile world, for it had been the birthplace in 1827 of the separate collar, the latest fashion statement in the country. Indeed, cuff and collar manufacturing soon became Troy's most specialized contribution to men's fashion, even though it was to be, for many years, a style symbolic of the well-to-dos, while being cut and sewn by the down-and-outs.

An ocean away, in Ireland, nearly 1 million people were dead of the horrid potato famine by the mid 1840s. A million more emigrated in desperation, but one in six bound for America died at sea. Many of the survivors, including Michael Kelly and Catherine Kylie, arrived in New York City.

They were drawn 125 miles up the Hudson River from their port of entry and settled into flats prescribed as worker housing. It was to this environment, in Troy, that the parents of Michael Joseph Kelly journeyed.

His father, Michael, and his mother, the former Miss Kylie, were both born in 1820. Their first son, James, was two when Mike was born.

We know nothing of other relatives or of the actual occupation engaged in by the elder Kelly. One report suggested that he was a paper hanger. Such are the misfortunes of attempting to piece together a working-class human life long after anyone has survived who could speak of the subject with firsthand knowledge.

We can, however, come to some reasonable inferences, based on what Mike himself told his ghostwriter when his autobiography was published in 1888.

We will infer that his parents took education seriously, and saw to it that Mike enrolled in school, both in Troy and later in Washington. This concern for education was apparently drawn from their strong feelings of British abuse in Ireland, suggested in Mike's autobiography, when he said of his parents, "They may not have had the advantages for an education themselves, British misrule prevents that, but they knew the value of education." We will later determine that while he may not have been a serious student, he thought enough of the practice to recommend it to youngsters when he was in a position to influence them. And while it became popular to call him an illiterate, it is unlikely that this was so. It is probable that he passed through at least a fourth or fifth grade education, which was not unusual for the times.

He was born on New Year's Eve—we don't know the hour of course, but it was December 31, 1857, and whether there is something astrologically presented to those born at such a time of merriment, so that they remain comfortable with a "good time" throughout their lives, one can only speculate.

The population of the 31 states was 31 million and James Buchanan, our only bachelor president, resided in the White House. Teddy Roosevelt was born ten months after Mike, if one is looking for a historical contemporary.

While early historians said that baseball was invented in 1839 in Cooperstown, New York, by Abner Doubleday, that view later passed from fact to myth. Greater credence is now given to the year 1845, in Hoboken, New Jersey, with a dashing young volunteer fireman named Alexander Cartwright credited as the man who set in print such things as 90 feet between bases, three strikes, three outs, etc. Still, Cooperstown, about 90 miles west of Troy, certainly experienced some form of bat and ball playing in the middle of the 19th century, and one can assume that the practice had drifted east during the time of which we speak. We know that in 1860 a club called the Victorys of Troy was formed as one of 62 teams in a loosely connected National Association, an amateur league which predated the first major league of the same name. The Victorys hosted the famed Excelsiors of Brooklyn in July of that year at Weir's Course, losing 13-7 in what would be the closest game of the Excelsiors northern tour. Brooklyn was led by a star pitcher, Jim Creighton, one of the game's first amateur stars.

In 1861, the Priam Club of Troy and the National Club of nearby Lansingburgh combined to form the Union Base Ball Club of Rensselaer County, but with many men departing for war duty, the plans for a schedule of games went astray. By the time baseball was revived in Troy, the Kellys had departed.

Troy's golden age of baseball began in 1871, after several years of well-regarded amateur play by a team that came to be known as the Haymakers. In 1869, the year the Cincinnati Red Stockings became the first openly professional team, the Haymakers were among those beaten by these undefeated wonders. But the score—32-30, on June 7, 1869—represented one of Cincinnati's narrowest calls. (The Reds' best pitcher, Asa Brainard, was a native of Albany. It is from his first name that we obtained the term "ace of the staff.")

In a rematch in Cincinnati on August 26, the score was actually tied 17-17 when the Haymakers president, James McKeon, pulled his team off the field following a protest over a close play, and the forfeit victory was awarded to the Red Stockings. Another close call for the Cincinnati team.

The Haymakers of Troy became a charter team in what is considered baseball's first "major league," the National Association. The Haymakers lasted just two seasons, 1871-1872 and the league lasted only three years more, ceasing operations at the end of the 1875 season. The first president of the league was a Troy native, James Kerns.

The Troy Trojans then appeared in the National League from 1879 to 1882, providing Kelly, first with Cincinnati and then with Chicago, with the opportunity to return to the city of his birth as a major league ballplayer.

The Trojans were neither very competitive nor very successful in the four years in which they faced teams from the likes of

Chicago, Providence, Syracuse, Cincinnati, Buffalo, Detroit, Boston, Cleveland and Worcester, and in 1883, they were no more, the franchise being moved to New York City. There, they played as the Gothams for two seasons before becoming the Giants in 1885.

It is unlikely that Kelly experienced much of a hero's welcome when he did pull into Union Station with his teammates during those three years of Trojan baseball. We assume there were no old friends or relatives to greet him, and as far as the fans were concerned, he had little identity with the city, if indeed there were enough fans to care.

In fact, when a historian of Rensselaer County named Rutherford Haynor wrote a history of the region in 1925, he made glowing mention of Johnny Evers, the native son who formed the middle of the Cubs' Tinker to Evers to Chance double play combination, but offered not a word on Kelly, who also went on to star in Chicago and was immortalized in rhyme with "Slide, Kelly, Slide." Of course Evers grew up in Troy, went from its sandlots to the big leagues, and as an adult called it home, while Kelly was only around for his early childhood. Whether he had any memories of those early years that made his homecoming nostalgic and sentimental, we cannot know.

A monument in Knickerbacker Park in Troy, dedicated in 1992, celebrates Kelly, Evers, and five men who played for Troy when it was in the big leagues—Dan Brouthers, Tim Keefe, Roger Connor, Buck Ewing and Mickey Welch, all Hall of Fame members. It also salutes the 32 Major League players born in Troy, the last being a journeyman infielder who debuted with the California Angels in 1971, Rudy Meoli.

As for Mike Kelly's childhood in Troy, it is unlikely he was touched by baseball at all. To be sure, however, there were some momentous events during his brief time there.

There was the meteor that came crashing in at 7:20 on the morning of August 11, 1859, perhaps awakening the 20-month-old child from his sleep. (With great irony, a Chicago newspaper, in writing his obituary years later, included a subhead that said "He Lived Like A Meteor.")

Perhaps Kelly's mother took her boys to Union Station on February 19, 1862, to see a hatless President Lincoln bowing acknowledgment to admirers from the platform at the rear of his train.

Three months later, on May 22, 1862, a devastating fire swept through the city, destroying 507 buildings, numerous barns and sheds, and uncounted personal property as people carted their belongings into small wagons and sought to flee the burning area. It began with sparks from a locomotive igniting a covered wooden bridge north of Federal Street, and a northwest wind helped to rapidly set the bridge aflame. Five adults and several children were killed, and the damage was estimated at more then $2.5 million. Among the buildings destroyed were the Second Presbyterian Church on Sixth and Grand, the North Baptist Church on Fifth and Fulton, the mansion of Jacob D. Vanderheyden, patron of Troy, and a building on State and Sixth belonging to Rensselaer Polytechnic Institute. The Kellys lived on Fifth, and the fire may well have claimed their home.

It had the impact on Troy that General Sherman's igniting of Atlanta had two years later, or that the great Chicago fire would have nine years later. There was an enormous economic impact on the city and its citizens. Wrote A. J. Weise in *History of the City of Troy* (1876), "The spectacle presented by the burning ruins at night was one of exceeding grandeur...the most feared ordeal that Troy ever passed through."

Although only four and a half years old, Kelly had to have kept the memory of the blaze with him for as long as he lived. And certainly, the fire must have contributed to some decisions the family would face in short order.

Whether of patriotic duty, not uncommon for an immigrant, or of economic necessity with his profession halted by the fires, Kelly's father enlisted in Union Army soon after the flames died off, ready to serve his country with a three-year enlistment during the Civil War. On August 13, 1862, about eleven weeks after the great fire, Troy proudly sent its 125th Regiment of the New York State Volunteers off to action.

Being a patriot and recognizing that there was live ammunition being used seemed to present two differing realities. In 1862, by way of example, Troy recorded 910 enlisted men among its contribution to the war effort. Thirty-nine died, while ninety deserted. Kelly's father was among those who stayed, fought, and survived. It would qualify him as a hero.

It is possible that the senior Kelly played some baseball while serving in the Union Army. Baseball's popularity spread quickly among soldiers. On Christmas Day in 1862, a game was played in Hilton Head, South Carolina, between the 165th New York Volunteers and a team made up of other Union regiments. Reports of the game had as many as 40,000 soldiers witnessing the action.

While their mother raised the Kelly boys and sent Mike off to school when he was five, news from the front was both grim and encouraging. There was no way to know immediately whether a battle had claimed the life of a loved one. But if there was no letter from the War Department, it seemed to mean that all was well. Only with the end of the war did a final letter from "the front" send confirmation home that the senior Kelly had in fact been a survivor. And not long after came the awful news of the assassination of Abraham Lincoln, that heroic figure of victory who had preserved the union, and who had once touched the people of Troy by waving to them from the back of the a Troy Union railroad car in Union Station.

The news was therefore even more personal in Troy, where Mayor Uri Gilbert led a mourning period that exceeded the prescribed thirty days. Homes were covered "roof to foundation" with wide strips of black and white cloth, and crowds thronged to the local bulletin boards for more news about the dastardly deed.

Imagine the day that townspeople read that John Wilkes Booth, the assassin himself, had been shot to death while on the run by a Seargent "Boston" Corbett, a native of Troy. What a cheer must have rung out! This early day Jack Ruby, while acting under the law and on the call of duty, had seen, to most people's thinking, that justice was done. There seemed to be little disappointment among the populace for the failure to have a criminal trial to judge Booth's actions and to learn of the conspiracy.

With the war over and hundreds of men returning home and with Troy still recovering from its inferno, it seemed that job opportunities would be limited in the capital district. The city had rebuilt much of its losses within a year, but Kelly and other vets faced an employer's market. And so having apparently enjoyed his time in the army, Kelly reenlisted, and was stationed in Washington, D.C., under the newly completed capital dome, with the administration of Andrew Johnson coming into power and the nation beginning a painful healing process.

It was time for Kelly to send for his family and relocate them from the banks of the Hudson to the banks of the Potomac. And it was time to play ball.

Washington, D. C.

In Washington, the Kellys were an intact family unit again, with school again a priority, this time with the influence of a heroic father figure to serve as role model.

A parade down Pennsylvania Avenue, featuring generals George McClellan and Judson Kilpatrick, captivated young Mike. "So much gold and gold lace I never saw before," he told his ghostwriter. "For years I remembered them, and it was the ambition of my life to go and do likewise."

Mike's budding athleticism seems to have taken hold around his ninth birthday, when he claimed he could outrun any boy in his school. At ten, he was introduced to baseball.

Baseball in 1868 was still a strictly amateur sport, played by differing rules from region to region. There were some men who received money "under the table" to help their teams, but by and large, the game was an informal, gentleman's recreation, a year away from the introduction of the first openly professional team, the Cincinnati Red Stockings. By today's standards it could be compared to pickup games of touch football, whereby the ground rules were easily adjustable depending on whose neighborhood one was visiting and what trees might be in the way.

The National Base Ball Club of Washington was an amateur club made up of government employees, which toured six states in 1867 and played nine well-talked-about games.

The baseball that Mike was introduced to in Washington was actually known as "burn ball." The slight rule variance in this game was that a runner, if hit by a thrown ball, was out. "Many a time have I been hit in the small of the back, and for a moment imagined that my back was broken," Mike recalled.

The rule was not unique to Washington. We know of its

occurrence in the northeast as well, and boys being boys, it seems to have been a natural act on a rough and tumble sandlot where gentility at times would give way to physical instinct if adult supervision was absent.

That "burn ball" had come to Washington was evidence that the Civil War had indeed carried the infant game with it as soldiers from different parts of the country met in new territories. The act of retiring a runner with a thrown ball was a part of the Massachusetts game, whose formal origins dated back to May 13, 1858, when Mike was just five months old. A group of ten clubs had met that day in Dedham, Massachusetts, to set a standard of 19 rules for this version of the game, which had been an outgrowth of town ball. (Rule eight had read, "If a player, while running the bases, be hit with the ball thrown by one of the opposite side, before he has touched the home goal while off a base, he shall be considered out." Burn ball.)

Seven weeks later, Williams College and Amherst played under those rules in Pittsfield, Massachusetts, in the first intercollegiate game.

Town ball itself had grown in the 1820s and 1830s, as an outgrowth of the British game of rounders. That Kelly found himself in Washington playing under rules which seemingly developed in New England was indicative of the spread of the game during the war.

Kelly found himself on a team organized enough to have a name—the Keystones—where he experimented with most positions.

Mike was particularly taken by a young teammate named Dave Walling, the best player on the team. Walling was a fine base runner, an able batsman, and an adept fielder no matter where he played. (Could this have been an ancestor of New Jersey's Dennis Walling, the Houston Astros all-purpose player of the 1980s?)

Kelly felt that Walling would have become a star had he stayed with the game, but instead, he teamed with a fellow named Reynolds, and as Reynolds and Walling, became a successful act on the variety stage. Whether Kelly's long-standing admiration for Walling was as a player or an actor is debatable, for Mike greatly admired the theatrical profession and was, in fact, obsessed with it throughout his life. As he matured into a very self-confident adult and was given the opportunity to stand on the stage through his fame as a ballplayer, there is no doubt he was enchanted by the feeling and would have been equally happy in that career.

The parallels between baseball and the theater were great in the 19th century. Neither profession was considered especially "respectable." They would be mentioned in the same breath when it came time for the finer hotels to discriminate against undesireables. No one from society's high levels would think of staying at a place that accepted actors or ballplayers.

With actors, Kelly always found kindred souls. Some of his greatest friendships would come from his entries into their world.

Paterson

The Kellys' stay in Washington did not last too many years. "Ill health," say his memoirs, "compelled my father to leave the army, and we moved to Paterson, New Jersey....My father's health didn't continue to improve any, and we had not been in Paterson very long before he passed over to the great silent majority. My mother followed him not long after. God bless them both, I shall forever cherish and bless their memory." (We do not know, of course, what Kelly's voice sounded like, but quotes attributed to him frequently suggest that he spoke with a bit of an Irish brogue, despite being American born. If so, it was obviously an inherited trait.)

The poor Kellys, who had only just passed 50, had survived the immigrant journey to America, the long absence of the father from the family during the war, and the movements from Troy to Washington to Paterson, the latter during a time of failing health. They would never know that from the meager, working class immigrant lives they were carving out for their boys, would emerge one of the nation's first great sports heroes. Or that they would have a son whose bronze plaque would hang in something called the Baseball Hall of Fame in Cooperstown, New York.

We do not know what caused their early deaths. Periodic outbreaks of epidemic often took lives prematurely in the 19th century. In 1866, a cholera epidemic wiped out 50,000 lives. But we now find Mike and his brother orphaned in a relatively strange city and left to their own wits. It appears Mike's schooling, by necessity, ended around this time. By his own admission, he was not a very good student, a fact he did not mind confessing with a likeable honesty from time to time.

Mike's days of baseball in Paterson began at age ten, when

he would play on "Forty-Acres Field" on Madison Avenue, a hotbed of local baseball until the Cooke Locomotive Works was built over it in 1888. The area, largely undeveloped, would house the daydreams of many Paterson youths getting their first experience at a game that would captivate the nation. Years later, Paterson would field a pro team in the Atlantic League; it would be the last stop for Honus Wagner before he entered the National League.

An ingenious device on Forty-Acres Field got the boys skilled at shagging fly balls. Six large boulders were located on one end of the field. On each was a long slat of hickory wood with two smaller strips nailed to one end. The ball was placed between the strips, and then a boy would bring a bat down hard onto the extended end, sending high fly balls to the waiting fielders.

What remained of Mike's childhood was a mixture of hard work and the continuing discovery of his baseball abilities. The mixture forced a responsibility and a maturity upon him before it was his time, but kept him young at heart throughout his years. As he would later write, "God bless the boys of America. I love them all. Why? Simply because I was a boy myself once. I'm a little older now, perhaps, and I might be looked upon as an old boy, but I'll remain a boy as long as I live. My boyhood days were a hard struggle for existence, but they were, nevertheless, the happiest and best days of my life."

These happy days often began very early in the morning for young Mike, who lived in the Sandy Hill district of the city. Paterson was the home of some of the nation's major silk mills. It was, in fact, "Silk City," the "Lyons [France] of the New World." Immigrant workers from Europe's textile centers had established themselves in Paterson in the early 19th Century, and by the time of the Civil War, hand looms were turning out cotton products. In 1857, the U.S. boosted the fledgling silk industry of Paterson by eliminating tariffs on imported silk from Italy and the Orient.

The nearness of the port of New York, the easy transport on the Erie Railroad, and the industrial entrepreneurism of men like Robert Hamil, George Murray, and James Booth, helped to speed the development of the industry in Paterson. The Hamil Mill on Market and Mill Streets, bordered by the Passaic Silk Works, and the nearby Phoenix Silk Manufacturing Co. on Van

Houten Street, provided thousands of jobs for skilled and semi-skilled laborers. It can be deduced that the move from Washington to Paterson by the Kellys was due in part to the opportunities for work in the familiarity of textile mills, in which the elder Kelly may have been trained prior to leaving Troy.

Mike got a job at the Murray Silk Mill on Mill Street earning three dollars a week hauling baskets of coal from the basement to the top floor. His boss was John Ryle, considered the father of Paterson's silk industry. Mike's developing strength and large physique allowed to him load the baskets with more coal than most of his coworkers, many of them adults, and he would often finish early. This would allow an early clandestine departure and time for sports or theatrics. At least once however, Mr. Ryle caught Mike jumping from a second story window to slip away for a ball game. It nearly cost him his job.

Mike was not one to slip away quietly anyway. Already a budding fashion plate, he could be spotted departing the mill on any given day sporting a handsome walking stick, strutting down Market Street as though he was the very owner of the mill.

One of Mike's good friends in Paterson was a boy named Jim McCormick, a couple of years older than Mike, and an immigrant from Glasgow, Scotland. Jim and Mike shared a common hero, a ballplayer named Joe Start who played first base for the Mutuals of the National Association.

Start, 5'9" and 165 pounds, had achieved a measure of fame with the Brooklyn Atlantics, a prominent amateur team during the 1860s, which had been undefeated in 1864 and 1865 and won what amounted to a "championship of the American continent" with a victory at the Rochester State Fair over a Canadian team in 1864. The Atlantics were one of the first teams composed of working-class players, many of them Irish. To this point, most teams had been populated by middle to upper class gentlemen meeting for a leisurely pastime. A match between the Atlantic and the Excelsior teams in 1860 was legend for a riot among the fans which caused a victory by forfeit for the Atlantics when the Excelsior captain removed his team from the field. While the Atlantics had worked with the police to try and restore order that day, they nevertheless developed a reputation for a less-than-gentlemanly brand of ball.

Start had a heroic sounding name and was known as "Old

Reliable" by his faithful. He is believed to have been the original first baseman to position himself to the right of the base, although some credit this to Charles Comiskey.

The Mutuals, the closest professional team to Paterson, played at the Union Base Ball and Cricket Grounds on Marcy Avenue and Rutledge Streets in Brooklyn. It was baseball's first enclosed park. Since travel did not seem to intimidate Mike, it is likely he and Jim might have journeyed there by rail, ferry and horsedrawn streetcar to watch their hero in action. Parks being intimate, perhaps they even met ol' Joe Start in person. There was a grandstand built expressly for the ladies which was capable of seating several hundred persons and, including those on foot and those who watched from carriages, as many as 8,000 fans could witness the more important holiday games. Could Kelly and McCormick have imagined that they might one day play professional baseball against Start?

Perhaps this is where the idea of playing ball for a living was first imagined. Kelly admited to talking about his future plans over whittling sticks with his friend Jim, and it is likely the glamour of Start's handsome uniform put stars in his eyes. But to this point, being paid for playing ball could only be a dream.

Still in contention for the boys' interest was acting and this idea took hold in McCormick's basement. "Mac's" father had a large cellar in his home, and the boys decided to make a theatre out of it. It was large enough to accommodate a crowd of 45.

The boys decided to stage a play called "Jack Sheppard," with Mac in the lead role. Kelly had lobbied unsuccessfully for a play called "Dick Turpin," and then lost the starring role to his friend when they settled on Sheppard. But, as Kelly acknowledged, "his father owned the theatre."

The boys were a hit, with a turn-away crowd, paying a penny each for admission. Unfortunately, the play seems to have lasted only one performance. In the final scene, Jack Sheppard was to be hanged. As the curtain closed, the block upon which Mac stood with a rope around his neck was kicked away, leading the audience to believe that the hanging was indeed taking place. In fact, it was. Mac turned blue in the face and only the rapid arrival of his father to cut him down saved his life.

"[Mac] was willing that I should play Jack after that," wrote Kelly. "But I wasn't. I didn't care to take any chances. That ended

our season of theatrical management. It also killed Mac's ambition to become an actor and partly killed mine. I still have hopes,
however."

McCormick also worked at the mill, holding the far more
important position of turning a crank that kept the mill's power
going. When he took a water break, the entire mill stopped until
he returned. That job lasted two days. Too many water breaks.

Perhaps the job that best demonstrated Kelly's youthful responsibility was one which required that he awaken at four each
morning and journey by rail to lower Manhattan to acquire a
stock of the morning's newspapers. He would then return to
Paterson by six and sell them to early arriving customers at the
rail station. No doubt he would glance at the sporting news in
the New York *Clipper* en route home, it being the best paper for
sports then published in New York.

"It wasn't very pleasant work, I assure you," said Kelly. "But
I had to do work of some sort, and I preferred that. It gave me a
chance to play ball in the afternoon."

Mike and his Sandy Hill pals first called themselves the
Haymakers, and they tried to imitate the exploits of two Paterson boys who had already become semipros, Jim Foran and
George Hueble. It was in 1873, when he was 15, that Mike found
himself on his first amateur baseball club sufficiently organized
so that it would face teams from other towns in higher levels of
competition. McCormick, 17, had already been recruited by the
team's captain, William "Blondie" Purcell, a Paterson native
who would go on to spend 12 seasons in the major leagues,
including holding down the captaincy of the Baltimore Orioles
in 1887-88. Another teammate was Edward Sylvester Nolan,
known as "The Only Nolan," a fourth Paterson native who would
go on to see major league service. Nolan, only a month older than
Kelly, was the team's best pitcher, and his departure for the
Buckeyes of Columbus in 1876 opened the door for McCormick
to show his off his newly perfected curve pitching.

McCormick went on to a 10-year career in the big leagues,
winning 265 games for six clubs, and serving a tour as a
teammate of Kelly's in Chicago for two seasons. He was 45-28 in
1880 and 36-30 in 1882, both for Cleveland. It was indeed a
fortunate thing he didn't hang himself in his father's basement

performing Jack Sheppard. Kelly and Mac remained lifelong friends.

The boys also played on the Olympic Grounds near Broadway and East 18th Street, an enclosed field alongside the Susquehanna Railroad tracks. The team was considered one of the best in the area, and also featured another Kelly, John "Kick" Kelly, as well as Billy St. Lawrence, Dummy Davies, and Dave Treado. Mike Kelly, McCormick, and Purcell were the three Sandy Hill contributions to the team.

It was on this team that Mike began to develop his crowd-pleasing flamboyance, complete with somersaults following outfield catches. He loved to play to an audience.

Kelly claimed to have persuaded his teammates to adopt the name "Keystones" as the team nickname, no doubt borrowing it from his first club in Washington. As their field was Olympic, they would at various times also be called the "Olympics."

Equipment was scare and often homemade, and the team owned but a single baseball cap among them. Mitts did not come into general use until 1875. Kelly, who by 1874 was established as something of a star on the club, insisted on wearing the cap lest he not play in match games. As with the selection of the team nickname, he got his way and wore the cap. "The day I wore it was one of the happiest of my life," he said. "I felt I was a bigger man than old Grant," that being Ulysses S. Grant, who was by now the nation's president.

With Nolan's departure in 1876, McCormick became the pitcher and Kelly the catcher, the position he would be most identified with throughout his career.

These were days in which catchers wore little protection, standing a safe distance behind the batter, but still forming a target, taking foul tips off all body parts, and running the game from behind the plate. The leadership role suited Mike.

In 1876, the Keystones defeated all opponents from New Jersey and several from other parts of the country. Occasionally there would be some money paid at the end of the day; anywhere from $1-$5 per player, based on how much the fans might have thrown into a hat, or at times, based on small wagers among the players. This would have been Kelly's first experience at playing the game for remuneration, however small.

If there was a "big game" in 1876, it would be the game

against the Stars of Covington, Kentucky, who traveled north expecting victory, but found McCormick too much. "We slaughtered them," noted Kelly. The Stars included Frank "Silver" Flint, 21, who would go on to share catching duties with Kelly in Chicago for many years. Dave Foutz, who would spend 13 years in the majors with St. Louis and Brooklyn, was with Covington as well.

The Keystones also recorded an impressive victory over the Buckeyes of Columbus, Ohio, where Nolan was now playing. McCormick bested Nolan in a thrilling contest, both being early and successful practitioners of curve pitching. But more important for Kelly was the impression he made on the visitors, considered to be an invincible club.

Paterson finally played a series with the Mutuals of Brooklyn, Joe Start's team, for the championship of the New York region. For McCormick and Kelly, it must have been quite a moment to share a field with their old hero, but the Mutuals won the series.

There was a strong camaraderie among the players, who would share beer and ale after a game, some of the players being as old as 20 or 21. Jim McCormick would develop a reputation as a big drinker in his own right and was likely an early "bad" influence on Mike. Drinking following games seemed to be *de rigueur*. An old photograph in the Paterson Museum shows a group of young men in a "team" picture, bats and catcher's gear visible, with many holding or pouring drinks, not just "German Tea" (beer), but whiskey as well. "Baseball and drinking seem to be the pastime on this outing sponsored by the Helveta Silk Mill," says the caption. One can assume that Mike was introduced to the pleasures of the hops at this stage in his life, a pleasure he would come to enjoy throughout his life. Few players would ever be able to recall the exploits of Mike Kelly without mentioning his love of alcoholic beverages.

Columbus

The road from the sandlots to the big leagues was not one of long hardship in the 1870s. If one had a measure of ability, a will to leave home, and a bit of good fortune, the opportunity was there. There was hardly a well-tiered minor league system in place. Any success in the early stages of pro baseball could easily lead to what passed for the big time.

Still, the haves could quickly be separated from the have-nots, and those who did succeed and emerged as the nation's first corps of big league ballplayers were generally more skilled than those who failed. Enough time had passed during the development of the amateur game for a wizened manager to discriminate between talent and the lack of it.

The National League had been born in 1876 while Kelly was sharpening his skills on the fast sandlots of Paterson. Then the weather turned cold and it was time to put baseball to rest until spring.

Nearly 19, and too old to be a paperboy, Kelly faced the inevitable fate of an honest living. He took a job at one of Paterson's silk mills to learn the weaver's trade. He wasn't quite ready to put aside his dreams of the stage, or the ball diamond, or perhaps the lure of the railroad, but practicality was dictating his moves. He had to eat.

With the coming of spring in 1877, he faced the decision of either continuing his apprenticeship in the mill or returning to baseball. His more responsible friends urged him to remain in the factory.

But "I was a crank on the game, and couldn't leave it alone if I wanted to," he said. "So I went at it again."

He began the year with amateur ball for a team in Port Jervis,

New York, a city at that point on the map where New York, New Jersey and Pennsylvania converge, about 45 miles northwest of Paterson. It was not a happy stay, or a very long one. It wasn't Mike's kind of town.

Jimmy McCormick had managed to get a job with the Buckeyes of Columbus, the team the Keystones had beaten the year before. He replaced Paterson's "Only" Nolan, as he had the year before with the Keystones. (Nolan had moved on to the champion Indianapolis Hoosiers, where his stay was marked by his expulsion for leaving the club to attend a funeral, which, it turned out, was fictitious.) McCormick was probably helpful in getting Kelly considered for an opening with the Buckeyes.

The Columbus experience marked the first time Mike received a salary for his play (although it was meager, and, he noted, they were sometimes lucky to get it). It was also his first test in pitting his skills against stronger competition and he met it well. "It was," he noted, "the first time that I really thought that I could play ball."

He got a single in his first game and was thrown out trying to steal second, earning big laughs from his teammates, and causing him to both question his confidence and learn to laugh at his own misfortune.

Profesional baseball in 1877 was played by six National League clubs, 13 League Alliance clubs, 16 International Association clubs, 13 clubs partly or wholly professional but belonging to no organization, and not less than 2,500 college, school, city, town, village and soldiers clubs. The National League included Boston, Louisville, Hartford, St. Louis, Chicago, and Cincinnati. The Buckeyes, members of the International Association, played about 90 games, but for league purposes, were grouped with teams from Lynn (Massachusetts), Pittsburgh (called Allegheny), Guelf, Ontario (called Maple Leaf), Manchester (New Hampshire), Rochester (New York), and Tecumseh, of London, Ontario. In the games deemed "league matches," Tecumseh was first with a 14-4 record and the Buckeyes last at 4-8.

Mike was listed 302nd among all pro batters, including National Leaguers, with a .156 average in 23 games in which statistics were recorded and submitted. The team was unsuccessful at the box office and disbanded on September 15. Minor league ball did not return to Columbus for another six years.

A number of the Buckeyes' games were played against National League competition, giving Kelly, McCormick, and their mates an opportunity to showcase their talents. These were not merely exhibitions; the so-called "minor" teams managed to defeat the NL clubs 72 times during the summer of '77, putting to question whether the talent was as properly distributed as it might have been.

As reputations apparently counted for more than sketchy statistics, Kelly found himself the recipient of a contract offer from no less than J. Wayne Neff, the president of the Cincinnati Red Stockings.

One day Neff had been sitting at a Columbus-Louisville game with John Chapman, who ran the latter club. Chapman later recalled that it was the first time he had seen Kelly play.

"He caught for the Bucks without hat, mask, chest protector or mouth rubber, and did great work," wrote Chapman. "The next day we played the Cincinnati club, at Cincinnati, and Mr. Neff...asked me what I thought of the new man Kelly, of Columbus. My reply was 'one of the best and most plucky catchers I have ever seen.' "

The glowing and accurate scouting report led to a major league contract. Signed as an outfielder and a catcher, Kelly now found himself as one of only ten reserved players on the Red Stockings winter roster of 1877-78, the reserve clause being the special genius of Arthur Soden, owner of the Boston National League team, and a man who would later figure prominently in Kelly's life. At 19, standing nearly 5' 10" and weighing about 157 pounds, just a year off the Paterson sandlots and a few months off whatever they played on in Port Jervis, he was a big league ballplayer.

Cincinnati

Despite Cincinnati's lofty beginnings in baseball as the first openly pro team back in 1869 and as a charter member of the National League in 1876, they were not a rousing success in the new league. Gone were the Wright brothers, George and Harry, who had brought such distinction to the city. In their place were a ragtag bunch of pretenders who seemed deeply out of place in this fast new league.

In the charter year of the league, they were an embarrassing 9-56, 42-1/2 games out of first in a 65-game season. In 1877, they were hardly much better: 15-42, dead last, 25-1/2 games out. The once proud Red Stockings were reduced to being laughingstocks. Even their outfielder, Bob Addy, was a source of amusement when he tried something new in 1877—he slid into a base. Had he gotten just a little more respect for this innovative action, there might one day have been a tune called "Slide, Addy, Slide."

The Red Stockings played their games at the Avenue Grounds, behind the stockyards on Hopple Street, just west of the Baltimore and Ohio railroad tracks. Because the grounds were also next to three pork packers, the team was sometimes humorously referred to as the Porkopolitans. It was the home of the first Ladies Day and, if you had an extra dime, you could get a nice lemon peel and water beverage from the concessionaire.

Cal McVey, one of the original 1869 Red Stockings, was the new Cincinnati manager, joined by only three holdovers from 1877—Bob Mitchell, Lipman Pike, and Charlie Jones. McVey, son of a piano maker, had earned $800 in the undefeated 1869 season playing for the Wrights. Pike, one of the game's first Jewish players, was a 33-year-old veteran of the National Association who had batted as high as .351 for Troy in 1871 and .346

for Hartford in 1874. His '77 season at Cincinnati would be cut short when he demanded his release in midseason, following a dispute with McVey over whether he was actually ill and unable to play. McVey complied. But now Pike was back.

Instead of the Wright brothers, Cincinnati now had the White brothers, Jim and Will, who made up the battery, with Kelly assigned to right field. The Whites were quality players. Jim, a 30-year-old teetotaler better known as Deacon, had led the National League with a .377 average for Boston the year before. He would go on to record a .303 lifetime average over 15 seasons. Will, seven years younger, the first major leaguer to wear glasses, would win 73 games over Kelly's first two years in Cincinnati, before he achieved even greater success with the Cincinnati franchise of the American Association in the '80s. In 1879, Will would work a remarkable 680 innings in 75 starts, never once being relieved. He did, however, have the advantage of pitching in an era when deliveries were made underhanded, the way nature intended an arm to swing. In addition, the pitching plate was only 45 feet from home plate and didn't go back to 50 until 1881. (The modern distance was still 14 years away.)

Kelly was billed as a "mid-west semipro" for the club, which debuted on May 4 with a home victory over Milwaukee in Mike's first major league game. When the Red Stockings won their first five, a large crowd of 3,000 turned out on May 11 to see their attempt at six. They failed.

By June 8, Cincinnati found themselves in first place with a 12-5 record, three games ahead of Indianapolis, which was led by Paterson's "Only" Nolan and by Silver Flint, late of Covington.

Boston, in third place, hosted Cincinnati on June 21 and 6,000 turned out at the South End Grounds on Walpole Street, all seats being filled including a "grandstand full of ladies." The Bostonians, whose stars included John Morrill, Jim O'Rourke, George Wright, Ezra Sutton, and Tommy Bond, took the game 4-2, and then shut out the Red Stockings 5-0 the next day. These would mark Kelly's first games in Boston, although his Columbus team had played in nearby Lynn the year before.

After the final game of the series, Boston, Cincinnati, and

Indianapolis all boarded the "Tunnel Line" train and headed west together to resume the season.

Cincinnati promptly dropped four in a row to Indianapolis and fell to second place, 2-1/2 games behind Boston. The race was on.

As the season neared its end, it came down to Boston and Cincinnati for the pennant. In reports of a number of big games down the stretch, Boston generally prevailed. By August 26, they had built a 7-game lead over Cincinnati. Kelly's name did not appear very often in the game highlights. He was not a rookie taking the league by storm.

By Saturday, September 7, Boston's lead was sufficient, if not mathematically so, to be recognized as the inevitable champions. Before 3,000 fans in Cincinnati for the final meeting between the two clubs, the Boston players formed a line near the outfield gate and marched, militarylike, behind a band, to the front of the grandstand. They were met by Kelly and his teammates, all raising their caps and shouting "hip, hip, hooray" three times to honor them as champions, even without the reality of a clinching. In fact, Cincinnati won 6-1 that day for their sixth straight victory.

But then Boston took three in a row from Indianapolis while the Red Stockings lost two of three to Chicago, and wrapped it up.

The final standings showed Boston 41-19 and Cincinnati 37-23, four games out. Kelly had been through his first pennant race. He played in 60 games, batted .283, scored 29 runs and delivered 67 hits, eight for extra bases.

As yet, he was hardly an impact player, nor had he secured his place in the majors by any means. He had, however, achieved a moment of glory by winning a contest sponsored by the Cincinnati *Enquirer,* which awarded him a silver bat for hitting the first home run at the Avenue Grounds. In later years, the celebrated bat trophy would be on display in a Paterson store window. (Despite this widely reported tale, official records do not credit Kelly with any home runs in his rookie season.)

Of all his rookie statistics, probably the most laudable was that he struck out only seven times in 237 at bats. He had established himself as a good contact hitter.

Mike was well-liked and seemingly a good-time fellow off the field and a "kicker" on the field; one who would raise his voice to cheer on his teammates or rile his opponents. A kicker later came to be called a bench jockey or a pepperpot, a sparkplug or a holler guy. For a former newsboy from the mill towns of Troy and Paterson, it did not seem all that unnatural.

In 1879, the decision was made to increase to nine the number of balls required to issue a walk. This rule change, which would last but a year (it went to eight in 1880), kept the batters at the plate longer and put more balls into play. One man the Red Stockings hoped would do just that for them was newly acquired second baseman Ross Barnes.

Barnes had won the league's first batting title in 1876 with a .429 average for Chicago, after twice topping .400 in the National Association.

Unfortunately, his specialty was the little bunt with a lot of topspin. He had a knack for dropping the bunts into fair territory and having them squiggle away from the fielders as they changed direction and rolled foul. The rules of the time said this was a fair ball and Barnes got a lot of hits.

The change in the foul bunt rule, combined with a long illness, saw Barnes' average drop from .429 to .272 in 1877, followed by a season in the minors. Thus the Ross Barnes who joined Cincinnati in '79 was not the same man who had averaged more than two hits a game in '76. Further, the local press described Barnes as possessed of a "big head." This may have also been due to his lawsuit against Chicago for withholding his salary during his 1877 illness. In an age before a disabled list and guaranteed pay, it was considered an indecent request.

The foul bunt rule also presented a dilemma for the catcher, and although Mike was not yet settled into that position, he would occasionally experience days of trial by fire because of the conditions caused by this rule change. Basically, by freeing the catcher from being on constant alert for these pesky bunts, he now had to decide for each batter whether to position himself nearly under the batter, as today, or further back, in greater safety. The tendency was to move forward only with men on base, the better to be able to hold runners close.

With the disappointing performance from Barnes (a .266 batting average), the Red Stockings never really got going in 1879. Providence, led by the pitching of young John Montgomery

Ward (47 wins), beat out Boston by five games, followed by Buffalo, Chicago, and then in fifth, Cincinnati, 43-37 and 14 games out. Eight of Ward's victories came against the Red Stockings.

Kelly almost didn't make it through the season. In fact, had fate played against him, it could have all ended for him in '79 and he would have been back in the silk mills of Paterson by summer.

In late May, the team began its first eastern swing of the season. The swing began with a trip to Troy, probably Mike's first return to that town since his family left nearly 15 years earlier. He stayed with his teammates at the Troy House hotel and probably had no reason to visit his old neighborhood.

The visit to Troy was marked by the sudden resignation of Deacon White as manager, discouraged over his team's bad play and feuding with influential sportswriter O. P. Caylor of the Cincinnati *Enquirer.* White, it seems, had brought in his brother-in-law from Corning, New York, to serve as the team's official scorer, costing Caylor the spot. (Caylor, a prominent early sports journalist, would later manage Cincinnati of the American Association, 1885-86.) Cal McVey succeeded the Deacon, returning to the leadership role he had held the year before, but the trip was a disaster. After leaving Troy, the team lost two of three in Syracuse, three straight in Providence and two straight in Boston. Kelly was not much of contributor, having gone 0 for his last 22, reaching base but once on an error. Certainly, he did not make a believer out of Caylor, the sportswriter who seemed determined to punish the Reds.

"[Kelly] had a disagreeable habit of stepping on himself, tripping up on his feet, getting his legs crossed and falling down at the most trying times," he wrote. "His only fault was a seemingly lasting weakness to fall down without any terrestrial cause, and often while actually waiting to catch a ball, his feet seemed to get into a panic and throw him."

There were, indeed, some early tales involving running blunders. He was said to have once bet a slowpoke teammate $100 (a huge wager) that he could give him a head start and win a 100-yard dash against him. In the end, Kelly tripped and lost the race. Said the victor, "I knew Kel couldn't run that far without falling down at least once, so I figured it was easy money."

McVey told close associates that he was going to bring in a new player, one Jack Leary from the Manchester team, to try and right things. It was McVey's plan to drop either Kelly or Buttercup Dickerson, an outfielder from Maryland who was a year older than Kelly. At the time, Dickerson was ill and out of the lineup.

Leary was to arrive for the final game in Boston and McVey had until game time to make his roster cut. Kelly was well aware that his job was in jeopardy.

As luck would have it, Leary was late arriving for the game, Dickerson was still too sick to play, and Kelly was penciled into the lineup.

Before a good-size crowd of Boston fans, Kelly went to bat five times, belting two doubles, a triple and, according to accepted statistics, his first major league home run. Knowing that he was playing for his very career, he rose to the occasion and delivered. It was the first time that he made such a glowing impression on the fans of Boston, and he was no doubt the talk of the Boston cranks for days.

The next game was back home in Cincinnati against the White Stockings and Kelly was again a hero, driving in all his team's runs in a Cincinnati victory.

"What might have been the result if Jack Leary appeared on the grounds in Boston?" he later mused. "I would have been laid off, and returned to Paterson in disgrace. Perhaps I never would have had nerve enough to play in a league club again."

The reprieve helped turn Kel into one of the team's stars. He took up residence in the spacious Gibson House on Fourth and Walnut and felt secure and at home in Cincinnati, at least for the balance of the season.

Secure? One day, while catching McVey, a fastball bruised Kel's hand and he promptly refused to handle catching duties any longer, particularly with McVey tossing "cannon balls."

McVey handled this crisis by bringing in Will White from the carriage gate, where he had been collecting tickets, and putting him in to pitch. As Kelly sulked off the field, holding his bruised hand, McVey put himself behind the plate. The 700 fans in attendance that day at the Avenue Grounds saw Troy beat Cincinnati 20-6. Kelly was none the worse for his deed.

On June 14, the Chicago *Tribune* reported that Will White had sprained his leg while practicing gymnastics in the hotel corridor prior to the game. But the Boston *Daily Advertiser,* possibly more investigative, reported that "Mike Kelly playfully tripped Will White while they were walking together a few hours before the game."

On September 11, the Syracuse club went bankrupt and disbanded. Some said they would have succeeded had they charged just 25 cents a ticket instead of 50 cents, as mandated for all clubs by the League. In any case, their players were dispatched around the league and Cincinnati wound up with Blondie Purcell, Kelly's old Paterson buddy. League officials decided the best way to handle a disbanded club was to throw out a selected number of games so as to even out the number of games each team played against Syracuse. This odd maneuver cost both Boston and Cincinnati five victories, more than anyone else. It was the kind of ruling that made much of the early records of the National League meaningless.

Kelly had righted himself just fine for the balance of the season. His .348 average was third in the league. He was fourth in runs scored, third in hits, third in triples, and ranked high in a lot of statistical categories that weren't compiled until years later, such as on-base percentage, slugging percentage, and so on. (Stolen bases were not recorded until 1886.) In addition to catching, Kelly played both the outfield and third base and handled himself well. The 1880 Spalding Guide noted that "The O'Rourke brothers, James and John, who are included in the list of Boston's players under engagement for 1880, are good examples of the free and effective use of the bat; as is also M. J. Kelly, of the Cincinnati Club of 1879."

It would be a long time before Mike Kelly might fear that his career was in danger of collapse.

With his success, he took on a charming cockiness to compliment his genial personality, feeling the growing acceptance among his peers that was transforming him into a crowd favorite. He was already getting a reputation as a big, if lovable imbiber. There was the story of his doffing his clothing and swimming across the Ohio River on a dare. Such tales made him

Tales of the King

One of the earliest baserunning tales of Kelly occurred in 1879 when Cincinnati was playing Chicago. It was a play that had to make Cap Anson take note.

Kelly smacked a double to left. The ball was fielded and thrown to second baseman Joe Quest. Kelly, having rounded the base, was, in the eyes of the Chicagos, tagged out before returning to the base by the quick-thinking Quest. The umpire called him safe.

This led to a great argument near the bag, with all the defensive players of Chicago joining in. Did someone call "time"?

Apparently not. Kelly dashed off to third and on to home as the argument ensued. One can only imagine the argument that followed—but score one for Kelly, one for the Red Stockings, and one for Anson's nose for talent.

a well-known character around the league. Despite the preachings of the league's founders that "anything in the way of intemperance which might interfere in the slightest degree with [a player] being able...to give to the public his best services," should be frowned upon, players admired a good-time fellow who could take a drink and enjoy life. A life of drink was encouraged and applauded; the more tales that came from it, so much the better. Reputations were made upon the stories told around the bars in the National League hotels.

The stories themselves, the first "legends of Mike Kelly," may have been exaggerated. Like the passing of folklore from town to town, just a little embellishment in each telling could have turned it into more than it was. Over the years, we will discover many tales of derring-do, mostly on the ball field, attributed to Mike. While there was certainly a pattern of adventure to his life and to his career, one most always bear in mind that without television playing video highlights on nightly recaps of the day's games, we have come to rely on storytellers, who may have heard the legends sixth or seventh hand. Always, one must assume that the truth was somewhere in the middle of "probably happened" and "probably didn't."

The disappointing season led to the resignation of Neff, the club's president, who claimed the team had lost $10,000, a third of it his. He was replaced by Justus Thorner. Efforts to win over the support of the press came with the inclusion of sportswriter Caylor, who along with Thorner, were the official representatives of Cincinnati at the annual league meeting in Buffalo that December. The Red Stockings were clearly in disarray. In fact, their refusal to cease renting their ballpark for Sunday games and their insistence on selling beer in the stands would lead an exasperated National League hierarchy to finally expel the once-proud franchise from the league following the 1880 season. But by then, Kelly was gone, probably delighted to be free of the poorly managed chaos that had become the Red Stockings.

Of greatest significance for Kelly was that Neff, on September 24, 1879, released all of his players, simply notifying them that their services would no longer be required after October 1. Although the season was the first in which the reserve clause was part of a signed agreement, Kelly and all of his teammates were free to look elsewhere for 1880. No one was minding the store when it came time to reserve players.

Chicago

It was not uncommon for teams to release players with a few days remaining on the schedule, if only to save a few dollars in salary where they could. It was generally understood that gentlemen do not sign other gentlemen's players during this lapse, as the beginnings of the reserve clause were taking hold.

But for Cincinnati to release everyone was another story. With the stockholders feuding and the scanty front office operation in disarray, no one seemed to consider the Red Stocking players sacred to their franchise. Surely, if this was to be the case, the good citizens of the National League who ran the Chicago White Stockings would not have interfered.

For in William Hulbert, Albert Goodwill Spalding, and Adrian "Cap" Anson, Chicago had three of the solid founders of the league, whose very names had already come to mean integrity and honor. In fact, they meant baseball. That Chicago had the good fortune of boasting of all three made them the league's most formidable and stable franchise. And without New York or Philadelphia entries in the National League, Chicago was also the biggest city in the majors.

Following the 1879 season, a group of disenfranchised Red Stockings combined with some Buffalo players and headed west to play ball against California semipro teams and against the proud Chicago White Stockings themselves. Kelly, ever with the sense of adventure a big trip might bring, was joined by his Paterson buddy Blondie Purcell and by Buffalo's Jim "Pud" Galvin, the "Little Steam Engine" of a pitcher who won 361 games in his career.

The assemblage reached San Francisco by rail on October 5

to begin a 12-week barnstorming tour which, according to Kelly, left them each with "a pocketful of money."

They were permitted to play Sunday baseball, fascinated the West Coast crowds with their level of skill, and played some exciting matches. Kelly, by now a very talkative presence on the field, delighted the fans with his bantering, with his "kicking" with the umpire, and with his overall, good-natured demeanor. These were now Kelly trademarks, and did not go unnoticed by Anson, the captain of the Chicago nine. A strict disciplinarian, Anson nevertheless had become captivated by Kelly's abilities, Mike having played so well during the '79 season.

One day in December, as the teams were nearing the end of this exciting tour, Anson approached Kelly and asked him if he might be interested in joining the Chicago club.

It was quite a moment for Mike. Anson had an unnerving presence about him, even during the lark of an exhibition tour. "I was a bit afraid of him when I first met him," Kelly later said.

But Chicago?

> As a matter of fact, it was the dream and ambition of my life to become a member of the Chicago club. I knew it meant lots of hard work, but I also knew that if I was a member of the club, and could play ball at all, Anson would be the one to give me a chance. He was always willing to push a young fellow ahead. He didn't know what professional jealousy meant.

Despite Kelly's delight at the suggestion, he was coy. Not yet 22, he knew a thing or two about bargaining.

A wily negotiation spread over a couple of weeks ensued. Anson wired Hulbert about the possibility and his boss replied, "Get Kelly by all means." (Interestingly, Hulbert is constantly spelled Hurlburt in Kelly's autobiography. Babe Ruth wasn't very good with names either.)

Still, a $100 difference in salary kept Anson and Kelly from an agreement. Each day they spoke and the difference didn't evaporate. Kelly remained firm, even without a secure contract for the 1880 season. It was a gutsy maneuver by Mike, and surely Anson felt he would cave in.

After two weeks, Anson went to Kelly's room in San Francisco, and said, "Well, Kel, are you going to sign?"

"No sir," said Mike, "not unless you give me the money I want. I am not at all particular to become a member of the Chicago nine, and unless I get the money I want, I would just as soon go somewhere else."

Anson left.

The next day, he returned again with the same question. And again, Kelly said yes, "providing you pay me what I think is fair."

"Well my boy," he quoted Anson as saying, "you can have it. Put your name on the contract."

And Michael Joseph Kelly was a Chicago White Stocking.

The barnstorming tour ended on December 19 and the players headed east by rail. They were forced to stay over at the Ogden Hotel in Council Bluffs, Iowa, on Christmas Eve—ten men in flannel shirts who hadn't shaved in days and all wore beards. The owner of the hotel, nevertheless thrilled to have the "great Cincinnati Red Stockings with us," invited them all to a big dance in the dining room, where they partied until dawn.

In the morning, they boarded the train for Cincinnati, and then Mike changed trains, celebrating his 22nd birthday on New Year's Eve en route back to Paterson.

He rested for a few weeks, and then received a wire to report to Anson in Chicago on April 1. The hard work was soon to begin.

Kelly met Anson on a Sunday and an introduction was arranged with the club president, "Hurlburt."

"I stood in wholesome awe of him," Kelly said.

A more thorough gentleman than he never lived. He was very kind to me at our first meeting, and told me just what the club expected. Our interview lasted but a few minutes, yet the impression remains with me still. He was a man in every sense of the word. During the few years that I knew him I was with him very often. He was a big-hearted, honest, straightforward man. He did more to build the national game than any one man in this country. He was a man of many resources, of great executive ability, and just as kindly and soft-hearted as a child. He was a noble man.

Hulbert, 48, was truly a major figure in the birth of the National League, yet he is barely recalled today. When the Hall of Fame properly installed Ban Johnson, the founder and first president of the American League, they also elected Morgan Buckeley, who was the first NL president. It must have seemed right and proper, but they erred badly. Buckeley, a distinguished politician, was no more than a figurehead president who served one year, if that, before turning over the reins to Hulbert. In fact, minutes of a National League meeting on December 10, 1880, included a salute to Hulbert that began, "Whereas Mr. W.A. Hulbert of Chicago, Ill., has been President of the League since its organization...." It is unlikely that everyone in the room completely forgot about Buckeley in just four years, yet Hulbert was so acknowledged. (He finally made the Hall of Fame in 1995).

Hulbert owned the White Stockings at their founding and gave them immediate credibility by luring Anson from Philadelphia and Spalding from Boston, both National Association teams. He ran a tight ship as league president, insisting on schedule fulfillment, the banishment of alcohol from ballparks, and the elimination of gambling on games. He was a pillar of honor whose dignity helped establish the National League and the White Stockings, as more than a pastime for gamblers and drunkards.

Born in New York State, he had moved with his family to Chicago when he was two. He was educated at Beloit College. At 18, he became a businessman and later a member of the Chicago Board of Trade. Persuaded to become an officer of the Chicago Base Ball Club in 1875, he attended the meeting that year in Philadelphia at which time he first saw the need for a league based on honesty and high purpose. He felt the game could not succeed on a professional level with the presence of gambling and the abuses of alcohol within the ballpark. If he was preachy on these subjects, he nevertheless had the respect of the likes of Kelly and that was perhaps his greatest attribute. He could sell the game to the ladies and gentlemen of America while still employing and earning the loyalty of those a bit more roguish than he might have the public believe.

Spalding, 29, had led Boston to four consecutive National Association championships before going to Chicago in 1876. By the time Kelly joined the team, his days as a star pitcher were past, and he retired in 1878 to open a sporting goods business, A.G. Spalding & Brothers. He made certain that his White Stockings were the best-tailored team in the game, and he became the official supplier of baseballs to the National League. A publishing end of his business produced instructionals and guides on all American sports.

Adrian Constantine "Cap" Anson, a nickname for Captain, was 29 when Kelly joined the club, seven years Mike's senior. He was the star first baseman of the team and its captain at a time when that position was perhaps more important than that of manager. He was the first player to record 3,000 hits and most considered him the best player of his long era. What he lacked in flamboyance he made up for in efficiency. His captaincy was augmented by the managing assignment of the White Stockings, which began in 1879. He would, in 1888, became a part owner of the team. One of the most popular players to ever call Chicago home, he was a towering figure of 19th century baseball.

On the other hand, Anson is fairly well exposed today as a racist and probably the man most responsible for baseball's color line. His sheer influence and stature in the game allowed him to impose his values on the rest of the sport and to refuse to participate in games as long as blacks were on the field. His own autobiography, published in 1900, made numerous references to "coons" and "chocolate-colored mascots." The best-known racial incident involving Anson took place in 1887 (after Kelly had left the team), when he refused to play a game against Newark of the International League because they fielded two blacks— Moses Fleetwood Walker and George Stovey.

As strong as Anson's position was on this, we can cite no evidence that it made Kelly into any sort of racist. There is simply nothing in print to indicate that Kelly had any particular view on the subject at all. If anything, we will see that Anson's strong, disciplinarian style was so in opposition to Kelly's pattern of behavior, that the two saw eye to eye on very little. It would be nice to believe that Kelly found little in Anson's views on race. By all accounts, he seemed to get on well with everyone.

Chicago's Irish resided in the fifth, seventh, and eighth wards on the southwest side of town near the stockyards and the lumberyards when Kelly arrived. His preference however, was for lodging at the majestic Palmer House, which had opened five years earlier.

Chicago had rapidly rebuilt following the devastating fire of 1871 that had swept through the city, and was the fastest growing major urban center in America as the 1880s beckoned. New York had a population of 1.2 million in 1880, with Philadelphia second at 847,000. As neither had a major league franchise at the time, that left Chicago, at 503,000, as the largest big league town in the land. Over the decade, Chicago would surpass Philadelphia, nearly double its population, and become "the second city," a position it would hold until Los Angeles finally moved beyond it some 80 years later. City historians will tell you that the fire, rather than setting Chicago back, launched it into a fantastic era of growth, partly through the attention it brought.

Twenty-two railroad lines converged on the city, with bustling Union Depot a central terminus. A fellow could go pretty much anywhere, transcontinental service having been made possible in 1869. The elevated railway, the "Loop," was under construction and would begin running in January of 1882.

There were 31,171 tenements and rented houses in Chicago, and 85 percent of them were considered defective in sanitary conditions. The city put many of its men to work in the grain, lumber, livestock, and meat-packing industries, as such giants as Swift and Armour flourished. Electric lights came to Chicago at the time Kelly did; telephones would be introduced the following year.

An Irish-American Club was formed in 1880 at 90 Washington Street; a good place to stop by and have a cold one from the Bemis & McAvoy brewery. The vice district was populated by intriguing places with names such as Little Cheyenne, the Badlands, Satan's Mile, Dead Man's Alley, the Black Hole, and Hell's Half Acre, all, as one might guess, places of gambling, whores and whiskey. You just might find a ballplayer there every now and then. There were over 5,000 saloons in town. Money could be bet on the ball games at any of the city's 30 legal gambling houses along Clark, Dearborn, Randolph and State Streets.

You could traverse the town on one of 80 horse-drawn buses, or dine at the Boston Oyster House, Henrici's, or Johnson's

Home Bakery. Marshall Field & Co., was being built at State and Washington, and the city proudly produced seven daily newspapers, including the *Tribune,* the *Times*, the *Herald,* the *Evening Journal,* the *Daily News* and the *Inter-Ocean.* The White Stockings office was at 108 Michigan Avenue. Spalding's sporting goods business was at 118 Randolph Street. Hulbert lived in grand style at 1334 Fortieth Street.

To witness wealth, one could admire the home of George Pullman, the railroad magnate, whose "castle" stood at 1729 Prairie Avenue, and whose office tower, at the corner of Michigan and Adams, was the most modern elevator building downtown.

The White Stockings played at the original Lake Front Park, which opened in 1878. Lake Front Park was built to become an attraction all its own, not just a place where you could see big league baseball. It had a capacity of 10,000, enormous for its time. Chicago had captured the first National League pennant in 1876 while playing at the 23rd Street Grounds. The "new" facility, near the foot of Randolph Street, covered land along Michigan Avenue to the area between Madison and Washington Streets. One of the beauties of the location was that it was just minutes from the retail center of Chicago, State Street, and could attract a crowd of pedestrians after their errands. The park would serve as home to Kelly for his first three seasons, before the success of the club forced a $10,000 renovation. With Spalding providing the handsomest uniforms in the league, the park seemed appropriate for its tenants. The renovation would include a "luxury" box above the third base grandstand, from which Spalding could place telephone calls, or summon an employee with a Chinese gong.

The outfield fences were only around 200 feet down the lines, a short poke, but one which would actually be shortened during the renovation. Still, the team was hardly a home run hitting club, as batters resisted the short porches to play the style of the day, smacking hard liners between fielders to advance runners one base at a time. The 1880 White Stockings hit only four home runs all season.

After Kelly's meeting with Hulbert, it was time to get down to the business of training for the new season, which to Anson was a business to be taken with great seriousness. Kelly weighed about 170 at the time, some 20 pounds more than when he first broke in two years earlier.

"Kelly," said Anson, "I want you to lose 20 pounds by the opening day."

Kelly could feel his jaw drop. He thought training meant some light workouts in a nearby gymnasium in between three hearty and protein filled-meals at the Palmer House.

Anson, however, had a training regimen that included a light breakfast, morning calisthenics, and a mile walk. That would be followed by a 15-mile "dog trot," Anson leading the way. Lunch at the hotel was followed by an hour's rest and then a return to the ballpark. Uniforms on, the team would then play intersquad games with local amateurs filling in at the needed positions. The games would be hard fought and the "old man," Anson, 29, would tear into anyone who didn't play to win.

In addition to Anson and Kelly, Chicago reserved nine other players for the 1880 season: Silver Flint, Ned Williamson, Fred Goldsmith, Abner Dalrymple, George Gore, Larry Corcoron, Tom Burns, Joe Quest, and Tom Beals. The basis for a dynasty was taking shape.

Kelly, Williamson, Dalrymple, Gore, and Burns were all born in 1857, so if not yet 23, they were nearly so; boys becoming men through the life of a traveling professional ballplayer. The man-ish part was the responsibility of showing up for games, whether hung over or not, and playing at a sufficient level so as to avoid being released. The boyish part was in finding ways around Anson's rules and regulations, thus insuring that the occupation would not be without its rowdy, childlike moments.

Kelly, Goldsmith, Corcoron, Burns, and Beals were all new to the 1880 club, while Flint, Williamson, Dalrymple, Gore, and Quest had arrived in '79. Only Anson had been there more than a season as the team gathered to begin the '80 campaign. It was a young team and a team assembled from scratch in a little more than a year. It would be a challenging managing assignment for Cap.

Flint, the Philadelphian, was 25. He was called "Silver" because of his light-colored hair. He would spend twelve seasons in the big leagues, almost all of it with Chicago, compiling a .239 average. He was the team's primary catcher through 1883, catching without gloves or a mitt and playing with broken fingers if necessary. Kelly would be Flint's backup, or "change" catcher until he took over more of the role himself in '83. Kelly had played against Flint as far back as 1876 when Paterson had faced off against the Covington Stars. Now they were teammates. Flint, it was written, could "catch a better game with a few swigs under his belt."

Williamson, nine weeks older than Kelly and also from Philadelphia, was the team's fine fielding third baseman. He hit .255 lifetime and is a statistical curiosity today with a sudden outburst of 27 home runs in 1884, the first year of Lake Front Park's renovation. He had eight in his six previous seasons. The 27 would be the all-time record in the game for one season until Babe Ruth came along and hit 29 in 1919. (For a time, it was thought Williamson had 26, and that Sam Thompson's 27 broke that mark.) Williamson was a favorite of Anson's, Cap citing him as "the greatest all-around ballplayer the country ever saw." He was "223 pounds of solid bone and muscle who could skip around...as lightly as a ballet dancer." He was a cardplayer and a gambler who enjoyed Chicago's nightlife and he later ran a Chicago saloon. He fit in.

Goldsmith, 27, from New Haven, played for Troy in his rookie season of '79. He had just a six-year career as a right-hand pitcher, but four of those were 20-victory seasons in which he completed all but nine of his 153 starts. He was one of the earliest practioners of curve pitching. Known as "Goldy" by his teammates, he was a 6'1", 200-pounder with a reputation for being somewhat on the lazy side. While he was certainly no hitter, one fine day against Buffalo he took no less than Pud Galvin's best offerings over the Lake Front Park fence—twice. Great laughter and kidding, including some from Galvin himself, coaxed Goldy to circle the bases, which he viewed as a tremendous exhaustion of energy. It was a riotous day at the ball yard.

Dalrymple, 14 weeks older than Kelly, was an outfielder and leadoff hitter from Warren, Illinois, (about 125 miles from Chicago), who had joined the White Stockings in 1879 after a year with Milwaukee. He was a .288 lifetime hitter who hit 22 of his 43 homers in that power-packed season of '84. He confessed to employing a "hidden ball" trick to rob an opponent of a home run, an extra ball tucked away in his uniform shirt.

Gore, eight months older than Kelly, was known as "Piano Legs." He was a swift outfielder and leadoff man from Maine who had broken in in 1879 with Chicago and who hit .301 over 14 seasons, later playing for the New York Giants. Hulbert and Anson had signed him after playing an exhibition series against him in New England, rather a replica of the Kelly signing, but on the other coast. A man who liked his ale and could work a town's nightlife as well as anyone, Gore is in the record books with seven steals in one game and five extra base hits in another. His nickname reflected his bulging calf muscles. He became one of Kelly's earliest and best friends in Chicago.

Corcoron, only 20 and from Brooklyn, was an ambidextrous hurler, which in the days of underhand pitching and form fitting gloves was not so difficult to imagine. He did not engage in this skill often; Tony Mullane would be better known for this art. Although listed at only 120 pounds, he was the team's big winner and most dependable starting pitcher, breaking in with a 43-victory season in 1880. He would only last eight years, but won 177 games in that time. He is considered to be the first pitcher to work out of a set position with men on base.

Burns, another rookie on the 1880 club, was a shortstop from Honesdale, Pennsylvania, who had played for Albany in '79. He would play 13 seasons and bat .264, all but his final campaign spent with the White Stockings. A heady player, who perfected the "blocking game" in the infield, he would later succeed Anson and manage the team (1898-99). He didn't drink or smoke, and he became the only regular on the team who didn't desert Anson when the Players League came along in 1890. He was not "one of the boys."

Quest was the second baseman, a 28-year old from New Castle, Pennsylvania, who didn't hit much (.217 lifetime), but he patched together nine checkered seasons in the National League and American Association. He later was hired as an accountant for the City of Chicago, but was implicated in an embezzlement scandal and left town in disgrace. Quest is credited with inventing the term "charley horse," after a "sure thing" horse named Charley at a local track went lame. When Gore fell running from first to second the next day, Quest, coaching at third, was said to have yelled, "There's your old Charley horse—

he'd have made it all right if it hadn't been for that old Charley horse."

The regular lineup would be Dalrymple lf, Gore cf, Williamson 3b, Anson 1b, Kelly rf, Corcoron p, Flint c, Burns ss, and Quest 2b.

Where, of all places, would the White Stockings open their 1880 season, but in Cincinnati on May 1. Welcome home, Mike!

The park was new; Avenue Grounds had been replaced by Bank Street Grounds, and most of the Red Stockings were new, with only the Whites and Blondie Purcell back from '79. Visiting clubs stayed at the Gibson House, and, as was becoming the fashion of the times, a parade accompanied the Chicago's horse-drawn bus from hotel to ballpark in an attempt to stir last-minute interest in the opening day festivities.

Chicago won, 4-3, over a lackluster team that would finish last with only 21 victories in 80 games. This was the first game in history played to a "sudden death" conclusion; prior to 1880, an inning had to be completed, even after the winning run scored.

And how did the winning run score?

A home run for Kelly! What a debut! It would be his only home run of the season on a team that hit but four, and he could not have selected a more auspicious moment.

The home opener was on May 7, again with Cincinnati, after Chicago had won two of three on the road. A nice crowd of 3,000 turned out to see Kelly make his home debut, as Gore delivered six hits and the White Stockings won 20-7. The crowd the next day was only 1,200, but Chicago won again, 15-1.

Chicago's first visit to Boston, on May 29, was a sampling of how avid the Beantown fans could be. Five thousand of them turned out, and they were happily surprised to see their old hero, George Wright, suddenly playing shortstop for the home team. Wright had managed Providence the year before to a 59-25 record, but was suddenly discharged and, at 33, found himself back in the city of his greatest stardom. He had one hit in four at bats that day, which turned out to be his only appearance of the season. Boston won the game 11-10, but by June 21, Chicago had a 24-3 record, losing only that early game to Cincinnati, the one to Boston, and one to Providence on May 13.

Both Goldsmith and Corcoron were pitching beautifully, the

latter running up a 13-game winning streak. On June 4, he hurled a complete game, 16-inning, 1-1 tie against John Ward of Providence. When the two squared off again on August 10, Corcoron hurled a one-hitter, and nine days later he pitched a no-hitter against Boston.

The defense was solid and Anson's training methods were bearing fruit. The men performed fundamentals better than any club in the league and showed daring and ingenuity on the basepaths. Kelly was recognized as the team's best base stealer and a fine practitioner of the hit and run. Some say he and Anson were the first to perfect the play, although most baseball historians credit the Baltimore Orioles of the 1890s with being the first true practioners of the art.

A good example of the precious economics of the game was demonstrated on July 1, when a rainstorm kept the Chicago crowd to 700. Still, that was $350 worth of receipts and when umpire Al Pratt halted the game in the first inning and refunds had to be made, Hulbert objected vigorously. Despite Hulbert's objections, the game was called.

Nine thousand turned out on July 4 for a holiday game against Providence, won by Chicago 3-2 in 11 innings to run the team's record to 33-3. The overflow crowd in right and left field forced a "ground rule single" into effect for the day covering anything rolling into the fans. It was reported that about 1,000 fans brought pistols and fired blanks to celebrate the holiday.

On August 19, Corcoron pitched his no-hitter, the first ever hurled in Chicago, as he beat Boston 6-0. (He would pitch two more in his career.) Some 2,000 fans saw the historic game, played with what was described as a "mushy and shapeless" ball. Flint's right thumb was dislocated in the final inning and Kelly would have to handle the catching for the next several days. But then Mike went down with an injury himself and Ned Williamson took over, catching without a mask.

On August 30, Chicago had a 51-11 record and a 13-game lead over Providence. The pennant was all but won, Anson looked like a genius, and the White Stockings were being toasted with raised steins of beer in every saloon along Rush Street. Each of the players was fast becoming a hero of the city. Never mind that so many were new; it was as though they were true "Chicagoans."

Chicago clinched the 1880 pennant on September 15 in Cincinnati, with the *Enquirer* praising "the executive ability of Anson, who commanded the respect and good will of the players and was a genius at field managing. Much admired was the shifting around of the Chicago players in the field when various batters were up, something that Cincinnati did not do once all season."

The White Stockings celebrated their triumph that evening, and still managed to come back the next day and whip the Reds 17-9, late night or not. But in the game, Flint reinjured his thumb and Kelly would catch the balance of the season.

The final standings had Chicago with a 67-17 record, 15 games over Providence, with Cleveland third, 20 games back. Their .798 winning percentage remains the best in major league history, and their 21-game winning streak is still a Chicago record (tied in 1935).

Gore won the league's batting title at .365, with Anson second at .338. Dalrymple, at .332 was fourth, Burns, .309 fifth, and Kelly, .292, eleventh.

Kelly played in 84 games and had 100 hits, 27 of them for extra bases, with one home run. He was third in the league in runs scored, and he even pitched three innings of emergency relief one afternoon, yielding no earned runs. (He would pitch 12 games in his career with a 2-2 record.)

The Chicago *Tribune* made an attempt to record runs batted in, a statistic which interested few, but which shows Anson and Kelly as numbers one and two in the league. As they were the fourth and fifth hitters in the lineup, fans were not surprised or impressed and seemed to simply make note that the stat had a direct bearing to the position in the batting order.

Chicago's success and the accolades placed on Anson served to sway public belief towards the benefits of hard work, rigorous training, and a clean life, all of which were espoused by Anson, if not practiced by his men.

If the 1879 season had given Kelly that certain swagger that went with self-achievement, the '80 season added to his great self-image and self-confidence. Now a three-year veteran, a man of individual success, and a member of the finest team in the land, Kelly could not have felt better. He was not quite yet "The Only Kel," or "King Kelly," but you would not have known this back in Paterson, where his friends hailed him as a conquering hero.

The fathers of Jim McCormick and Blondie Purcell, who took pride in their own sons' accomplishments, looked to Mike's championship season as though it was one of their own.

On the field, Kelly was establishing a singular reputation for daring baserunning. The little successes on the base paths, encouraged by Anson, gave way to an occasional tip of the hat to the fans, and in his right field position, Kel loved bantering with the crowds. One who attends minor league games today, particularly the Rookie League or Class A ball, can better understand the interaction between players and fans. When attendance is only a couple of thousand and the parks are small, players can be heard and the intimacy is contagious. A smart player would win the fans over to his side and discourage jockeying. Kelly was obviously a very good player, but he was clearly going to enjoy a long career with intelligence as much as with natural ability.

He claimed, for instance, to be the first catcher to use finger signs to the pitcher, although Flint was using body signals and body positioning for the same purpose. He was only the backup catcher at first, and it is not possible to determine what year he claimed to have done this. We certainly would not recognize the catcher at work in the 1880s; not until 1909 did Jimmy Archer of the Cubs become the first to crouch down under the batter.

Kelly would have worn an unpadded catcher's glove—a padded version did not come along until 1890. The catcher's mask, disdained by Williamson, goes back to 1875. Chest protectors were introduced in 1885, a couple of years after Kelly's work behind the plate increased. Shin guards were not invented until 1908. It would be nearly 70 more years before catchers wore helmets, and then throat protectors.

As for Kelly on the bases, he would have worn leather shoes with heel and toe plates, but would not have worn his first pair of spikes until around 1888.

The Chicago uniforms, as noted, were the finest in the league, particularly since Spalding manufactured them.

"We always wore the best uniforms that money could get," Kelly wrote.

Tales of the King

"There was no trick in baseball that Kel didn't know," wrote Maclean Kennedy, an early baseball historian, whose clipping file went back to 1884 and who spoke with many of Kelly's contemporaries when he started covering the game in 1905. "Yet there was never a better or more brilliant player. Colorful beyond description, he was the light and life of the game. Equal to all demands at the bat, on the base lines, behind the bat, or playing the outfield.

"King Kelly always pulled off tricks. It wasn't necessary for him to do these stunts, for he possessed excellence to such an extent that he didn't have to resort to trick play, but he liked that part of the game.

"[He] was one of the quickest thinkers that ever took a signal. He originated more trick plays than all players put together. There were rules and amendments passed by the powers to frustrate many of the tricks Kelly had in his repertoire that he constantly introduced into the game.

"As a drawing card, he was the greatest of his time. Fandom around the circuit always welcomed the Chicago team, with the great Anson and his lieutenant, King Kelly."

Spalding saw to that. He had big wide trousers, tight fitting jerseys, with the arms cut out clear to the shoulder, and every man had on a different cap. We wore silk stockings.

The White Stockings wore handsome white uniforms with a bold CHICAGO across their chests and that exuded tremendous, puff-out-your-chest pride among the players. (The following year, Spalding put them in, of all things, lavender uniforms with white trim.) Every player had a mustache, with Kelly's being perhaps the bushiest of them all.

Off the field, with a little money in his pocket, Kelly was becoming a fashion plate. He was known to dress in pointed, patent leather, high-button shoes and to wear a high silk hat, jauntily cocked off to one side.

The success of the White Stockings did not necessarily make its players "household names" throughout the land, but their reputation was growing. True celebrity was difficult to come by in an age where newspapers, letters, and word of mouth were the only means of communication.

America did have its heroes in the early 1880s. Everyone placed George Washington and other founding fathers in a special category, and fiction provided the great adventures of Horatio Alger, a street urchin turned entrepreneur. Alger novels took hold late in the 1860s. Aside from the names of Civil War heroes (dependent on which side you were on), most of the nation knew Buffalo Bill, Lillie Langtree, Jesse James, Wyatt Earp, Billy the Kid, Wild Bill Hickok, Annie Oakley, Sarah Bernhardt, John D. Rockefeller, Joseph Pulitzer, Thomas Edison, Andrew Carnegie, John Philip Sousa, General George Custer, Sitting Bull, Mark Twain, Alexander Graham Bell, and P. T. Barnum. The most celebrated sports figure was heavyweight boxing champion John L. Sullivan. The exploits of baseball players were soon to grow as the game's popularity increased. And the White Stockings, playing in the nation's third biggest city, were helping. In 1883, when the National League finally landed in New York City, major league baseball was exposed to millions of new fans in the biggest city, and the celebrity status of the Chicagos was further enriched.

Chicago II

Although Anson was dismayed, if not angered by the drinking habits of a number of his players, particularly Kelly, Gore, and Flint, the 1881 team remained basically intact. If the truth be told, Anson could, on occasion, take a drink himself. He had a one-time arrest record in his past to prove it. But older than his teammates and a "well respected man about Chicago," he felt compelled to lead by example.

Kelly had no problem at all in flaunting his marauding nocturnal habits. It was considered manly. As his fame grew, he was able to wean himself off beer and onto straight whiskey, which seemed ever available from some admirer at a local tavern. A shot of the hard stuff was pretty cheap anyway, even if Kel had to pay for it himself.

Hulbert led the enactment of a written rule that prohibited the sale of alcohol in ballparks in 1881, an effort to bring continued civility to the games and to attract female customers.

Also new for 1881 was the relocation of the pitching plate from 45 to 50 feet, and the determination that it would now require only seven balls to earn a walk. In addition, a pitcher could be fined for deliberately hitting a batter. This rule was difficult to enforce, and because all pitching was still underhand, with the batter able to request high or low deliveries, it was dropped after a year.

Wintery weather kept the crowd under 1,000 for Chicago's home opener on April 30, an 8-5 victory over Cleveland. Following a loss the next day, the two teams met again on May 3 in a game highlighted by Mike McGeary trying to trip Kelly between third and home. It was a primitive trick (something Kelly himself might try) that promptly drew a $10 fine from the umpire, to the fans' delight.

Later, when Williamson hit a foul ball into the stands behind right field, outfielder George Schaffer stood with his arms folded and refused to retrieve it. The fans booed him as Anson and Kelly left the bench to hunt the ball down so that the game could resume.

On May 18, diminutive Tommy Burns shocked his teammates by hitting a drive towards the Chicago clubhouse in deep left field. Hilarity followed when the ball approached the sleeping dog owned by Hulbert. Buttercup Dickerson, Kel's old Cincinnati teammate and now Worcester left fielder, was afraid of the large black dog and refused to run down the ball. Burns circled the bases to the roar of the crowd.

Two days later, when Boston came to town, second baseman Jack Burdock demanded that the dog be removed from the clubhouse platform and that the doors be closed, lest a ball roll into them. Hulbert laughingly agreed.

Kelly's baserunning was the story that day, not the dog. One newspaper described it as such:

> It was strongly suspected that Kelly, in his eagerness to reach the plate from second base, somehow forgot to go by way of third, slighting the bag entirely by 15 feet, thereby saving much valuable time and distance. The umpire [Alfred Barker], of necessity, was fixing his attention on first base where Burdock and Deasley were disposing of Anson and hence could not possibly know whether Kelly touched third or not.

Chicago won the game, 5-4. This was no "legend" story. This was witnessed by the journalist and duly reported. What did become legend was the belief that this was now a common procedure for Mike, taking full advantage of the use of one umpire on the field. Whether he pulled this stunt as often as people would come to recall is a matter of debate. But most recountings of Kelly's career made references to his "ignoring bases."

On June 6, Chicago had a 14-8 record, just a game ahead of

Buffalo and two-and-a-half ahead of Worcester and Cleveland. This was not 1880 all over again.

The next day, Detroit's Lou Knight attempted the "Kelly racket" of skipping third base, but the umpire, Herman Doscher, wouldn't have it. Knight was ruled out.

Returning home on June 24, Chicago debuted their new lavender flannel uniforms, which one reporter said was "no improvement over the time-honored white." But the team played well with the new garb and began to build a lead in the standings.

On July 4, they drew over 10,000 to a game against Boston, with the overflow crowd again forcing a one-base ground rule for balls hit into the outfield fans. The fans dealt with the blazing heat, but bad fielding by the White Stockings brought about a disappointing 11-10 loss. The 18 players consumed four gallons of ice water. If there was any distraction caused by the shooting of President Garfield in Washington two days earlier, it was unnoted, and seemed not to detract from the holiday mood of the crowd. (When Garfield died on September 19, no games were postponed.)

On July 11, Chicago was 29-11, 5-1/2 games ahead of Buffalo, but then the White Stockings dropped three straight at the home park of their second-place rivals, where Pud Galvin was enjoying a 29-victory season.

The losing streak ran to five in Detroit before they finally won 9-4 on the July 26. Corcoron was having a difficult stretch of pitching, which came to be attributed to a "lame arm."

Another defeat, 6-3 to Cleveland, featured

> Kelly [commiting] an act of folly in the third inning when he tried to steal across the diamond to the plate without touching third and was detected by umpire Doscher. It broke up a Chicago rally. Kelly needs an admonition that this sort of baserunning is too much of a cheap-and-nasty description to give satisfaction.

On August 1, Chicago was 33-18, and the lead over Buffalo was three games. Buffalo then came to town and the White Stockings took three in a row to put some distance in the race. It proved to be the decisive series of the season.

Chicago got another boost on August 23 when Goldsmith was injured in the third inning, pitching against Detroit, and Anson had to summon Corcoron in to pitch. Larry went nine innings and led the White Stockings to an 8-6, 12-inning victory. And where had he been summoned from? From his post at the turnstile, where he was in charge of monitoring the day's attendance count.

The final home game of the season in Chicago was played on August 25, with 3,000 in attendance. To the delight of the fans, Hulbert's beloved black dog was brought out of retirement before the game to resume his watchful place from the clubhouse platform.

At the grandstand entrance, "handsome illuminated scorecards" were distributed, and the players collected $200 among themselves to present Hulbert with a gold watch and chain with a locket attached, containing a team picture.

The standings on August 29 showed Chicago 42-22, eight games over Buffalo. The White Stockings played the entire final month of the season on the road.

On a mid-September day in Boston, Kelly again skipped third base as Anson was retired at first. This time he got away with it, and Chicago won the game 4-3. The umpire was one "Honest John" Kelly, a New Yorker, no relation, in his first year in the league. As Mike always invested a lot of time in befriending the umpires, he found in Honest John a warm relationship. The two would go on to become close friends and later business partners, a practice which would never be tolerated today. He was also some years later, a manager in the American Association.

"Honest John" was not a tongue-in-cheek moniker. He was selected to work in five of the first World Series played, more than any other man of his era, and he was a respected figure despite the relationship with Mike which might have raised eyebrows.

"Kelly...ran unmindful of third base," wrote a reporter. "He got away with it as umpire Kelly did not see it." There was no suggestion of dishonesty.

The White Stockings clinched their second straight pennant with a 4-0 victory at Boston on September 16. The season ended on September 30 with Chicago 56-28, nine games over Providence, which had won 24 of its final 34 games to slip by Buffalo.

Anson won the batting championship with a .399 mark, with Dalrymple and Kelly both hitting .323 to tie for fifth. The 5-foot extension of the pitching distance was not believed to have measurably helped the hitters.

Kelly was second in the league to George Gore with 84 runs scored in 82 games and he tied Paul Hines of Providence for the league lead with 27 doubles. He was third in total bases, third in runs batted in, and fifth in slugging percentage despite hitting only two home runs.

It was believed that Chicago had profits of as much as $40,000, far ahead of any other team in the league. Only Detroit was also thought to have made any money.

At the close of the season, Mike returned to Paterson. Now 23, he had been seeing a local girl, one Agnes Hedifen. Mike was a "man's man" in every sense of the word: he liked his liquor, his tobacco, his card playing, the race track, and sports. But there was another side to him. He was described as a "fairly good dancer," and an "admittedly bad singer," and we can speculate that he brought some social graces from the sophisticated city of Chicago with him. He was known to be a grand fashion plate and had a winning personality, money in his pocket, and the confidence that reflected his success and the admiration of others.

Agnes was 21, the daughter of John Hedifen and the former Mary McGill, both natives of Scotland.

Mike and Agnes were married on October 25, 1881, in Hackensack, New Jersey. The witnesses were John Ryan and Jimmy McCormick. By all appearances, the couple led a happy life together for the remaining 13 years of Mike's life. They were childless until the last year, but enjoyed winters on the farm at Agnes's brother's place in the sleepy Hudson River town of Hyde Park, New York, in Dutchess County. While it is hard to believe that Kelly would enjoy the quiet of this community, he often reflected on the beauty of the area.

If Hyde Park has a familiar ring to it, it is indeed the birthplace of the nation's thirty-second president, Franklin Delano Roosevelt. He was born on January 30, 1882, three months after the Kelly wedding. He was the son of James Roosevelt and the former Sara Delano. James, vice president of the Delaware & Hudson Railroad, was a lawyer and financier with roots in

Dutchess County back to the early eighteenth century. It seems unlikely that the socially correct Roosevelts ever had the Hedifens or the Kellys over for tea or to meet baby Franklin.

At the winter meeting, it was voted that each team be required to wear a different color stocking for 1882: Chicago white, Cleveland dark blue, Providence light blue, Worcester brown, Buffalo gray, Troy green, Boston red, and Detroit yellow. Further, each position was to wear a different color shirt, belt, and cap, although black and white photographs do not bear this out as having come to pass: catcher scarlet, pitcher light blue, first base scarlet and white, second base orange and blue, third base blue and white, shortstop maroon, left field white, center field red and black, right field grey, and substitutes green and brown. All pants and ties would be white. By May, the rule was rescinded for the following season, giving in to the player's charges of wearing "clown costumes."

Significantly, the club owners took the substantial step of discarding ten players whose conduct was felt to be detrimental to the game; translation: men who were suspected of throwing games or other shady actions. Among the players were Lipman Pike, Buttercup Dickerson and "The Only" Nolan, men whose names we have encountered before. Pike, for example, was accused of "selling" the game of September 3, when he made three errors in centerfield and cost his team a 3-2 decision.

If Kelly ever needed a message to stay away from baseball gambling, this was surely it. No doubt the honorable presences of Hulbert, Spalding, and Anson provided frequent threats about the penalties for such action. But Kelly, filled with other vices, might have been easy prey without stern warnings. The roots of the game in which he had been raised were steeped in friendly wagering. He was better to direct his propensity for the wager to two of his other vices: the card game of faro and the nation's many racetracks. Both were great passions.

At the track, Kelly was a familiar face, greeted as a special guest whenever he arrived. He had a particular fondness for Salvatore, the best-known race-horse of the latter half of the 19th century. Salvatore was owned by James Ben Ali Haggin, the biggest operator to that point in the history of racing. It was not surprising that Kelly and Haggin would become acquainted, and Mike took every opportunity to watch Salvatore race at the nation's finest tracks: Sheepshead Bay, Monmouth, and Saratoga.

Great as Salvatore was, he could break your heart. He had a habit of losing some big races to a horse named Proctor Knott. If Kelly bet Salvatore, he probably lost some big stakes races. But he never lost his affection for the handsome beast, for, to Mike it was the sport, more than the purse. He was never one to cry in his beer over a wager.

Just as a pop tune would one day be written for Kelly, a stirring poem by Ella Wheeler Wilcox helped carve the legend of Salvatore:

...One more mighty plunge,
and with knee, limb and hand
I lift my horse first by a nose past the stand
We are under the string now the great race is done
And Salvatore, Salvatore, Salvatore won!...

The 1883 opening of a fine new track at 61st and South Park Avenue in Chicago—Washington Park—afforded Kel not only many fine afternoons of wagering, but one off-season, employment as a starter.

In the days before starting gates, two men would stand on ladders and hold a string in front of the horses until it was determined that they were in an even line and ready to begin the race. The string would be lifted to signal the start. Kelly had a grand time strutting on the track and determining when to hoist the string. And the track rightly felt his presence brought in a lot of baseball fans.

Spalding represented Chicago at the preseason meeting of club owners held on March 7, 1882 in Rochester, New York. Hulbert was home in Chicago. He never missed league meetings; few worked as tirelessly as he did in moving professional baseball toward success. The fact that only Chicago and Detroit had turned profits in 1881 indicated that the game was not yet in healthy order. Much work was ahead. But for Hulbert, the time to lead was passing. He died on April 10 of heart failure. He was 50. How special it must have been to him to have received the gold watch from his championship players in the closing days of the 1881 season.

All the members of the White Stockings attended his funeral and accompanied his coffin to its final resting place at Graceland Cemetery, where both his family, and the National League erected monuments.

Spalding, a quasi-official of the White Stockings to this point, now became the owner, purchasing the team with John Walsh from Hulbert's widow.

There were no significant rules changes for 1882 and the team roster was untouched, although Kelly found himself playing half a season, 41 games, at shortstop. Not a particularly graceful player, he seemed out of position and much more suited to right field, where he played 36 contests.

Chicago went after a third straight pennant, with Providence the toughest competitor. Recalled Kelly, several years later:

> I was playing with the best ball team ever put together
> —the Chicagos of 1882. I bar no team in the world when
> I say that. I know about the New York Giants, the
> Detroits and the Big Four [Dan Brouthers, Deacon
> White, Hardie Richardson, and Jack Rowe, 1886-88],
> the 1886 St. Louis Browns and all of them, but they were
> never in it with the old 1882 gang that pulled down the
> pennant for Chicago. Then was when you saw ball
> playing, away up in the thirty-second degree. [A Masonic
> expression.] That was the crowd that showed the way to
> all the others. They towered over all ball teams like
> Salvator's record dwarfs all the other race horses. Where
> can you get a team with so many big men on its payroll?
> There were seven of us six feet high, Anson, Goldsmith,
> Dalrymple, Gore, Williamson, Flint and myself being in
> that neighborhood. Larry Corcoron and Tommy Burns
> were the only small men on the team. Fred Pfeffer was
> then the greatest second baseman of them all. All you
> had to do was throw anywhere near the bag, and he
> would get it—high, wide, or on the ground. What a man
> he was to make a return throw; why, he could lay on his
> stomach and throw 100 yards then. Those old sports
> didn't know much about hitting the ball either; no, I
> guess they didn't. Only four of us had led the League in
> batting—Anson, Gore, Dalrymple and myself....When

we marched on a field with our big six-footers out in front
it used to be a case of "eat 'em up, Jake." We had most
of 'em whipped before we threw a ball. They were scared
to death.

Scared to death or not, it was an awfully close race. And as
for Kelly's great remembrances of the '82 team, Pfeffer didn't
come aboard until '83, so the King's memory failed him. Still, his
observations are worth preserving, flawed though they might
be. He was clearly caught up with the physical size of his team,
even if he, at 5'10", was one of those "being in the neighborhood"
of six feet.

The rivalry between Chicago and Boston was by this time
already a strong one. Both were large, populated cities with loyal
and vocal fans, and Kel was extremely popular in Beantown. A
gregarious Irishman, who could give as well as take tough
bantering with the fans, he relished his visits there for the
intensity of the rivalry and the competitiveness of the games.

On Chicago's first trip to Boston in '82, newspapers suggested
that the rivalry had become too intense, that Kelly, in particular,
might be singled out for "special notice" by the Boston fans.

Mike loved the press. He could dish it out to them on occasion,
more or less saying "just as long as they spell me name right,"
but in this case, the Boston writers were suggesting that Kel
might be subject to actual physical abuse by the fans. Mike's
teammates found this irresistible. Gore and Williamson took
him out the night before the trip to Boston, got him good and
drunk, and laughingly told Anson that he was too sick to make
the trip.

"Forget it," was the basis of Anson's reply.

So Williamson went to Kelly and suggested that he perform
"in disguise," by shaving off all of his hair. Mike, who would do
pretty much anything for a joke, went along with it and was
shaved bald by a barber. The next day, Silver Flint suggested
that the big mustache was still too much of a giveaway—and
Kelly had that shaved off too.

The disguise didn't work—everyone in Boston knew Kelly by
now—but the fans loved the theatrics and had a great time with
Mike, treating him exceptionally well.

The Providence Grays had a 13-6 record for May, and Chicago

was a disappointing 9-9, 3-1/2 games back. The teams didn't face each other until June 9 at Providence, by which time Chicago had fallen six games back. But the White Stockings took two out of three to set a nice race in motion. By the end of June, Chicago was 21-15, one game behind Providence. A month later, Providence was still clinging to the one game lead. In August, the Grays pulled ahead by three games. Eighteen games remained for Chicago and 15 for Providence with a month to go.

The Providence team, managed by the venerable Harry Wright, featured old Joe Start, now 39, at first base, hitting .329, fourth best in the league. George Wright, 35, Harry's kid brother, was the shortstop. It was his last hurrah as a player, but a disappointing one for the old Red Stocking, his season yielding but a .162 average.

The Grays in fact, had only the fourth highest batting average in the league. It was their pitching that kept them on top, with two future Hall of Famers sharing the work—John Montgomery Ward, and Ol' Hoss Radbourne.

Ward, 22, was already a five-year veteran who had won 47 games in 1879 and 39 in 1880, including a perfect game. In this season he would make 32 starts and post a 19-12 record. When he wasn't pitching, he was playing the outfield or shortstop. He was a Columbia law student, who would, in a few years, help found the game's first player's union, the National Brotherhood of Professional Base Ball Players.

Radbourne, was a player more in the mold of Kelly. A 27-year old righthander who stood only 5'9", he broke in in 1881 with 25 victories and in '82 made 52 starts, had 51 complete games, and a 33-20 record. He led the league in strikeouts and shutouts.

But that was nothing. He won 48 games the following year, and then a remarkable 60 in 1884, a record certain not to fall under current conditions. He completed each of his 73 starts that season, worked 679 innings, struck out 441, and had an earned run average of 1.38. Yes, it was a season of underhand pitching, but it was still a height to which no other ever soared, before or since.

The 60 wins went a long way towards his career total of 310, compiled in only 11 seasons.

Radbourne would not go out in glory. Through at 36, partly due to a case of syphilis, he returned home to Bloomington,

Illinois, and opened a pool hall. In 1894, he blew off part of his face in a hunting accident, and became a recluse, ashamed to be seen in public. By 1897, he was dead.

But in 1882, he was on top of his world, leading the Grays to what looked like a possible pennant. On August 17, he and Detroit's Stump Weidman were locked in a 17-inning scoreless pitching duel, the game of the season. A newspaper said the fans awaited the outcome "as though awaiting the outcome of a presidential election."

In the 18th, before the hometown fans, Radbourne hit a home run to give Providence the victory. The deep hit became lodged in the rear hoof of a horse, tethered innocently in the deep recesses of the outfield, and the weak-hitting and exhausted Radbourne dashed around the bases as the fans went wild with joy. It was one for the ages.

The season was not going well by Chicago's recent standards. If there was to be a third straight pennant, it would have to be hard fought and time was running out. Anson, the stern taskmaster, was going to be a tough trail boss for the next few weeks. There were to be hard workouts, tight curfews, strict enforcement of training rules. If the White Stockings were going to go down, it would not be without a fight.

They began September with a 7-1 home victory over Boston, but the next day, they fell to the Beaneaters while Providence was winning in Buffalo. They were back to 3-1/2 games behind.

That was the first of four straight wins for Providence, and Chicago took their next three to hang tight at 3-1/2. Now, the two teams met in Chicago for a three-game series on September 12, 13, and 14, a series Kelly would recall as "the three most exciting games of ball I ever played in."

Baseball fever was running high in the Windy City. This series would be the most critical series of the year, and likely Chicago's last chance to defend its championship. Kelly, meeting Harry Wright before the first game, offered to bet a new hat that Chicago would finish the year ahead of the Grays, but the gentlemanly Wright wouldn't hear of a gamble, even a friendly one.

At last, when the dust had cleared and Corcoron and Goldsmith had pitched their magic, the White Stockings had emerged with three consecutive victories, 6-4, 6-5, and 6-2.

The first game went right to the final inning, tied 4-4, when
Kelly, on first, was faced with a moment in which a double play
could leave Chicago on the short end of the game.

Burns hit a hot grounder to George Wright at short. Instead
of tossing the ball to the second baseman, Wright decided to take
the putout at second himself.

"I never ran so hard in my life," said Kelly.

> I reached the bag a second before George, and then, like
> a flash, he raised his arm to send the ball to first, to cut
> off Burns. Somehow or other an accident occurred at
> that moment. My arm went up in the air, and it caught
> George on the shoulder. The result was that when the
> ball left George's hand it went away over into the grand-
> stand. I scored first and Burns followed me a moment
> later. The cheers from a thousand enthusiastic specta-
> tors proved that the Chicago club had won the first great
> game.

Harry Wright, gentlemanly Harry Wright, "was the maddest
man in Chicago when the series had finished." He blamed it all
on "Kelly's infernal tricks," and said, "if not for Kelly, the Providence club would have won the series and the championship."
Kelly later went to Wright and innocently said, "Harry, when I
saw George raise his arm, I knew that if something didn't occur
we would be defeated. I didn't think of George or myself, only of
the Chicago club." Harry forgave him and the two remained good
friends.

How could you not forgive Kel?

But intentional or not, Kelly had made the play that defined
the series, and perhaps defined his win at all costs approach to
the game.

The sweep cut the lead to a half game, and two days later,
Chicago beat Worcester 5-4 and Providence lost to Detroit 6-2 to
fall into second.

The Grays, though, stayed right in the race. They won three
straight and moved back into a tie for first on September 22,
when Chicago's nine-game winning streak ended. On the 25th,
Chicago went back on top by a game and never again relin-
quished the lead, clinching it on the 28th with an 11-5 home

victory over Buffalo. For the month, Chicago was 16-2. Anson had rallied them to a third consecutive pennant and a collective "whew!" no doubt accompanied the clinching in what had been a great, great pennant race. When it came time for the key three games, head to head, Chicago had risen to the task. Long before Chicago enjoyed the "three-peat" championship years of Michael Jordan and the Bulls, the White Stockings had rocked the town with three years of glory.

As usual, Chicago players were prominent among the league leaders—Gore leading in runs scored and walks, Anson in runs batted in, and Kelly in doubles with 37. Goldsmith won 33, Corcoron 27, and the latter had a 1.97 era to top all National Leaguers.

Kelly's average was .305, third on the team and eighth in the league. His lifetime mark to this point was .312, ninth on the "all-time" list, which now covered seven National League seasons.

The year 1882 also marked the first season of the rival American Association, which featured teams in Brooklyn, Philadelphia, Cincinnati, St. Louis, Pittsburgh, and Louisville. Beer was sold in their ballparks, making for more rowdy crowds, but their existence was tolerated and about 20 interleague exhibitions were played with National League clubs. There was no championship officially scheduled between the two leagues. However, at the end of the season, Chicago played two exhibitions against Cincinnati, champions of the American Association, in what would be another homecoming for Kelly. These exhibitions were, in a manner of speaking, the first "world series"; that is, the first time two league champions met in post-season play.

Cincinnati still featured Will White, Kelly's old teammate, and played their games at the new Bank Street Grounds. In Cincinnati, the games were much heralded; the Cincinnati *Commercial* hailed the return of "Kelley [sic]— our Kelley of old.

"If there be anybody who is not going out to see to-day's game, he was not to be found last night," wrote the *Commercial*.

In Chicago, the games were barely noted. In fact, the White Stockings were squeezing in the two games while on an East Coast exhibition tour. They came in from New York and were to return there after the second game.

Twenty-seven hundred people turned out on October 6 for the first game. A coin toss was won by Pop Snyder, the Cincinnati manager, and they chose to bat last. The strategy was sound; the offense was weak and Corcoron was in fine form. Chicago won 4-0, in the days when a shutout was called, coincidentally, a "chicago."

Previewing the second game, the *Commercial* said,

> The game of to-day therefore, will be the most intensely interesting ever played on this continent. With heavy laurels on their brows, which nothing can take from them, the Cincinnatis go into to-day's game with nothing to lose and the world to win. The Chicagos, on the contrary, have nothing to win and all to lose. That it will be a bitter struggle nobody has reason to doubt.

A capacity crowd of 3,500, largest of the season in Cincinnati, turned out. They paid 50 cents for the grandstand, 35 cents for the pavilion. Many stood upon the "earth banks" down the left field fence. Corcoron pitched again, and this time, beat the Red Stockings 2-0 to leave few doubts as to the superior team, if not league. Corcoron would have driven away in a new car if they had been invented and a series MVP had they been selected.

Hearing of the games, the American Association president, Denny McKnight, sent a rush telegraph to Cincinnati, threatening the Red Stockings with a heavy fine ($100) if they played again. There was, remember, no plans for a post-season series, and no truce yet existed between the leagues. In any event, the Chicagos had an exhibition engagement back in New York and the series was to have ended anyway. Even with the two victories, Chicago didn't seem to make much of the importance of these games.

And what was Kelly's contribution to this unheralded, historic first meeting of two major league champions in post-season play in this city of his major league debut?

He did not appear in either game. Goldsmith played right field and Flint caught. News accounts provide no explanation for Mike's absence, even though he had been "previewed" as returning to Cincinnati.

He may have been injured or he may have been AWOL, but

Anson on Kelly

"He was a whole-souled, genial fellow with a host of friends, and but one enemy, that one being himself. Time and again I have heard him say that he would never be broke, but money slipped through Mike's fingers as water slips through the meshes of a fisherman's net, and he was as fond of whiskey as any representative of the Emerald Isle."

---

in any case, it was obviously decided that there was nothing to report in the press. Today, a baseball player failing to show up for a game creates an incredibly scandalous story. When Darryl Strawberry missed an exhibition in spring training of 1994, the police were called to find him. No matter how irresponsible a player might be today, he is always at the park at game time.

Kelly played in a time when rules were not quite as tight. Anson was a stickler for rules all right, but there certainly could have been times when Kelly was hung over and simply couldn't get his body to the park. It is speculative, but his capacity for drink certainly leads one to this conclusion. His absence from a lineup makes one wonder if he was simply drunk and out of commission. He might have been. At a time when little was thought of pitchers working nearly every day, the absence of Kelly, a big gate attraction, was always laden with suspicion.

Mike again returned home to Paterson, his pockets containing his remaining salary and wagering dollars, none of the latter, presumably, coming from baseball. That which remained, he was all too happy to spend on his friends in the Paterson taverns, telling tales of the mighty White Stockings and the thrills of the National League race.

At a "Harmony Conference" in February 1883, dictated as usual by economic necessity, a "National Agreement" was worked out which effectively put a $2,000 ceiling on salaries to prevent jumping for better offers. Although no post-season series was played in '83, the mechanism was in place for future competition.

The year 1883 also saw the addition of National League franchises in both New York and Philadelphia, the nation's largest cities. Troy and Worcester were out. The league now included the two newest franchises, along with Boston, Buffalo, Chicago, Cleveland, Detroit, and Providence. All were connected by the Michigan Central Railroad, the travel of choice for most clubs, with its sleeping cars, smoking cars, dining cars, and scenic passage over Niagara Falls en route to Detroit. Kelly could often be found enjoying a big cigar and some friendly games of faro on the long but convivial journeys.

Ward moved from Providence to New York, whose roster also included pitcher Smilin' Mickey Welch and slugger Roger Connor. The Gothams' presence would mark the first time in which Kelly could perform before his hometown fans of Paterson, which was just a short hop to the Gothams' ballpark located on 110th Street in Manhattan, near Fifth Avenue. (The American Association's New York Mets continued to play at the same site, only on a different diamond, separated by a canvas fence. At times both diamonds would be in action at once, and balls rolling under the canvas were "in play." You could find a Met scurrying after a ball in the distant outfield of a Gotham game and vice versa.)

Chicago added the German-speaking second baseman, Fred Pfeffer to their lineup for '83, replacing Joe Quest. Pfeffer was the last link to what would become the best infield of its time, the "Stonewall Infield," with Anson, Pfeffer, Williamson, and Burns.

Pfeffer, 23, had played for Troy the year before, hitting only .218, but Spalding saw defensive prowess there that he felt would bolster the White Stockings. He would become a close friend of Kelly, which usually meant someone with whom Mike enjoyed running with in the evenings. He also became one of the most quoted of Kelly admirers.

Pfeffer was of "the old school" even when that school was but a few years past. He was one of the last of the bare-handed fielders, disdaining the "modern" glove, which was barely more than a skin covering with no fingers. The tales of his defensive play and his throws to first while on his backside, his knees, or on the run were many. He is credited with being the first infielder to cut off a catcher's throw to second and return the ball to whence it came from in order to stop the double steal.

Pfeffer would become a very popular player in Chicago, and

although he moved onto other teams beginning in 1892, he called Chicago home for the rest of his life, which took him to 1932. He operated a successful saloon in the city's theater district which became a major watering hole for both the theatrical and the baseball crowd.

Although overhand pitching was technically illegal, it was used without penalty more and more as the 1883 season wore on. For some hitters, it was as difficult a transition as actors would find decades later when talkies replaced silent movies. It turned careers around.

Kelly found 1883 to be more of a struggle than he had previously experienced in Chicago. At times, his frustration would get him into heated "kicking" with umpires, which, while entertaining to fans and admired by the rougher segment of players, was considered boorish by the more statesmanlike leaders of the game. The practice was especially criticized by the revered journalist Henry Chadwick, who edited the annual Spalding Guides. One can assume that to reach print in a Spalding volume, it bore the approval of no less than Albert Goodwill Spalding himself.

Spalding knew that Kelly was a crowd pleaser. His baserunning, both daring and wreckless, drew crowds to the park. His bantering with the fans and his good nature were great assets to a man concerned with ticket sales. But there were times that his good nature was as much a product of good whiskey as natural charm. And it continued to disturb both Anson and, to a lesser but significant extent, Spalding. The Spalding Guides would not continue to preach mightily against intemperance if Spalding did not have some particular suspects in mind.

Anson chose to skip a series of exhibitions with American Association teams in April, games which got the New York and Philadelphia teams acclimated to playing as a unit. Chicago continued to work out in a local gymnasium, employing medicine balls, Indian clubs, dumb bells, and other forms of calisthenics for conditioning. (All the equipment could also be purchased at Spalding & Bros., 108 Madison Street, Chicago.)

Chicago lost four of its first six, perhaps an omen that a fourth straight title would not be automatic. Still, through the first two months of the season, they were locked in a good race with Providence and Cleveland, the latter benefiting from good early season pitching from Paterson buddy Jim McCormick, coming off a 36-win season in '82, and 26-year old Hugh Ignatius Daily, whose nickname, "One Arm," closely described his handicap. (Actually, like Jim Abbott, he was missing a hand, not an arm, having blown it off in a gun accident.) In underhand pitching days with soft gloves on both hands, his handicap was less severe than it might be in another time, but his 23-19 season for Cleveland was certainly a remarkable accomplishment, highlighted by no less than a no-hitter against Philadelphia on September 13. But the advent of overhand pitching would spell his doom, and his only future success came in the Union Association, a one-season, third major league.

Entering the eighth week of the 20-week season, Chicago and Providence were in their familiar positions, tied for first, with Cleveland third.

Then came the worst road trip the team had been on since Kelly joined them. They spent nearly the entire month of June in the East, battered and bruised at each stop.

On June 3, they began a four-game series in New York; their first visit ever to the nation's biggest city. Friends of Kelly's came from Paterson to watch their local hero in action, but they saw the White Stockings drop three of four in embarrassing style, including a 22-7 trouncing in the first game and 16-8 in the last. For the series, the Gothams outscored the defending champions 50-23. Kelly, who was having a tough year in the outfield (32 errors), was not much help, but neither were his two superb fellow flychasers, Gore and Dalrymple, who each made 34 errors. It is true that outfield defense was much different then, with the small gloves and lack of fences, but 100 errors by the Chicago outfield in the 98-game season was a major lapse for this well-drilled club.

From New York, the champs went to Providence where the rivalry was as strong as ever. Radbourne still did most of the pitching (this was the 48-victory season), and Charley Sweeney started the 18 games which Ol' Hoss didn't, replaced Ward on the roster.

The Grays took two of three from Chicago and then it was on to Boston, where the White Stockings again dropped two of three, with a 12-1 pasting in the finale.

Things got no better in Buffalo, where two games resulted in two losses, 12-0 and 6-2. That marked nine losses in 12 games on the trip, which was only salvaged by splitting a pair at Cleveland and then winning a single game at Detroit. Anson's club pulled into Union Station on the 28th with a 5-10 trip and a shaky third place tie in the standings.

The good home cooking that the players found at the Clifton House, along with the support of their loyal, if puzzled fans, helped. They regrouped against Buffalo and swept four straight, with the final providing a 31-7 laugher, unusual even for the 1880s.

The White Stockings won 13 of 19 in July, including 3 of 4 from Providence and Boston in successive series. These helped put Chicago back in the close race and by the end of the month they were right in the thick of things, with Cleveland setting the pace and Providence and Chicago right behind.

August found the team playing just over .500 ball, but still holding on, with six straight wins to conclude the month. Entering September, the standings were:

Cleveland	49-30	
Providence	49-32	-1
Chicago	47-33	-2.5
Boston	46-32	-2.5

It looked like it would be just as exciting as the 1882 race, except this time, four teams were involved.

Home games were still a decided advantage for Chicago. They began September with five more home victories, including three from Cleveland, to run the winning streak to 11 and look like the champions of old. On September 6, they beat Detroit 26-6, scoring a record 18 runs in the 7th inning. In that one inning, Tommy Burns went 3-for-3 with two doubles and a homer.

But on September 10, they opened a four-game series in Boston, and the old road trip blues struck hard again.

The night before the first game, a man approached Kelly at the United States Hotel, where the White Stockings were staying.

"Kelly," he said, "I have it on pretty good authority that Chicago is going to throw the championship to Boston this year. Is it so?"

Kelly, relating the story five years later, said, "You had better ask Anson. He knows more about it than I do." Replied the man, "Look here, Kelly, what Anson knows in regard to this affair doesn't matter. You fellows can win it, if you want to. There isn't any doubt about that in my mind. Now, I'm in this thing to make money, and I am willing to help you do the same. I understand that you are to catch in the coming games. If you will promise me that the Bostons will win, I will give you $2,500. You can fix the pitchers."

Kelly tells the rest of the story:

> The proposition stunned me for a moment. Anson was in the office. I called him over, and told him what the man had said. He just stood there like a dummy, but looked as though he would like to be present somewhere else. I thought Anson would get mad, but he didn't. He said, "My friend, you cannot buy the Chicago club. There isn't enough money in Boston for that. Now, I will give you a straight tip. If we can win, we are going to. We're going to make the great fight of our lives. I heard, on the very best authority, tonight, that the Bostons were going to do the same thing. One thing I will admit. This week settles whether it will be Boston and Chicago, or Chicago and Boston. Good night, sir. I'll play you a game of billiards, Kel."

Wrote Kelly,

> On one thing I will risk everything I have in the world— there is no dishonesty about baseball. The games are played for all they are worth; and of the many players at present in the league, I am sure there is not one dishonest one. There may have been a few in the past. Let us thank God that there are none in the present, and hope that there won't be in the future.

The White Stockings dropped four dismal games in Boston, 4-2, 3-2, 11-2, and 3-1 and never recovered. A crowd of 3,500 fans saw Kelly in bad form, for as the press reported the next day, "Chicago catcher Kelly was as conspicuous and farfetched in his conduct as ever. He was the only one of the visiting Chicago players who found any delight in making himself ridiculous. Too bad that such a good player has to act so little like a gentleman."

Boston, in seventh place in June, had staged one of the great National League rallies.

Only eight games remained for Chicago—in Providence, New York and Philadelphia—and although they took six of them, they were done. Dethroned. Boston had won their last six. The new champs were the Boston Red Stockings, whose sweep of Chicago catapulted them on to first place. They were not unlike their descendents, the 1914 Braves, who went from last to first in the same season with a team of unknowns. For that matter, their distant heirs, the 1991 Atlanta Braves, also staged a "worst to first" revival from 1990.

As for the White Stockings, they might have well understood the fate of their distant heirs, the 1969 Chicago Cubs, a far more talented team on paper than the '69 Mets, but a team doomed to step aside for a miracle in progress.

That Boston could win over the star-laden White Stockings was rather remarkable. They had not a single player on the team whose name is well recalled today. The regular lineup featured manager Honest John Morrill at first, Black Jack Burdock at second, Sam Wise at short, Ezra Sutton at third, Mike "Ubbo Ubbo" Hornung, Shorty Radford, and Charlie Buffinton in the outfield, Mike Hines catching, and a pitching duo of Grasshopper Jim Whitney (56 starts) and Buffinton (41 starts when he wasn't in the outfield).

This was the first season that saw as many as 100 games played (Cleveland and Detroit played that many, the rest 98 or 99) and Chicago's good finish had given them second place, four games back. But after three pennants, second was nothing to celebrate.

Kelly had his worst season to date, a .255 year, with all of those errors and his name nowhere to be found among league leaders. There can be little doubt that after the Boston sweep and his boorish behavior, Spalding and Anson had to think about whether this was the kind of man they wanted on their club for 1884. Yes, he was popular. But no, he was not "their kind of player."

The month of October brought a series of exhibitions against

Association teams. There had been plans for a "world series" at the end of the month between Boston and the Association champions from Philadelphia, but the Athletics lost seven of their eight exhibitions against National League teams, and politely declined after all. Chicago won four post-season exhibitions, beating Cincinnati, St. Louis twice, and Columbus, and lost two, both at Cincinnati. They called it a season on October 11, long before the other teams disbanded for the winter.

Kelly's salary for 1884 remained as it had been, $2,000, which was the agreed upon maximum; agreed upon by the owners, of course. The reserve clause was working, and teams were holding their players without signing others. Wrote Chadwick in Spalding's 1884 *Guide,*

> Here is a ball player, who, as a street car driver or conductor, a brakesman, a porter or an assistant at some ordinary trade in which, at his work as a common day laborer he can only command ten dollars a week for his services, and to earn that has to work laboriously from ten to fifteen hours each day; and yet, this self-same individual is taught by unscrupulous or short-sighted rival clubs to believe that he is treated badly if he is not readily given $2,000 as salary for six months' services as a ball player, in which his work is comparatively a pleasant recreation, requiring but two or three hours of easy work each day. This is the rational view of the situation so far as equity is concerned, in estimating a ball player's real value.

So there.

For 1884, overhand pitching was made legal and the number of balls required for a walk was reduced to six.

The Union Association, in its only year of existence, attempted to attract National Leaguers without much success. One of their signings, Larry Corcoron, with the Chicago Unions, had a change of heart and returned to the White Stockings in January. The big signing for the league turned out to be Jim McCormick.

Chicago beefed up its winter roster to 18, with the most notable addition being a fast outfielder named Billy Sunday, who had passed a 14-game test in '83. Sunday was thought to be as swift a runner as Kelly, and he was a crowd pleaser as well. An Iowan like Anson and just 21 in 1884, he could take a drink with this teammates and was welcomed as "one of the guys." His five-year stay in Chicago never saw him play regularly, but when he got in, his speed excited the fans.

Lake Front Park was reconfigured at this time to produce the shortest outfield dimensions in major league history. Left field was brought in to 180 feet, just twice the distance of home to third, and right field measured 196, 100 feet shorter than the famous old Yankee Stadium right field. Dead center was marked off at 300. Spalding continued to make the park attractive for fans, employing eight musicians, three cushion renters, and six refreshment boys, along with a staff of 25 ushers, security people, ticket takers, gatekeepers, and grounds crew.

The alteration of the outfield had an immediate and dazzling impact on White Stocking power production. After the team hit only 13 home runs in the 1883 season, they hit 142 in 1884, a number that would hold its own even by today's standards. The next highest total in the league was 39 by Buffalo. The top four home run hitters in the league were all White Stockings, with Williamson hitting 27, (25 at home), Pfeffer 25, Dalrymple 22 and Anson 21. Kelly had a career high of 13, but the right-hander maintained a Ty Cobb style of batting stance in which his left hand was at the bottom of the bat and his right hand considerably up the bat, reducing any significant power potential. Kelly never abandoned that style of hitting. (The following year, it was decreed that any ball hit over a fence less than 210 feet would in fact be a double.)

Like the 1947 Giants (221 homers, 4th place) and the 1956 Reds (221 homers, 3rd place) the power outburst did not necessarily translate into a good season for the White Stockings.

There being no true "spring training" as we know it, the White Stockings convened in late March of '84 for gymnasium work, which Anson favored over exhibition games against American Association teams. There was a certain snob appeal to this, not unlike John McGraw's refusal to recognize the American League in 1904 when it came World Series time. Anson did not wholly boycott the Association, but he waited until April 28 to play his one and only preseason game, an 8-4 win at Indianapolis. Other

teams had been playing since April 5, with Boston having played
five games and Providence seven.

Perhaps Anson misjudged the importance of the warmups, for
the White Stockings lost their first three regular season games,
15-3 and 13-6 to New York, and 9-8 to Philadelphia. Chicago was
only 9-15 in May, a horrid start, made all the worse by a 21-4
start by Boston and a 20-4 start by Providence. In a way, the
race was over before the White Stockings could even regroup.

Behind the sensational pitching of Hoss Radbourne, who was
rolling off an 18-game winning streak, the Grays stayed on top
of the league, with Boston the only serious challenger. Chicago
had its best month in July with a 14-6 record, and in September
they made a bit of a run with a 14-5 mark, but only a nine-game
winning streak to end the season gave them the appearance of
respectability. The win streak allowed them to tie New York for
fourth place, but a hefty 22 games behind Providence.

Season highlights included a three homers in three days
performance by Sunday, three homer games by Williamson and
Anson (the first in baseball history), an ambidextrous pitching
performance by Corcoran on June 16 against Buffalo, a third
no-hitter by Corcoron on June 27, and an exciting 5-4 victory
over Providence on June 30 with Kelly homering with two out
in the last of the ninth. On August 14, Kelly hit the tenth grand
slam homer in history (the fourth of the season) and the only one
of his career.

The season did not end until October 15, and this time, a
"world series" was finally held, under the name "championship
games." The Grays opposed the New York Metropolitans, the
American Association champs, and took three straight, 6-0, 3-1,
and 12-2. Kelly and his teammates followed the account of the
games, if they wished, in the local newspapers back in their
home towns. It was not a proud year for Anson's men.

Kelly however, had staged a magnificent comeback from his
.255 showing in 1883. Facing more overhand pitching than he
had ever seen, he led the league with a .354 average, beating out
Boston's Jim O'Rourke (.347) and Ezra Sutton (.346). Unfortunately, these averages were computed only in recent years when
researchers found errors in old box scores and recalculated. In
1884, Kelly was denied the glory of the batting championship,
for it was believed at the time that he hit .341, trailing O'Rourke

(.350) and Sutton (.349). *The Baseball Encyclopedia* and *Total Baseball* give Kel four more times at bat and seven additional hits, while *The Sporting News* recognizes the original numbers. Alas, if the revised numbers are correct, poor Kel never knew that he was the batting champ.

Kelly also led the league in runs scored with 120, was fourth in hits, fourth in total bases, and second in bases on balls. He played 63 games in the outfield, caught 28, played shortstop 12 times, third base 10 times, first base twice, and pitcher twice.

Another bright ray of sunshine in the Chicago season was the debut of John Clarkson late in the season. Clarkson had pitched three games for the National League's Worcester franchise in '82, and then spent '83 and '84 with Saginaw until he was purchased by Chicago in September. He was a 5'10", 155-pound right hander from Cambridge, Massachusetts, 23 years of age, and in 13 late season starts, he was 10-3 with a 2.14 earned run average, as Goldsmith's talents began to fade.

A "quiet, modest gentleman," according to Kelly, Clarkson "had more curves and shoots than any pitcher in this country." Anson found Clarkson sensitive and not much use if "scolded." He was apparently quite scientific about his approach to the game, studying hitters' weaknesses and pitching with a slow but steady pace to keep the intimidation edge in his control.

Meanwhile, the concerns of officials continued to focus on the drinking habits of some of its players. The Spalding *Guide,* recapping the '84 season, named no names, but stated that

> ...the evil of drunkenness in the ranks...is still in exist-
> ence, it being the most conspicuous evil that was con-
> nected with professional ball playing during 1884. This
> trouble has proved to be not only destructive to the
> morale of every club...in which it exists, but it is a
> powerful barrier to the financial success of the club
> whose team is injured by drunken players among them.

> As for the class of habitual drinkers they should be
> driven from the ranks of the fraternity forever, just as
> Jim Devlin, Al Nichols, Bill Craver, and others were for
> their proved dishonesty.

Tales of the King

The White Stockings were playing Detroit one day, with the score 2-2 in the 9th and Stump Weidman pitching for the Wolverines. Kelly beat out a bunt and Williamson walked. The two then engineered a double steal, but as Kelly slid into third he howled with pain and called time. Williamson rushed over to help his teammate. As he approached Kelly, Mike said, "Ned for the love of heaven, pull my arm. Faith, I think it's out of joint." Williamson proceeded to pull, and as he did so, Kelly whispered to him from under his mustache, "Say Ed, soon as Weidman raises his arm I'm going to break for home. You sneak along behind, see. They'll play for me, sure and forget about you. But when I'm close, I'll straddle my legs and you slide under." Kelly then returned to third, still writhing in pain; Williamson resumed his position at second. In a second Kelly was roaring down the base path, and even Weidman was fooled by the miraculous recovery of the injured player. Kelly closed to within ten feet of home plate before Weidman, still unbelieving, threw the ball to catcher Charlie Bennett, who made ready to tag Mike. By that time Williamson, who later confessed he had cut third by some 15 feet, was near at hand. Bennett had the ball and was waiting for Kelly, but the King stood still and Williamson dove through his legs for the winning run. Today, Williamson would be called out for passing the runner in front of him.

Devlin, a star pitcher for Louisville in the National League's first two seasons, was bounced out for drunkenness and dishonesty, and he died destitute at 34; a symbol to all players to practice temperance.

Chicago III

The biggest promise that Spalding could offer Chicago fans for 1885 was that Clarkson would be available for the full season and that the White Stockings, two years removed from a championship, would not disappoint again.

Fred Goldsmith was through. He finished '84 with the Baltimore Orioles of the American Association but didn't get a contract with anyone for '85.

The other shock was the dispatching of Larry Corcoron to the Giants early in the season. A 35-game winner (with his third no-hitter) in '84 and the franchise's best pitcher since 1880, Corcoron, a tobacco-chewing workhorse, was suffering from a strained shoulder muscle. He would have no further success in baseball; not with the Giants, not with Washington in '86 or Indianapolis in '87, or in the minor leagues after that. In fact, he was suffering from Bright's Disease, which would claim his life in 1891 at the age of 32.

Corcoron's replacement was none other than Jim McCormick. After six years with Cleveland, he had jumped to the doomed Union Association in '84, and managed to get a contract with Providence for '85. At first, the National League's position was that they would not sign Union League jumpers, but fortunately for McCormick, they weakened and signed him and two others just before the '85 season began. Spalding then managed to get him over from the Grays in May when Corcoron was deemed useless and later released.

As good as the Chicagos had been in the years prior to 1883 with Corcoron and Goldsmith as the pitchers, the 1885-86 teams with Clarkson and McCormick were even better. Anson called them "the strongest team that I ever had under my management

but, taken all in all, one of the strongest teams that has ever
been gotten together in the history of the league...."

Perhaps learning his lesson from the late exhibition start of
the previous year, Chicago was the first team to begin play in
'85, defeating Louisville of the American Association 11-9 on
April 2, four weeks before opening day. They played a hefty
schedule of nine additional games that month as Anson whipped
his men into shape. Kelly and Gore remained his biggest problems when it came to late night carousing, and when McCormick
joined them the problem only worsened. Anson was no fan of his
big drinkers, but the talent pool was only so big, and Anson's
desire to win was bigger.

The team got off to a fast start, winning 14 of 20 in May. All
the more remarkable was that they lived out of suitcases and
played a full road schedule for the entire month and into early
June, awaiting completion of a new ball park to replace Lake
Front. They played 28 consecutive road games, and still would
have owned first place had they not lost three of four to the
Giants in New York, bringing the Giants to the top of the
standings with a 17-4 record.

The new ballpark, West Side Park, also called the Congress
Street Grounds, opened on June 6. The park was long and
narrow, 216 feet down the lines, and had a bicycle track sur-
rounding the field. Chicago beat St. Louis and One Arm Daily,
9-2, before a good-size and enthusiastic opening day crowd.

In their first month in their new home, the White Stockings
were not to be believed. They won 21 of 23 games, including an
18-game winning streak. They didn't lose a game at home until
June 25, 2-0 to Philadelphia. McCormick, new to the team,
began what would be a 14-game winning streak. Clarkson, on
his way to a fabulous season, would run up a 13-game win streak
during the campaign, which included a no-hitter over Providence on July 27. The combined 27-0 stretch, "unanswered
points" in modern basketball parlance, would prove insur-
mountable.

At the end of June, Chicago was 35-8, New York 32-9, two
games back. Providence, seeking to defend its title, was in third,
6-1/2 games back, and losing ground.

New York was managed by Jim Mutrie. (Who this year had
coined the nickname "Giants" when speaking of his big players.

"My boys are not only giants in stature but in baseball ability.")
Mutrie had managed the American Association's New York
team, the Mets, in previous years, winning the association
championship in '84. But he no doubt welcomed the opportunity
to move to the better field at the Polo Grounds in New York
where his team was not treated as secondary citizenry.

Mutrie inherited a future Hall of Fame pitcher in Smilin'
Mickey Welch and brought another one with him from the Mets
in Tim Keefe. They would win 44 and 32 respectively. The lineup
was also laced with Hall of Fame futures Roger Connor at first,
Jim O'Rourke in center, Buck Ewing catching, and John
Montgomery Ward at short. The National League was enjoying
a maturity in terms of the caliber of its players.

Both New York and Chicago won 18 games in July. That put
it at 53-14 for Chicago, 50-16 for New York, both remarkable
winning percentages, and Chicago 2-1/2 games up. With more
than two months to go, this was already just a two-team race.

In August, New York was 18-3 to move to 68-19, while Chicago, 15-4, went to 67-18. The Giants won three of four from
Chicago early in the month to tie the standings before pulling
ahead, the final game being a 12-0 romp on August 10 which left
the Giants fans full of belief in their new powerhouse as they
exited the Polo Grounds. Huge crowds were watching their
games, including a record 13,427 on August 1, when they beat
Chicago 7-6.

Once again, Chicago was having its problems on the road. One
could argue that the night life of New York was taking its toll on
the likes of Kelly, McCormick, Gore, Williamson, Flint, and the
bunch. Still, even when at home, you could usually find them
down at Mickey Finn's Lone Star Saloon, hardly observing
training rules.

The good news for Chicago was that if they remained close,
they had a great chance to win the pennant. They closed the
season at home with four games against the Giants. The potential was there to make up even a four game deficit.

Sure enough, going into the series, anyone could turn it into
a pennant. Chicago was 83-21, New York 81-23, two games back.
While four games would remain after this series (New York
would play St. Louis and Chicago would play Philadelphia),
everyone felt that these would be decisive.

The first game was played on Tuesday afternoon, September 29. The Giants made their way from the Clifton House to West Side Park in the manner of the day, parade-like, with crowds lining the streets to howl and hoot at the enemy. The practice was encouraged as an attendance builder, but one hardly had to get the Chicago faithful into the spirit for these games.

The rides from the hotels to the ballparks, intended to rouse the fans' interest, were usually fun; sometimes the rides back were dangerous. One year in Detroit, the White Stockings were on their way back to their hotel when their carriage became the target of stones along Woodward Avenue. Anson told his troops to keep their heads low, but as he was speaking, the captain himself was pelted by a pellet of chewing tobacco, right in the face.

Burns and Kelly immediately leapt from the carriage and began swinging their fists in the crowd. Burns got a broken wrist in the melee; Kelly survived.

Chicago was at full strength, with Anson, Pfeffer, Burns, and Williamson in the infield, Dalrymple, Gore, and Kelly in the outfield, Flint catching, and Clarkson and McCormick on the mound. The only substitutions came when Kelly relieved Flint behind the plate, and Billy Sunday played right. Kelly's bat was hot, but he was having trouble catching and would be charged with six passed balls during the four game series, even with limited action behind the plate.

The Giants had an infield of Connor, Joe Gerhardt, Ward, and Danny Richardson, with Pete Gillespie, O'Rourke, and Mike Dorgan in the outfield, Ewing catching, and Welch and Keefe pitching. Connor was on his way to the league's batting title, with Dorgan third. Dalrymple and Kelly were 1-2 in home runs. Anson and Kelly were 1-2 in runs batted in. Kelly and O'Rourke were 1-2 in runs scored. Welch, Clarkson, McCormick, and Keefe had the best pitching records in the league, and Clarkson and Welch were 1-2 in strikeouts. Anyone you would have wanted to see in 1885 was pretty much going to be playing ball at West Side Park in these four games.

An overflow crowd of some 10,000 cheered the White Stockings on to a 7-4 victory in the opener, as Kelly belted three triples. A three-game lead with seven to play.

On Wednesday, the 30th, the White Stockings won a thriller, 2-1, to go four up with six to play.

And on Thursday, October 1, it was Chicago again, this time 8-3. A five-game lead with five to play meant they had clinched a tie for first, running over the Giants in 72 hours of championship-level baseball excitement. The "magic number," a term not used in those days, was one. Any Chicago win or New York loss over five more games would wrap it up. And as far as the fans were concerned, wrapped up it was.

The park filled again on Saturday, October 3 after a scheduled off day, with the fans hoping to see the pennant clinched. Unfortunately, the Giants were not about to be swept, and they salvaged the final game, 12-8.

For the four games, Kelly and Dalrymple had each come through with seven hits off Welch and Keefe to lead all batters, with Kelly scoring 5 of Chicago's 25 runs. His fielding was sloppy, but he was an offensive key to the Chicago success and the pride in the White Stockings was back.

Three days later, in their next games, the Giants lost to St. Louis 7-4, and Chicago, playing at home, beat Philadelphia 9-4 to win the 1885 National League pennant. How they celebrated the night away! The fact that they lost the final three games to Philadelphia may be indicative of their hangovers, and in the end, they won the flag by two games over New York, who managed to win their last three when it no longer mattered.

Kelly hit only .288 for the season, 17th in the league and third on the club, but led the league with 124 runs scored in only 107 games. Stolen bases were still not a compiled statistic, but it is likely he ran wild on the bases to run up such a total.

His nine home runs were second only to Dalrymple's 11, and his 74 RBIs second only to Anson's remarkable 114. Clarkson had a sensational year off the pitching plate, appearing in 70 of the team's 112 games, with a 53-16 record, a 1.85 earned run average, 308 strikeouts in 623 innings, ten shutouts and a no-hitter.

A championship series of games had been played in 1884 between Providence (NL) and the New York (AA) team (led by Mutrie), with the Grays winning all three games played in what is generally regarded as the first true "world series." Now, Chicago was ready to take on the champions of the American

Association, Charles Comiskey's St. Louis Brown Stockings, who had won their pennant by an easy 16 games. This one was called "The United States Championship" in the '86 *Spalding Baseball Guide;* "world" being too pretentious for what it truly was (but of course, hardly any more so than it is today).

The championship, on the surface, was to be a showcase of top flight baseball for the benefit of the Association. It was intended to bring the mighty White Stockings to Association cities to enhance the game in those towns and, with any luck, provide some proud moments for the Browns.

Anson and Comiskey worked out a schedule of 12 games, with only the first, on Wednesday, October 14, to be played in Chicago. There would then be three in St. Louis, followed by a five-day interruption while the Browns played the St. Louis Maroons of the National League for the "city championship." Imagine!

The "United States Championship" would then resume on the 22nd at the neutral Association site of Pittsburgh, followed by two games in Cincinnati, one in Baltimore, two in Philadelphia, and two in Brooklyn, bringing the series to a conclusion on October 31. At least these were the grand plans.

Anticipating a modest fan reaction, the owners put up a winner-take-all purse of $1,000 to be distributed among the players: less than $100 a man for nearly a month of extra play, with nothing for the losers, but nevertheless, an incentive to play to win.

Unfortunately, the series was an embarrassment for both sides, and inferior umpiring made it hardly a model for the maturity of major league baseball.

The first game began with a carnival of stunts for the amusement of the spectators, not uncommon for the era, but perhaps demeaning to the magnitude of a championship series. Throwing and running contests were staged, with Fred Pfeffer circling the bases in 15.75 seconds to edge Kelly by half a second. Williamson had the longest throw—400 feet, 4 inches—a rather spectacular performance for the third baseman.

The game began at 3:15, and St. Louis ran up a 5-1 lead after four innings, Chicago's run provided by Kelly who singled and came around on two errors.

The White Stockings who won the coin toss and elected to bat first in their own park, came up in the top of the eighth with darkness falling. Bob Caruthers, the Browns's pitcher, gave up a walk to Gore (who was playing "under the influence"), and singles to Kelly and Anson. Pfeffer then hit a home run over the left field fence to tie the score.

Clarkson held the Browns scoreless in the last of the eighth, at which point the umpire, David Sullivan, called the game for darkness and ruled it a 5-5 tie.

Anson was furious. He felt his club was on the verge of victory. He also felt the team had not played as well as they should have against an inferior team from a lesser league in front of his hometown fans. Further, the performance of the drunken Gore so angered him that he suspended him for the balance of the series.

On a team of such heavy drinkers, this was a shocking move. But such was Anson's command that it went unquestioned. A lesser man might have faced the threat of a walkout by Gore's drinking buddies, Kelly among them. Young Billy Sunday was assigned to Gore's centerfield post.

Gore, a man of much ability, was breaking down. He would spend just one more year in Chicago and then Anson would be rid of him. "Women and wine brought about his downfall," Anson would later write. "The last time I saw him in New York he was broken down, both in heart and pocket, and willing to work at anything that would yield him the bare necessities of life."

The second game was a terrible show for baseball. The teams went by train to St. Louis and arrived early in the morning. At two o'clock, they arrived at Sportsman's Park, on Grand and Dodier, along with Sullivan, the umpire.

Three thousand fans turned out, a disappointing crowd. Chicago won the coin toss and batted first, and play began again at 3:15. McCormick pitched and Kelly caught (the old Paterson battery), with Clarkson in right. Kelly and Flint would alternate throughout the series behind the plate.

To the delight of the fans, the Browns scored three runs in the first. To Anson's obvious disgust, the Sox fielding just fell apart. There was a grounder through Williamson's legs, and a throw home by Pfeffer to Kelly that reached the plate with the runner long since on his way to the bench. A stolen base by Comiskey included a boot by Pfeffer on Kelly's delayed throw, and Commie

scored when Kelly was charged with a passed ball on a McCormick fastball.

As the game moved forward, a number of Sullivan's calls were
going against the Browns and the fans were getting hostile. In
the sixth, with St. Louis up 4-2, Sunday doubled and went to
third on a wild pitch. Kelly grounded to Kid Gleason at short
and was retired easily at first. But with Sullivan watching
Sunday score, and unable to keep his eyes on two places at once,
he called Kelly safe. For the next 15 minutes, Comiskey led a
huge, crowd-inciting rhubarb on the field, cursing Sullivan and
threatening to take his team off the field if the call wasn't
reversed. Sullivan gave Comiskey two minutes to get his team
back in position, and took out a pocket watch to make his point.
He prevailed.

Anson came to bat and Kelly stole second. The captain then
singled to tie the game at 4-4. Pfeffer hit a pop to short right
which was dropped by Hugh Nicol, but recovered in time to force
Anson at second. Pfeffer then stole second and went to third on
a passed ball.

Up came Williamson. He grounded foul beyond first, but the
ball spun back into fair territory. Comiskey fielded it and threw
to first, but Williamson beat the throw as Pfeffer scored, making
it 5-4 Chicago.

Now realizing what had happened, Comiskey claimed that
Sullivan had already shouted "foul ball" and that even though
he had played it, the ball should be considered foul and Pfeffer
returned to third base.

Sullivan agreed, which was the correct ruling. But this
brought Kelly and Anson out onto the field, and, in modern terms
"into Sullivan's face."

Properly intimidated, poor Sullivan then switched his call
again, allowing the run to score. Bedlam! The police had to jump
onto the field as some 200 fans cleared the fences and headed
for the hapless umpire. The outpouring of the 200 led to a second
wave. The White Stockings, sensing physical danger, grabbed
their bats to stand ready with weapons if need be. The police
escorted Sullivan and the White Stockings from the field and to
their hotels. The game was over. Perhaps the whole series
should have been over.

That night, Sullivan decreed (from the safety of his hotel

room), that the game be forfeited to Chicago, as St. Louis had left the field.

Comiskey, burning, reminded the press that games were to be decided on the field, not from the hotel room of a weak umpire, and that it was actually Chicago which had abandoned the field first.

Sullivan admitted that he had had an "off day."

For all the shouting, it now stood, one tie, and one forfeit for Chicago. Some series.

For game three, the next day, Sullivan was replaced by Harry McCaffrey, a former American Association pitcher, acceptable to Anson.

In the first inning Gleason singled for St. Louis and Curt Welch hit a pop to Kelly in right. Mike dropped the ball, but managed to force Gleason out at second. An error by Dalrymple in left allowed Welch to score and instead of there being three out, St. Louis went on to a five-run inning, and won the game 7-4. One suspects that it was a good idea to avoid eye contact with Anson after this one.

The fourth game found Anson now refusing McCaffrey as umpire, and instead, settling on William Medart, a local fan who was in the stands to watch the game. And this was the world series!

Medart, having witnessed the Sullivan show in game two, seemed to make every call in favor of the Browns. Anson at this point, might not have even cared. In fact, he decided to rest Clarkson from outfield duty, and handed the position to a 17-year old amateur named James "Bug" Holliday, the only amateur to ever appear in a world series game. Holliday, who would eventually have a pretty good major league career, was 0-for-4 on this day with an error. Does the word *mockery* come to mind?

Trailing 3-2 in the ninth, Burns reached on an error with one out. Comiskey then dropped a popup behind first off McCormick's bat, and Chicago had two on.

Before returning the ball to his pitcher, Comiskey playfully tagged McCormick at first. Jim clearly had one foot on the bag, but Medart, to everyone's amazement, including Comiskey's, called him out!

McCormick turned angrily on the amateur ump, but Anson quickly ran out and stepped between them. Sunday, who had not yet found salvation and became an evanglist, curled up his fists and threatened to hit Medart. Only Kelly's intervention prevented him from doing so. And who should be the final batter in this 3-2 world series game?

Bug Holliday, 17, who fouled to third. Two wins for St. Louis, one tie, one forfeit for Chicago. Ugly.

Game five, on the 22nd, was played in Pittsburgh, but only about 500 fans turned out, a huge disappointment, and hardly worth the trip. The National League's respected "Honest John" Kelly, Mike's buddy, was brought in to umpire the rest of the series. And the fifth game was won by Chicago 9-2 on a four-hitter by Clarkson which was called after 7:00 P.M. due to darkness.

The sixth game was played before 1,500 fans in Cincinnati and Chicago won again by a score of 9-2 despite sloppy fielding by Anson, who made four errors. Prior to the game, facing diminishing interest and an embarrassment to the game's good name, it was announced that the series would end with the seventh game, the following day, October 24.

With the two 9-2 Chicago victories, the series now stood two legitimate (?) victories each, one tie, and the game two forfeit which had been awarded to Chicago. If that was to be recognized as a Chicago win, the White Stockings would now go into game seven up 3-2.

On the evening of the 23rd, Comiskey and Anson met. They came out of the meeting agreeing that the forfeit in game two would instead be a "no contest," that the series was now tied 2-2, and that the seventh game would be the decisive one. Anson now had his team playing well, a good umpire out there, and the confidence that his team would win. "We will not even claim the forfeited game," he said to the press. "We each have two victories now and the winner of today's game will be the winner of the series." Twelve hundred people showed up for the big game.

One would not think that Clarkson would show up for the championship game five minutes after it began on the day he was to pitch, but he did. And of course, he found McCormick in the pitcher's box, as he had been the day before. Anson must have been beside himself to have his 53-game winner a no-show at game time.

In the first, Sunday singled, Kelly doubled, and Anson reached on an error to put Chicago up 2-0. But then St. Louis unloaded on McCormick for four in the third and six in the fourth to go up 10-2 as Anson looked on helplessly, perhaps tearfully. Cap himself made two errors, Williamson made a wild throw, and Flint had two passed balls in the fourth inning alone. The box score showed 17 Chicago errors, although passed balls and wild pitches were usually so credited. Eliminating the three charged to McCormick and the three to Flint, the team still made at least 11 errors in this championship showing. (In fairness, St. Louis made ten, five charged to its battery.)

By the end of the long afternoon, St. Louis had a 13-4 championship victory, delivering 13 hits off McCormick, who also walked three and struckout but a single batter. Kelly's two doubles were the only extra base hits managed by Chicago. McCormick, pounded, proved to be a decent sport, responding to a fan's cry of "buckle up your harness, Mac" with a broad smile.

So did St. Louis divide up the $1,000 purse?

Well, not exactly.

Chris Von Der Ahe, the autocratic owner of the Browns, met with Spalding after the game and decided that, well, yes, that second game was actually a Chicago forfeit after all, and thus the series ended in a 3-3-1 tie, with no champion. How convenient. Poor Spalding and Von Der Ahe would thus be unable to award the purse, and would have to keep their $500 each. They certainly could have divided the money among both teams, even at less than $50 a man. Comiskey was a victim; he was out his ninety bucks, or whatever the share would have been. But when he later became a club owner—with the Chicago White Sox of the American League—he too would take his place among the game's tightwads, with a salary scale so paltry that most consider it the very root of the Black Sox scandal of 1919.

What a horrible show was the 1885 United States Championship. And there could be no doubt that players of good education, like John Montgomery Ward of New York, were paying close attention to these doings.

Providence and Buffalo were out of the National League in 1886, the league's tenth anniversary season, replaced by the Washington Statesmen (for whom Connie Mack would play), and the Kansas City Cowboys. Detroit managed to secure the "Big Four" from Buffalo—White, Rowe, Richardson and Brouth-

ers—greatly changing the makeup of the team and its competitive strength in the league.

It would now take only six balls to receive a walk, and Anson
pushed across a rule change saying that the home team did not
have to announce its lineup prior to the game, giving him a
chance to see how his first inning went before deciding who
should bat. It would also be the first year in which stolen bases
were officially logged.

To the roster, Anson added a pitcher named John "Jocko"
Flynn, a 21-year old "one year" wonder who would go 24-6 with
a 14-game winning streak in his only major league season. "His
arm gave out while he was with us," wrote Anson, "and besides
that he got into fast company and, attempting to keep up the
clip with his so-called friends, found the pace much too rapid for
him and fell by the wayside." Do we see the hand of Kel in here?

Rather than work out indoors at a Chicago gymnasium or play
exhibitions in chilly weather against American Association
teams, Anson introduced a most revolutionary training concept
prior to the 1886 season. He took his team south for spring
training. It was the first foray into the American South for a
major league team and remains, of course, one of the game's
most enduring and endearing rituals. Anson selected Hot
Springs, Arkansas, as the site for his preseason conditioning,
becoming the first manager to make the southern preseason
journey an annual ritual.

Prior to departing, Spalding gathered his team together at
his sporting goods store on Madison Street, both to wish them
well and to have them raise their hands in a solemn oath that
they would practice temperance. Anson administered the "oath."
In an act that would create great acrimony in the months to
come, Spalding further proclaimed that he was withholding
$250 from the pay of Kelly and McCormick as an "incentive" for
them to curtail their drinking. Should they play through the
year sober (fat chance), they would receive the money back as a
"bonus" at the end of the year.

While there was no major league competition for the White
Stockings to play, the training camp was considered to be a
success, and the team headed north to provide the competition
for Kansas City's home debut in the National League on April
29. (This would be the one and only National League opener for

this one-year franchise; the game itself was rained out and played on the 30th.)

The three game series thus found the White Stockings out of town when, on May 1, the city of Chicago was witness to a major labor demonstration, as 40,000 workers, armed with anger and signs, marched through the streets calling for an eight-hour workday. The White Stockings home opener was not until May 6, but 32 hours before, in the section of town known as Haymarket Square (on Randolph Street between Desplanes and Halstead), a bomb exploded killing seven policemen. It happened at 7:30 in the evening as the ballplayers were at dinner in St. Louis. Attention could hardly have been on opening day in the city of Chicago.

Chicago had been the center of the growing American labor movement, which began two years earlier and led to the formation of the American Federation of Labor in 1886. On May 3, a highly charged union meeting was held at McCormick Harvester where a strike was in progress. A frail line of police kept strikers from scabs as the factory struggled to remain in operation, but the protection broke down, one striker was killed, and tempers ran high. A meeting was called for the evening of the 4th to protest police brutality.

The rally began quietly, with only about 3,000 on hand to hear a series of speeches from men identified in the press as "mostly communists and anarchists." The mayor, Carter Harrison, was there early and left, even stopping at the nearby police depot to say it was rather tame. But antilabor police captain "Black Jack" Bonfield sent his own men to disperse the gathering. Someone set off a bomb, and seven policemen died, with many injured. The Haymarket Square Riot remains an important part of the history of the American labor movement. Eight alleged anarchists were eventually convicted; seven were sentenced to hang, and four did. The trial, June 21 to August 20, would occupy much of Chicago's attention during the summer of '86. The baseball players, no doubt still talking about the lack of payment to the winning team in the '85 Series, must surely have been feeling the reaches of the movement under their noses.

The ballplayers of America were not a militant group in 1886, but the first stirrings of labor versus management were beginning to bubble.

John Montgomery Ward had earned a law degree from Columbia in 1885 and a political science degree the following year. He stood tall over his brethren when it came to intelligence, and he was the drafter of the charter of the National Brotherhood of Professional Base Ball Players in late 1885. While the Brotherhood fell short of stepping into America's budding labor movement, declining to join the Knights of Labor, there was a growing care among players for each other's treatment by management.

Said the charter, "[it] will protect and benefit its members collectively and individually, to promote a high standard of professional conduct, and to advance the interests of 'the National Game.'"

With the Brotherhood in place and the scepter of the Haymarket Square Riot looming over Chicago, the White Stockings went about the business of defending their 1885 pennant and looking for revenge in post-season play.

The '86 season was extended to 126 games, 18 against each of the seven opponents in the league, up from 112 games the year before.

Chicago won five of its first six, but the newly strengthened Detroits surpassed their May performance and finished the month 20-4 to Chicago's 18-4.

In St. Louis one day, demonstrating his affable banter with the cranks, Kelly told his Irish fans in the bleachers, "So yer Kerry Patchers, eh? Well, this is the twenty-fourth of May [Queen Victoria's birthday]. God save the Queen! I'm coming up yer way tonight and start an Orange lodge. I expect all of yez ter join up. Let me hand in your name!" Mike would move in and out of his position, whistling "The Boyne River," and occasionally removing a slip of paper and a pencil and saying to some fan, "Let me have your name, please." After the game, it kept all the police and ground help busy explaining to the Kerry Patchers that Mike was himself a Catholic, and was only kidding with them.

While Kelly was noted for his trickery, Anson was not above being a partner to it all if it could win him a game. One day in New York, McCormick was struggling with a tired arm. By the last inning, he had pretty much had it. But Anson had no relief to turn to and needed Mac to finish.

Anson picked a called strike to charge at the umpire from first base and begin an argument. It went on nearly ten minutes, at which point, Anson signalled to Kelly, the catcher, to "hurt your finger on the next one." With the next pitch, a ball, Kelly dropped to his knees and grabbed his finger. Forced to go to the clubhouse to care for himself, the game was delayed another ten minutes. Anson had his men toss the ball around while awaiting Kel's return, and what do you know, Pfeffer then got hurt too, and had to get some first aid. The end result—almost a 30-minute delay, a rested McCormick— and a Chicago win.

As July 4th approached, Detroit was 35-8, two-and-a-half games over Chicago; four-and-a-half over New York. By the end of the month, Detroit's lead had grown to four and a half over the White Stockings.

The White Stockings were taken by surprise in late July when Spalding hired detectives to follow his players, and seven of them were fined $25 each for excessive drinking. This action would most certainly include the men whose salary was with-held pending their good behavior. Trouble was "brewing."

Perhaps the most unusual story involving the temperance movement involved Billy Sunday himself.

One Sunday afternoon in the summer of '86, Billy sat with teammates at the corner of State and Madison in Chicago. Kelly was one. They were drunk. From across the street came a gospel choir, singing hymns that reminded Billy of his childhood. It was as though he was receiving a message from God.

He began to cry, rose, and accompanied the choir to the Pacific Garden Mission. To his teammates, he said, "Good-bye boys, I'm through. I'm going to Jesus Christ. We've come to a parting of the ways."

Well, not exactly. He continued to play for another four seasons, but he did clean up his act. He no longer drank, smoked, played cards, or attended vaudeville shows. He began delivering inspiration talks at local Y's, and the following year married a devout Presbyterian woman with whom he had four children. He went on to become the nation's best-known evangelist.

This story had a Kelly moment.

Wrote Sunday in his 1914 memoirs:

Twenty-seven years ago I turned and left that little group of the corner of State and Madison Streets and walked to the little mission and fell on my knees and staggered out of sin and into the arms of the Saviour.

The next day I had to get out to the ball park and practice. Every morning at ten o'clock we had to be out there. I never slept that night. I was afraid of the horselaugh that gang would give me because I had taken my stand for Jesus Christ.

I walked down to the old ball grounds. I will never forget it. I slipped my key into the wicket gate and the first man to meet me after I got inside was Mike Kelly...he said, "Bill, I'm proud of you! Religion is not my long suit, but I'll help you all I can." Up came Anson, the best ball player that ever played the game; Pfeffer, Clarkson, Flint, Jimmy McCormick, Burns, Williamson and Dalrymple. There wasn't a fellow in that gang who knocked; every fellow had a word of encouragement for me.

It was Kelly who broke the ice and led the way.

The White Stockings rallied for a 17-6 record in August and passed Detroit, building a two-and-a-half game lead. Thirty-three games remained for Anson's boys; but only nine would be at home, where they were traditionally very strong. Kelly's hitting and daring base running were keeping the Chicagos atop the league, but it would be another tough finish.

By September 20, the race was still up for grabs, and very close. On that day, the White Stockings, accompanied by a multitude of ardent fans and by their new boy mascot, traveled to Detroit for three big games. The fans carried brooms, symbolic of a "sweep" of the series, although Detroit was on an 18-game home winning streak.

Chicago promptly snapped the streak, winning the first game behind McCormick, but Detroit came back to win the next two. The race was virtually tied at this point. The teams both went to Chicago; this time with Detroit accompanied by some 500 loyal fans aboard a special train. But Chicago, tough at home, took all three games, for four clutch victories in six head-to-head meetings. It was nearly over.

It fell to Philadelphia to decide it. Fighting for third position most of the season, the Quakers were poised to serve as spoiler as the season wound down. And when the White Stockings left Philly after September 28 with just nine games left, it appeared the Detroit Wolverines and their Big Four were going to edge them out, the Quakers having done well at Chicago's expense. But Detroit followed Chicago into the City of Brotherly Love and lost two, won one, and tied one, and the White Stockings moved back in front.

Taking a respite from the tension of the race, Anson, through a local congressman, arranged for the White Stockings to visit the White House and meet President Cleveland, when the club went to Washington on September 30.

Anson then led his team from their hotel to the White House, where they were greeted by a presidential aide, Dan Lamont.

Kelly tells the story in his autobiography.

> President Cleveland wore a Prince Albert coat, tightly buttoned, and he looked much stouter than the photographs we had seen of him led us to believe. While Lamont was talking to him, Captain Anson was puzzling his brain for a few words to say, suitable for the occasion. But the President didn't give him or any of us a chance for formal words. He was as affable and as courteous as it was possible for a man to be.
>
> "President Cleveland, this is Captain Anson, of the Chicago Base Ball Club," said Colonel Lamont.
>
> "I'm happy to meet you, Captain Anson. You have the champion ball club, I believe."
>
> Anson gripped his hand. Then I was the second man to be introduced. The President's hand was fat and soft. I squeezed it so hard that the President winced. Then George Gore did the same. Burns gave the President another warm grip, and Dalrymple did likewise. When it came to McCormick, the President's good right hand was almost doubled up. McCormick shook his hand warmly; so warmly indeed, that President Cleveland

looked glad and happy when it was all over. He would
rather shake hands with one thousand people than two
ball nines, after that day. He conversed with us for a good
half hour. He spoke of early days in Buffalo, when he
used to be a great admirer of base ball, and how, when
young, he used to toss the ball himself, occasionally. He
said laughingly, that he was so stout then that he didn't
think there was a fat man's nine in the country which
would care to make him a member. The President didn't
shake hands again when we parted. He remembered the
grip of a few minutes before. He wished us all good luck
and prosperity. He impressed me as being a charming,
courteous gentleman, who has considerable backbone,
and democratic enough to be a Democratic President of
our glorious country.

Kelly's tale may well explain why White House visits by
baseball teams pretty much ceased to exist until the Nixon
administration.

The season went to the final day. Chicago was 89-34, Detroit
87-34. Chicago's final game was to be in Boston and Detroit was
back in Philadelphia with a doubleheader, the first game to be
played in the morning.

The White Stockings waited at their Boston hotel for news of
the game in Philly. It came by telegraph; Philadelphia, behind
Charlie Ferguson, had won. Chicago was now ahead by 1-1/2
games, and only a Detroit win and a Chicago loss in the afternoon would cut the lead to a half game and force Detroit to play
their one remaining makeup game to go for a tie.

It wasn't necessary. Chicago took care of that themselves by
beating Boston to win a second straight pennant and their fifth
in Kelly's seven years with the club. Ferguson, going for his 30th
win, beat Detroit anyway for good measure. (Ferguson, who was
99-64 in four seasons, died just before opening day of 1888 of
typhoid pneumonia. He was only 25.)

In the end, Chicago had a 90-34 mark, a terrific .726 winning
percentage, and a two-and-a-half game edge over Detroit, who
played .707 ball themselves. New York was third, Philadelphia
fourth, but not close. Boston, in fifth, suffered 30-1/2 games back.

Anson had a new suit of clothes sent to every member of the Philadelphia club with his compliments.

Kelly and Anson carried the day for Chicago. Cap hit .371 with a sensational 147 runs batted in, while Kelly hit .388 for the National League batting title. It was as we now know, his second, but of course, all believed it to be his first at the time.

What added to Kelly's grand season was his daring baserunning, leading to a league-leading 155 runs scored, 53 stolen bases, and his wonderful versatility. He played 56 games in the outfield, 53 behind the plate, 9 at first, 6 at second, 5 at short and 8 at third. It was one of the few times in which one could argue that a utility man had won a batting title.

The defense of the club was weak, with Anson, Pfeffer, Williamson, Flint, and Clarkson all leading the league in errors— five of the nine positions on the diamond. But the team scored 900 runs, 345 more than their opponents.

Clarkson was 35-17 with 340 strikeouts, completing 50 of his 55 starts. McCormick was 31-11 and ran off a 16-game winning streak early in the season. Flynn, of course, added his surprising 24-6 season.

Meanwhile, in the American Association, the St. Louis Browns were playing a remarkable season of 175 games including exhibitions, and ran away with another pennant, besting second place Pittsburgh by 12 games. Dave Foutz was 41-16; Bob Caruthers 30-14, and when he wasn't pitching, Caruthers led the team with a .334 batting average while playing the outfield.

Would there by a rematch of the '85 championship? On September 26, Chris Von Der Ahe wrote Al Spalding:

Dear Sir:

The championship season is fast approaching an end, and it now seems reasonably sure that the Chicago White Stockings and St. Louis Brown Stockings will win the championship of their respective associations. I therefore take this opportunity of challenging your team, on behalf of the Browns, for a series of contests to be known as the World's Championship Series. It is immaterial to me whether the series be composed of five,

seven or nine games. I would respectfully suggest, however, that it would be better from a financial standpoint
to play the entire series on the two home grounds, and
not travel around as we did last season. I would like to
hear from you at your earliest convenience, in order that
the dates and other details may be arranged. I am yours
respectfully,

C. Von Der Ahe
St. Louis
September 26, 1886

Even before clinching the pennant on the last day, Spalding
accepted the challenge. It was arranged to make it a best-of-
seven series, with three in Chicago, three in St. Louis, and the
seventh, if necessary, on neutral grounds, perhaps Cincinnati.
In the event of a four-game sweep, a fifth game would be played
for exhibition purposes. The winner (ahem) would take all prize
money.

The first game was scheduled for Chicago on October 18. The
Browns arrived from St. Louis by train, a banner reading, ST.
LOUIS BROWNS CHAMPIONS OF 1885 AND 1886, hanging on its side.

To the musical accompaniment of Austin's First Regiment
Band, the Browns took the field before 5,000 chilly, but heckling
spectators at 3:00 P.M. One umpire was in place.

Chicago got two in the first off Foutz and that was all they
needed as Clarkson hurled a 5-hit shutout and Chicago won 6-0.
Kelly caught, batted second, and went one-for-four.

In the second game, three umpires were used for the first
time. Two were positioned behind home plate—one to call balls
and strikes, the other to handle all other calls. The third man
was stationed behind the pitcher. He was called a referee and
would be asked to decide matters not decided unanimously by
the two men behind home. A novel experiment.

With the warmer weather, 9,000 packed the Congress Street
Grounds to watch McCormick face Caruthers, the 138-pound
wonder of St. Louis. This time it was again a one- sided affair,
St. Louis winning easily, 12-0, as Chicago managed just one hit,
a single by Gore, leading off the first inning.

Evidence of Kelly's heady play came in the first when speedy

Arlie Latham, sometimes called the "Association's answer to Kelly," stole second with Caruthers at bat. When Caruthers struck out, Kelly dropped the ball, perhaps intentionally. Instead of throwing to first, he fired it to Pfeffer at second, who tagged out the daydreaming Latham. Kelly was 0-for-4 in the game, now 1-for-8 in the series, but as always, his play was team play, not individual. He had a lot of ways in which to beat you.

It was suggested that too much drinking and late night carousing was hurting Chicago after this embarrassing slaughter, and both Anson and Pfeffer had to publicly issue denials.

The third game, the final one of the season in Chicago, had Clarkson against Caruthers, who had asked Comiskey to pitch again. But again, it was one-sided, this time in favor of Chicago, 11-4, and they took a 2-1 lead in the series.

In the fourth inning, Yank Robinson stood on third for the Browns as Doc Bushong lifted a fly to George Gore in center field. After the catch, Robinson raced home. Gore fired in to Kelly, who received ball and Robinson at once, flying to the ground. Kel took a spike in the face amidst the pileup, but held on to the ball for the out to the screaming delight of the 6,000 fans. The next inning, Mike hit a home run to really get the crowd rolling.

The journey to St. Louis was notable in that Spalding chose not to accompany the team and McCormick was absent as well, "rheumatism" being listed as the cause. In the midst of the world championship series, Anson added a pitcher named Mark Baldwin and a catcher named Lew Hardie to his roster.

The fourth game, Clarkson against Foutz, was an 8-5 St. Louis victory, tying the series at 2-2. This game featured the first intentional walk in world series history, apparently ordered by Kelly in conversation at the mound with Clarkson while Tip O'Neill batted. Tip had hit two home runs in game two.

Back at the Lindell Hotel after the game, the Chicagos, excluding Anson, stood around smoking cigars, drinking champagne, and laughing with the press. Kelly was especially engaging. Clarkson, the losing pitcher, was in a great mood. The laughter caused more than a few raised eyebrows among the journalists.

The fifth game, as the second, was another embarrassment for Anson's men. With McCormick out, Anson decided to start Baldwin.

But Comiskey protested that "we're playing the '86 White Stockings, not some team of the future." Anson backed down, and could have used his rookie right fielder John Ryan, but instead, handed the ball to Ned Williamson who had pitched three innings all season. Ryan, at least, had pitched 23.

Williamson was no pitcher and the result was a 10-3 St. Louis victory, in which they jumped off to a 7-2 lead after three.

St. Louis led the series three games to two.

Rheumatism? Is that what bothered McCormick? What was going on here? Was Anson trying to extend the series to seven games, or was he trying to make light of the games in case Chicago lost.

The sixth game was played on October 23 before 10,000 fans at Sportsman's Park. Bob Caruthers would make his third start for the Brown Stockings and Clarkson would go for Chicago in their must-win effort. Kelly was behind the plate for the fifth time, Flint seemingly a forgotten man.

Spalding arrived from Chicago and talked Von Der Ahe into a 2:15 starting time so as to avoid calling the game early for darkness, as had occurred in games four and five.

Chicago jumped on top in the second on a walk to Pfeffer, a steal, a passed ball, and a single by Ryan. Pfeffer homered in the fourth for a 2-0 Chicago lead, and then in the sixth, it was Pfeffer again, scoring on a sacrifice fly by Williamson, to make it 3-0.

Clarkson, meanwhile, was at his best. He walked O'Neill in the first, but otherwise, had a no-hitter through six. St. Louis failed to score in the seventh when O'Neill broke up the no-hitter with a double, but was thrown out trying to stretch it to a triple.

In the eighth, Comiskey singled and Curt Welch, the center fielder, grounded to Tommy Burns at third. But Burns's throw to Anson went wild, putting runners on second and third. A sacrifice fly made it 3-1, and Clarkson then walked Bushong to put the tying runs on with Arlie Latham up.

Latham proceeded to hit a triple down the right field line just out of Dalrymple's reach, to clear the bases and make it a 3-3 game. St. Louis could now win the championship with one more run.

Neither team scored in the ninth, and the first extra inning game of the series was in order. In the tenth, Caruthers fanned Clarkson and got Gore and Kelly on flyouts. Kelly, despite his heady defensive play and earlier home run, was now just 5-for-24 in the series, a .208 showing—not much for the NL batting champion.

Curt Welch led off the last of the tenth. It was nearly 4:30 in the afternoon.

Welch was best known for his shallow defensive play in center field, for his umpire baiting, and for his hard-kicking play on the diamond. He drank heavily (including sips of beer during games, from bottles he would store beneath the outfield billboards in Sportsmen's Park), was crude and rough, and would in fact be dead of alcoholism just three years later. But he was about to have his moment of glory.

He was hit by Clarkson's first pitch to put the winning run on first. When Anson protested that he had made no attempt to get out of the way, the captain won the argument. Welch was sent back to bat.

Unfazed, he singled to center.

Foutz, the right fielder on nonpitching days, got an infield single sending Welch to second. Yank Robinson sacrificed the two men to scoring position.

Welch danced off third. Clarkson faced Bushong. Encouraged by Kelly, he tried to "quick pitch" Doc, but the ball sailed high over Mike's head. He barely got his gloved hand up in time to feel it grazing by.

Oh no! Here came Welch, and there went the ball. There was no point in chasing it—and Kelly didn't. Welch made a wholly unnecessary slide into the plate and raising himself from the cloud of dust, delivered the winning run and a St. Louis World Championship!

The St. Louis fans went wild. The play came to be known as the "$15,000 Slide," representing the winning share to be divided among the Browns players. (It was actually $13,920.10 or $580 a man; pretty good in the days of the $2,000 maximum salary.) The crowd stayed on the field and cheered each player as the dejected White Stockings began to depart for their hotel.

The Chicago players were quick to blame Dalrymple, who had failed to get Latham's big triple. Even Spalding said, "Dal ought to have caught that ball." He looked at Kelly as he spoke it, but Kel wouldn't take the owner's side, only saying "I don't know about his catching it."

Tales of the King

Said Fred Pfeffer of Kelly, "He was a creator....His strongest playing point was that he was always ready. He could take advantage of a misplay which others wouldn't see until afterward....He played the umpire as intelligently as he did the opposing nine. He would make a friend of him, engage his confidence, and in various ways get the best of close decisions.

"The greatest ball player who ever stepped upon the green was Michael J. Kelly, and the title of 'King Kel' is justly his. I have seen him make plays that others never dreamed possible, and many things he did with the Chicagos have never been duplicated, and I doubt if they ever will be. In every department of the game, batting, fielding, baserunning quickness, decision and judgement, he was the peer of them all. He played not by rules or instruction, but by instinct, and to him belonged the degree of perfection, that faculty known as base ball sense. I never knew Kel to hesitate in a close play. Before the play ever came up he seemed to have anticipated it, and instantly did the right thing."

The next day, the Browns played their National League rivals, the St. Louis Maroons, in an exhibition game. Many of the White Stockings stayed to watch it. In the fifth inning, play was halted so that a silver trophy and floral arrangement could be presented to the champions. Kelly, who was sitting with Williamson and Flint, went on the field and made the presentation.

"Ladies and gentlemen," he said. "It is my honor on this occasion to present to your champion club this floral tribute. They have earned it. They have beaten our club, the Chicago club, fairly [applause] and they have beaten us on the dead rattle [applause]. I can say you have treated us well here, and we hope to meet you again in the future. [Cheers].

Mike and Agnes left for a winter in Hyde Park, far from the baseball wars. Did he know at the time that he would never

Early drawing of Kelly, about age 22, with Chicago, circa 1880. (*National Baseball Library and Archive*)

William Hulbert, Kelly's first boss in Chicago, the owner of the White Stockings. (*National Baseball Library and Archive*)

Lake Front Park in Chicago, site of five championship teams during Kelly's term with the White Stockings. This is a view after its 1883 refurbishing, showing the "luxury suites" atop the grandstand. (*Harper's Weekly*)

Kelly's first season with Chicago, 1880, featured (clockwise from top) Cap Anson, Fred Goldsmith, Ned Williamson, Tommy Burns, Larry Corcoron, Tommy Beals, Joe Quest, and Silver Flint. In the center (clockwise) are George Gore, Mike Kelly, and Abner Dalrymple.

Anson, with bat, before his 1885 champions. Kelly, cap jauntily tipped, is seated at the left.

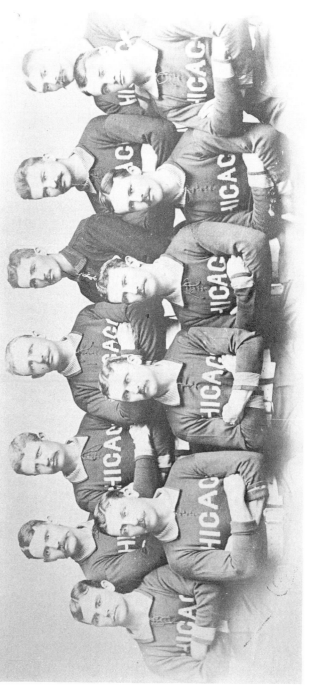

The 1886 champs. At the top (l-r): Gore, Flint, Anson, unknown, Kelly, Pfeffer. At the bottom (l-r): Corcoron, Williamson, Dalrymple, Burns, Clarkson, Sunday. The "unknown" player has been superimposed over Jim McCormick, perhaps in a fit of anger by Anson over Mac's inability to play in the post-season championship due to rheumatism. It could be Mark Baldwin, who replaced Mac in the series without having appeared in a regular season game. (*National Baseball Library and Archive*)

M. J. KELLY,
BOSTON BASE BALL CLUB.

141 TREMONT ST.
COR. WEST ST.
BOSTON. MASS

A portrait of Kelly shortly after he joined the Boston Beaneaters. (*Ken Felden*)

An unknown artist's portrayal of Kelly, circa 1887. (*National Baseball Library and Archive*)

The South End Grounds on Walpole Street in Boston, scene of some of King Kelly's greatest days. (*National Baseball Library and Archive*)

A series of three trading cards featuring Kelly.

The 1889 Boston Beaneaters. At the top (l-r): Joe Quinn, Tom Brown, Pop Smith, Dan Brouthers, Charles Ganzel, Charlie Bennett. Seated (l-r): Hardie Richardson, Ol' Hoss Radbourne, John Clarkson, manager James A. Hart, captain Mike Kelly, Dick Johnston, Billy Nash. At front (l-r): Bill Daley, Kid Madden. Note Kelly's catching gear on the ground. (*Ken Felden*)

The 1890 champion Boston Players League team. At the top (l-r): Charlie Bennett, Matt Kilroy, Dan Brouthers, Harry Stovey, Tom Brown, Joe Quinn. Seated (l-r): Billy Nash, Pop Sweet, Arthur Irwin, manager and captain Mike Kelly, Ol' Hoss Radbourne, Ad Gumbert, Hardie Richardson. Front (l-r): Bill Daley, Morgan Murphy, Kid Madden. (*Ken Felden*)

Boston fans presented Kelly with this horse and carriage when he returned as captain of the Cincinnati Red Stockings of the American Association on May 6, 1891. (*Ken Felden*)

This Agreement, made this *14* day of *April* 189*1*, between ~~the~~ *M. J. Kelly in behalf of the Cin* Base Ball Club, a corporation under the Laws of *Ohio the organized* _____ party of the first part, and *N. E. Mains* party of the second part, Witnesseth:

1st—Said party of the second part agrees to devote his entire time and services as a ball player to said party of the first part during the period of this contract.

2nd—Said party of the second part agrees to conform to all the rules and regulations now adopted or which may be hereafter adopted by the party of the first part, appertaining to his services aforesaid.

3rd—Said party of the second part agrees not to render any services as a ball player during the time of this contract to any other person, corporation or association, other than the party of the first part.

In consideration whereof the party of the first part agrees

1st—To pay to the said party of the second part the sum of $ *17,50* per year, to be paid in equal semi-monthly installments, upon the first and fifteenth of each and every month during the season, which shall commence April 1st and terminate November 1st of each year, unless the ball team shall be away from home, playing games, in which event the installments falling due, shall be paid within the first week after the return home of said ball team.

2nd—Said party of the first part agrees to pay the traveling expenses, board and lodging of said party of the second part whenever said party of the second part may be traveling in the service of said party of the first part and when not so traveling, the party of the second part will pay all of his own expenses; and the party of the second part agrees to furnish at his own expense his uniform and outfit as a ball player, the same to be designated by the party of the first part, and in case the party of the first part shall pay for the uniform and outfit, it shall have the right to deduct the amount so expended from the salary of the party of the second part.

This contract shall be in force during the year *1891* .

In Witness Whereof, The party of the first part has caused ~~its seal to be~~ ~~hereto affixed and~~ these presents to be subscribed by *W. J. Kelly* of the said Club, and the said party of the second part has hereunto set his hand and seal this _____ day of _____ 18____

and said Kelly shall have the right to transfer this contract to said corporation when organized

In Presence of

H. C. Bancroft

Cincinnati BBC

By *M. J. Kelly*

N. E. Mains

Kelly's contract with the ill-fated 1891 Cincinnati "Kelly's Killers" team of the American Association. The $1,750 payment, which makes no mention of his additional duties as manager, includes the standard clause whereby the player had to pay for his own uniform. Kelly's signature is one of sports' most coveted autographs today. (*Leland's Auction House*)

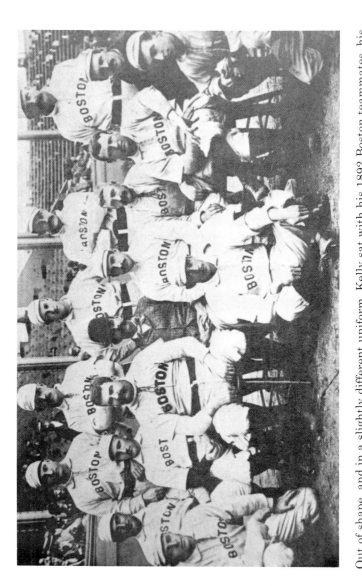

Out of shape, and in a slightly different uniform, Kelly sat with his 1892 Boston teammates, his last championship team. Hugh Duffy is on Kelly's right, and in street clothes, on his left, is manager Frank Selee. Clarkson, in the dark sweater, is at the far right.

The Elks cemetery plot at Mt. Hope in Mattapan, and Kelly's grave. (*Marty Appel*)

St. James the Greater on Harrison Avenue, as seen today. It was the site of the funeral service on November 11. (*Marty Appel*)

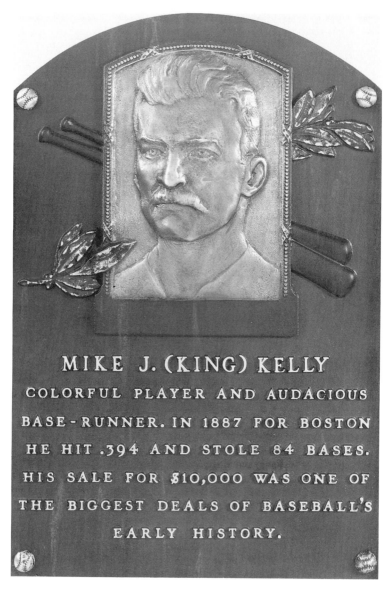

MIKE J. (KING) KELLY

COLORFUL PLAYER AND AUDACIOUS
BASE-RUNNER. IN 1887 FOR BOSTON
HE HIT .394 AND STOLE 84 BASES.
HIS SALE FOR $10,000 WAS ONE OF
THE BIGGEST DEALS OF BASEBALL'S
EARLY HISTORY.

Kelly's Hall of Fame plaque, 1945. (*National Baseball Library and Archive*) again wear a Chicago uniform? Did he know that the $15,000 Slide would lead the way to the $10,000 Beauty?

The Sale

The serenity of Hyde Park, with its ice fishing, tobogganing, snow-shoeing, and horseback riding should have served as a welcome respite to Kelly after the season. At first glance, the thought of Mike and Agnes relaxing on her brother's farm, hardly presents an image of the Kelly we know. Picturing Mike taking a leisurely ride on a horse-drawn carriage up the state road, a narrow and curvy dirt road which is today Route 9, conjures up the image of a retired country squire, not a 28-year-old hard-drinking ballplayer.

Still, that is where Mike chose to spend his winters. And there he could be found at the Hyde Park Club with its billiards, or at Pop Hornung's to tell baseball tales to the locals, or at dances with Agnes at the firehouse.

Trouble had been brewing in the minds of many key parties within the great Chicago organization. Anson, ever the stern disciplinarian, was growing increasingly weary of his player's late-night activities. Kelly, indeed, would occasionally miss a game, or simply take the field drunk. One day he muffed a fly-ball in right, and cheerily said to Anson at first, "By God, Cap, I made it hit me hand anyhow!" Cap would not have been amused.

Spalding was always more tolerant. He didn't have to live it day-to-day on the road. He saw Kelly as his best gate attraction, both at home and on the road, and Mike was, arguably, the game's best player. The .388 average in 1886 had brought his career mark to .315, tied for fifth on the all-time list, which now covered eleven seasons. Ahead of him were only George Gore (.326), Roger Connor (.337), Dan Brouthers (.349) and Anson (.350).

But the loss to St. Louis, a huge moral victory for the American Association and as equally huge an embarrassment for the National League, weighed heavily on Spalding. It was time to listen to Anson's pleas. He told Spalding of the breakdown of discipline, marked by McCormick's inability to play in the series, the poor performance by Kelly, the suspension of Williamson, and overall defensive lapses by many of the team's stars. If Spalding would go along with him, Anson was prepared to remake the club with more sober men and restore its glory.

If Kelly truly wanted to remain in Chicago, he didn't help matters. He was still bitter over being fined back in July after being trailed by the detective into the Clark Street saloons. He had boastfully set the press straight when the report was "cleaned up" for public consumption by stating that his infraction was being out too late drinking lemonade. He retorted, "I have to offer only one amendment. In that place where the detective reports me as taking a lemonade at 3 A.M., he's off. I never drank a lemonade at that hour in my life! It was straight whiskey!"

After a bad game a few days later, Kelly played his performance on "too much temperance."

A few weeks later, Mike mistook a stranger at a train station for yet another Anson detective and walloped him. He boarded the train feeling much better about himself, only to learn that he was not being followed at all. Late in the season, Kelly told Spalding, "I'm going up to Hyde Park for the winter. If I'm not a member of some other club next season, you will find that farming is good enough for me during the summer. I will not play again in the Chicago club, under any circumstances, and don't you forget it."

What was only publicly discovered after the season was the $250 Spalding had withheld from Mike's 1886 salary of $2,000, promising to restore it should Kelly stay sober during the year. That was of course, impossible. And so Mike played for $1,750 while winning the batting title and leading the White Stockings back into the world series, all the while influenced by the growing antimanagement sentiments being heard all around Chicago since the Haymarket Square riot. The $250 was finally paid back to Mike at the end of the season as a "bonus for winning the League championship."

The White Stockings began to break apart. Said Spalding, "we shall no longer endure the criticism of the respectable people because of drunkenness in the Chicago nine." Gore was released to the New York Giants. Dalrymple and McCormick were sold to Pittsburgh, which was to replace Kansas City in the National League for 1887. With the departure of Gore and Dalrymple, two-thirds of the regular outfield was gone. The lone survivor was Kelly, who was of course, also the team's change catcher.

On December 27, Kelly sent a letter to Spalding. He was bitter over the withholding of part of his salary and, now, over the general treatment he was hearing about. He wrote,

> I cannot understand why you think it necessary to speak of me in such a belittling style whenever you find an opportunity to do so. Certainly you can say that I will play with you next season if the saying gives you any pleasure. Words cost but little, especially to the management of the Chicago club. But I think it altogether unnecessary for you to take pains to lead the public to think I cannot survive without your well known generosity. Again, I fail to see why you think it necessary to always speak unkindly of me. I have always done a man's part for the success of your club. That you have paid me much or little, early or late, in parts or whole, I understand it. It is nobody's concern but our own. Every poor man's capital is his ability, and if this is not made the most of by the owner of it, then he is a fool. I have played ball for you for much less than I could have had anywhere else, but did not shirk from my knowledge of this fact. I have never taken one advantage of you, while you have taken advantage of me. This fact could be shown in many ways. I have told you that I would not play ball with you, and I will not.

Spalding professed surprise at the letter. "I always thought that Kelly was satisfied with the treatment he received here," he told a reporter from the Chicago *Herald,* as the feud began to play out in the daily press. "But I am determined that there be no drinking on our club, no matter what the consequences are, and all the players must be treated alike in that respect."

Spalding said he answered Kelly's letter in a "kindly manner" and argued with him in the hope that he would alter his decision. "His silence led me to infer that he was determined not to play with us. We could keep him off the field entirely this year, but we will not do that."

In his planning, Spalding was already thinking of getting Jack Glasscock from the St. Louis Maroons to fill the catching spot. He still had the aging Flint and a rookie, Tom Daly, a 21-year old prospect from Philadelphia (who would go on to play 16 years, mostly with Brooklyn.) So too, did Boston have their eyes on Glasscock.

If Kelly did any daydreaming about playing for another team, his two prime candidates would have been New York and Boston.

New York was "home." He still had a residence in nearby Paterson, his wife was from there, and he had opened a saloon on Sixth Avenue and 30th Street in Manhattan with Honest John Kelly called, "The Two Kels." New York was the nation's largest city, had plenty of vaudeville and stage opportunities for the dashing Kelly, and would certainly be a place where he could laud his celebrity.

Boston was an equally strong candidate. It too had a theater industry, and it had a huge Irish population that would no doubt embrace Mike and his elegant style. He was already a very popular visiting player there and enjoyed some of his greatest games there. One might say that there was no telling how popular Kelly could be in Boston, or to paraphrase Reggie Jackson, circa 1976, "if I played in Boston, they'd name a candy bar after me."

On February 9, 1887, a report appeared in a Chicago newspaper stating that Mike Kelly, "the crack fielder and the leading spirit of the Chicago ball club, will not wear the uniform of the White Stockings next season, and that 'he hoped his arm would drop off,' if he should ever be persuaded to have anything to do with Spalding's nine."

To this, Spalding said,

I read the dispatch on my way to the store this morning, and regarded it then as I regard it now, the work of some newspaper man who was pushed for news. I do not believe Kelly ever said anything of the kind.

There have been a number of such dispatches published
of late. May not New York, or some other club wanting
Kelly's services, be directly or indirectly responsible
through a desire to make Mike dissatisfied with Chicago?

Possibly. But Mr. [John] Day of the New Yorks has
denied any such intention in a personal letter to me. The
New York public and the New York press undoubtedly
want Kelly, and as most of those dispatches have ema-
nated from New York, I am inclined to think them the
work of overzealous baseball editors in the metropolis.

"Could New York buy Kelly's release?" asked a reporter.
"No, sir. New York could not buy him at *any* price."
"Could any other club?"
"It depends on how badly they wanted him. I think you can
say however, that Kelly will play with Chicago next year. I stated
that belief some time ago and have not yet changed my mind."
Spalding was careful to focus the attention on New York so
that his credibility would hold up. Only at the end, when pressed
on other clubs, did he have to hedge, with "on how badly they
wanted him." He was already talking to Boston.
There was a certain irony in the conversations with the
Beaneaters. Spalding had been a pitcher for the Bostons in the
National Association from 1871 to 1875. He won 56 of 60 deci-
sions in that final season. With the formation of the National
League in 1876, Spalding personally engineered the move of
Boston's "Big Four" to the outstretched arms and deep pockets
of Hulbert in Chicago. Spalding persuaded Cal McVey, Ross
Barnes, and Jim White to join him in Chicago, and also coaxed
Anson and Ezra Sutton to move from Philadelphia. The four
from Boston came to been known as the Four Seceders.
Now, the management of the Bostons began to think of what
popularity Kelly could bring to them. J. B. Billings, one of the
owners, proposed buying Kelly in conversation with his partners, William Conant and Arthur Soden. They told Billings to
see what he could do—"Kelly's your boy," they said.
Telegrams began to move back and forth between Boston and

Chicago immediately after the new year. An offer of $5,000 was made to Spalding.

Spalding contacted Kelly and asked if he would consider being sold to Boston. In the meantime, Boston offered $7,500 to St. Louis for Glasscock, but the league's supervisory committee held up the transaction. Spalding was a member of the committee and thus helped stall for time while he was trying to peddle Mike.

Spalding told Billings it would take $10,000. Boston offered $9,000. Spalding replied that if Boston would make a bona fide offer of $10,000 and give him until mid-March to discuss it with his other shareholders, they could have Kelly. The timing wasn't good for Billings. He said the $10,000 would be okay, but he needed to know at once. On Friday afternoon, February 11, Spalding accepted the offer. On Sunday, the 13th, Billings left for Poughkeepsie, New York, to meet with Kelly and attempt to persuade him to sign. If Kelly didn't agree, all bets were off.

Kelly just didn't want "out" of Chicago; he wanted more money wherever he wound up. And from his earliest, youthful contract negotiations with Anson, we know he could drive a hard bargain.

On 9:30 A.M. on Monday, Valentine's Day, February 14, Billings, accompanied by Boston *Globe* sports editor Billy Sullivan, journeyed to the Nelson House in Poughkeepsie, a few miles down the Hudson from Hyde Park, where Kelly had agreed to meet. Kelly would describe Billings as "rather nervous at times, but good-hearted."

Billings asked Kelly to guess what his playing ability was rated by Chicago, in terms of sale price. "I don't want the Chicago club to make anything out of me," he said. Then he guessed $3,000.

"No," said Billings, "guess again."

Kelly raised his guesses by $500 increments, then gave up at $7,000. Billings then showed him Spalding's letter, accepting the terms of the sale.

The sale price of $10,000 was a previously unimagined figure. For sheer impact, it rivaled the free agent signing of Catfish Hunter in 1975, which was some $3 million, all for Hunter. In this case, Kelly's salary was still to be negotiated. And there still existed an agreement by which the "maximum" salary was $2,000.

Wrote Sullivan, a witness to history,

> They began a philosophical discussion on the value of
> ballplayers. Mike sat in the corner of the reading room
> and a right-fitting Prince Albert coat set off his finely
> built athletic figure, while he told why "diamonds cannot
> be bought with shoestrings." He toyed with a diminutive
> cane and puffed a cigarette. For an hour and a half the
> discussion went on. But just soon before noon it came to
> an end. Mr. Billings had come here to sign Kelly and was
> not going away without doing so.
>
> The contract was drawn up for two thousand dollars, the
> limit, and then Mr. Billings said that the Boston club
> wanted a picture of their new player and would pay well
> (three thousand dollars) for it.

"Well, I am with you," said Kelly to Sullivan. Billings got Kelly
to sign the contract with Sullivan as a witness. Said Billings,
"Ten thousand dollars is quite a sum for one player, isn't it? We
thought so, and considered the price decidedly high. Good things
come high, but we must have them."

The $3,000 for use of his picture in advertising was, of course,
a smokescreen—pure hogwash. It was simply a way around the
salary limit. Teams always used player's pictures as they
wished. But the solution was Solomon-like for the moment.

The reactions left much unspoken, particularly regarding the
place Kelly's lifestyle played in the dramatic decision to release
him to Boston.

Said Spalding:

> Of course I know that this will be a great surprise to
> everyone in view of what I have said. Still, I will explain.
> Although we received more money for his release than
> was ever before paid for a player, it was not the money
> that made us consent to his release. I have been inves-
> tigating the matter for some time, and I became con-
> vinced that Kelly would be of no use to us, even in case
> he consented to play with the Chicago club. He had
> worked himself into a sort of frenzy about the matter,

and had fully made up his mind not to play with Chicago. Boston has been after him for some time. Several weeks ago they made us an offer and we sent back word that they would have to raise it considerably. They did so, and now Kelly is theirs. I'll tell you another thing. Kelly had the captain's bee buzzing in his cap. He wanted to be captain, and that he could never be in Chicago as long as Anson was playing ball. In Boston, I understand, he stands a good show of being made captain of the team. Kelly has gone, but we have got a good price for him and that settles the matter. I'm mighty glad too, that the thing is settled at last.

Asked a reporter, "How much did Boston pay you for him?"

Said Spalding, "More than has ever been paid for a player before, and more, I believe than will ever be paid for a player again."

Said the writer, "It must have been about $10,000 then."

Spalding looked thoughtful for a moment, and then a contented smile crept over his face. "That's just exactly it," he said, "$10,000. Kelly was a rattling good player, but $10,000 is a pile of money, and since Kelly was determined to not play with us next year it looks to me as if we had made a pretty fair bargain."

The sale price and the salary made Kelly the first player whose celebrity rose on the basis of his earnings. (Soden had the certified check photographed and displayed in the press and in store windows.) The instances would become rare; Babe Ruth's $80,000 was the next heralded salary and then the $100,000 mark scaled by Joe DiMaggio. (Hank Greenberg was actually first, but the finances were complicated and not publicized.) Then came Catfish Hunter's breakthrough free agent contract for 1975, Nolan Ryan signing the first guaranteed million dollar contract, and now the annual lifting of the unbelievable by a million or so seemingly each winter. But Kelly-Ruth-DiMaggio-Hunter pretty much defined the "shock value" pacts that made all America stand and notice.

Kelly sent a telegraph to a good Boston friend, Nat Goodwin, an actor, with the big news: "I shall play in your town all next summer."

The amount of the sale price amazed Kelly, but he said:

Well, that beats me, but take my dying oath, I'll play hard enough to be worth every cent of it to you. Why, I can do as much playing as two men. I'm not one of your fancy players who can catch today but will have to lay off tomorrow to get in condition. I play every game and when I ain't catching I'm always ready to fill some other place. I was taught to play for every man in the Chicago club, and last year I played in all but two or three games, I've forgotten which. [It was six]. That man Anson is all terror. Why, he made me go in and catch when my hands were in frightful condition. I could hardly hold the ball, but it made no difference; I had to play all the same.

Asked how he liked the idea of being captain (John Morrill already was), he hesitated. But told that Morrill wanted him to be field captain, he "expressed his delight at the confidence shown in him and said the team was "bang up" and offered the opinion that they [Kelly and Morrill] would "make the boys hustle this season."

The headlines passed along the sad news to shocked Chicago fans:

Chicago *Herald*:

MIKE GOES TO BOSTON
The Only Kelly Leaves Chicago
President Spalding Releases the Old Right
Fielder in Consideration of a Certified Check for $10,000
Anson as a Strict Disciplinarian.

Chicago *Times*:

Chicago Releases Mike Kelly, and That Ball Player Signs a Contract With Boston. Ten Thousand Dollars the Sum Which the Puritan City Paid for the Fielder.

***Inter-Ocean*:**

Kelly sold for $10,000

Chicago's Great Ball Player
Transferred to Boston for
Quite a Large Consideration
Mike Signs With Hub Management, and Is to
Receive $5,000 for the Season—

Chicago Daily News:

MIKE KELLY RELEASED
Boston Pays $10,000 For Him
President Spalding Springs a Complete Surprise

A popular tune in Chicago, to the tune of "Climbing up the Golden Stairs," went

Arab Kelly's gone and left us
Of his presence he's bereft us—
Kelly of the diamond bold
He's deserted us for Boston.
Although Albert laid the cost on,
Ten thousand clear in Puritanic gold.
We surely have the pity
Of every sister city,
In our loss of Kel,
the tricky and the bold.
But we've entered for the pennant,
And we'll win—depend upon it,
Notwithstanding Mike has left us in the cold.
Just hear those bank notes rustle,
Ten thousand crisp and clean.
True Boston's got Mike Kelly,
But Spalding's got the lengthy green.

The fans of Chicago were indeed devastated. But for the fans of Boston, they were preparing to welcome the "King of Baseball," to name him "King Kelly," and to bestow upon him an adoration and a celebrity such as the city had never seen.

Five days after the sale, Spalding wrote to Kelly.

Dear Sir:

I am in receipt of your picture, in costume and batting position, and the same has been handed to our engraver, with instructions to get out as good a cut as possible for the forthcoming *Guide*.

I congratulate you on the magnificent salary that I understand you will receive from the Boston club next season, and I hope you will not disappoint them, but will make yourself not only worthy of the amount that you will receive from them, but also of the very large bonus they have paid the Chicago club for your release. I am just in receipt of a letter from Mr. Billings, from which I quote as follows:

"Kelly did not say a word against you; said the Chicago club was a good one to get money of, when wanted. Anson worked him pretty hard sometimes, when not in condition, and there is where the trouble lies, I think."

I am very glad to know that you have no personal feeling towards me, for I certainly have none towards you, and I do not believe you can truthfully say that either myself or the Chicago club have taken any advantage of you, but have always treated you right and fair. I have placed no credence in the rumors and alleged interviews, that have been published in the New York papers, from time to time, knowing, from my own experience, how these interviews are manufactured. And you will, no doubt, be captain of the Boston nine, you will find it necessary, or at least it will be advisable, to set examples to your men in the way of habits and deportment, that will be an incentive for them to follow.

Wishing you every prosperity and success in your new position, I am

Yours truly,
A.G. Spalding

One tantalizing and intriguing postscript to the sale appeared nearly a quarter of century later. It was a little hint about a long-lost connection between Kelly's sale, and the equally shocking sale a year later of Clarkson.

In his book *Touching Second,* Chicago star (and Troy native) Johnny Evers wrote, "The cause of that sale never was made public, but the real reason was a woman, and the club was compelled to sell the men, although the act brought down the wrath of the city upon them."

What a statement!

This may have been culled from the benefit of a quarter century of clubhouse rumors; there is no other evidence to validate this one, but whatever could Evers have been hearing?

One woman?

Two players?

We will never learn the story behind that one.

Boston

There may never have been a better pairing of a player and a city than that of Michael Joseph Kelly and Boston, Massachusetts.

Boston was a great sports town which embraced its heroes warmly. When its team won the 1883 pennant, roaring from seventh to first between June and October, the fans gave the players rings, watches, and engraved shaving cups. The team had not fared quite as well since then, but Honest John Morrill was well liked as manager and captain, and the fans supported the club nicely. Further, the population was going through a tremendous growth spurt, moving from 362,800 in the 1880 census to 448,400 by 1890, a 24 percent jump. Even now, more than a century later, it is not yet 600,000. The new citizens were happy to welcome an exciting new baseball star to their community.

While James Billings had negotiated the Kelly purchase, it was the other two partners, Arthur Soden, 44, and "Uncle Bill" Conant, 53, who really ran the club's business. Soden, father of the reserve clause, was a well-rounded businessman who operated out of the offices of Chapman and Soden at 150 Oliver Street. It was in the loft, upstairs, that his club prepared for the new season. It was a far cry from the White Stockings heading off to Hot Springs.

Soden and Conant would operate the club until 1906, and then would both live until 1926, telling tales of Kelly long into their old age. He would give them more than a few gray hairs over the coming seasons.

The coming of Kelly to Boston led fans and newspapers to begin calling him the "King of Baseball." From this came the natural progression to "King" Kelly. It was not a rapid process. None of the stories of the purchase, or those immediately after, used the word *king*. There were early references to "His Royal Highness" in the Boston press as the 1887 season unfolded. The publication of his book a year later referred to the author, Mike Kelly, as "The King of the Diamond." King Kelly was thus an evolution during the late 1880s.

So immediately popular was he with the Boston fans that he was quickly dubbed the "$10,000 Beauty," and on occasion, the "$15,000 Beauty," blending the sale price with his salary. (The name seemed to come from an actress named Louise Montague, who was also known as the "$10,000 Beauty.") The salary, of course, included the money for the use of his picture on club advertising and Messrs. Soden and Conant wasted no effort in maximizing their new star's drawing power.

Truth was, Kelly was always a big draw in Boston. The Irish faithful often made a point of waiting for the Chicago games, just for a chance to see Kelly. Frequently, he gave them some memorable times on the ball field. And of course, his lively banter with the crowd made him a darling. Kelly needed no special persuasion by management to "earn his keep" by treating the fans well. That came quite naturally to him.

The Boston team that Kelly now worked for was emerging as the Beaneaters, after some years as the Red Stockings or the Reds. Kelly referred to himself as a Beaneater while preparing to join Boston, and as the year passed, the name generally surpassed all others. Still, as was the custom of the time, the team was more popularly known as simply the "Bostons" or the "Boston Nationals," as was the case in most league cities.

Boston had finished fifth in 1886, five games under .500. For 1887, the regular lineup featured Morrill, 33, at first (in his 12th campaign); Jack Burdock, 35, at second (in his 9th season); Sam Wise, 29, at short (in his 6th year); Billy Nash, 21, at third (in his second full season); Dick Johnston (24, 3rd season), Joe Hornung (30, 7th season), and Kelly, in the outfield; Ed Tate, 26 (2nd season) catching when Kel didn't; Ezra Sutton, 36, (11th season) as an oft-used change player (utility), with pitching being shared by veteran Ol' Hoss Radbourne, 32; in his second year with Boston, Bill Stemmeyer, 22, in his second season in the majors, and another Michael Joseph, this one "Kid" Madden, just 19.

Morrill, Burdock, Wise, Hornung, and Sutton had all been part of the '83 champs. Radbourne was two years removed from his 60-win season for Providence.

Kelly would play 61 games in the outfield, 30 at second base, 24 at catcher, 2 each at short and third, and 3 on the mound. It was not a stirring lineup; certainly not a team which could remind Kel of Chicago's great glory.

Home games for the Bostons were played at the South End Grounds on Walpole Street, which had been in use since the National Association's Boston Red Stockings began play in 1871. The park was showing its age, and this would be its final season before a remodeling.

John Francis Morrill, was the town's baseball hero until Kelly arrived. A Boston native, an old amateur star, he received a five-year contract when he joined the new National League franchise in 1876, to begin a long career in his hometown.

It was at a Fast Day Game in '76, while playing for the "Picked Nine," that he so outclassed the older, professional players that he earned his first contract. (Fast Day was a religious/secular holiday in Massachusetts each April that had its origins in 1649. In 1894, it became Patriot's Day, which continues today with an annual morning baseball game on the day of the Boston Marathon.)

Three years later, he replaced George Wright as the team's captain and, in 1882, succeeded Harry Wright as manager, wearing both crowns for a year until Burdock took over as captain the following spring. But in July, Morrill once again assumed both roles and led the team to its '83 pennant, hitting .319 along the way. When he had told writers that "I thought we would finish fourth or fifth," they tabbed him "Honest John."

Kelly's arrival forced Morrill to yield the captaincy of the team, while retaining the managerial assignment. Despite all the assurances that the passing of the team's captaincy would move smoothly from Morrill to Kelly, the inner politics of the team were not nearly so tranquil. It had been three years since a pennant, but the fans were patient and Morrill was popular. When it was decided to split the duties for 1887—Morrill as manager, Kelly as captain—the move was laden with problems.

The role of captain was a far more visible one, and Kelly was still the reckless, incorrigible one, hardly a perfect selection to set an example.

Despite playing against each other for years, Kelly professed to not knowing Morrill very well until he joined the team, but found him to be a "pleasant, affable gentleman, and I do not think a man ever played ball in the Boston nine who doesn't say the same thing."

Wrote Kelly,

> I heard in certain quarters that Morrill and Kelly were not good friends. This statement is false in every particular. [We] are and always have been, the very best of friends....It was also said that there was rivalry between Morrill and Kelly; it was hinted that Morrill wanted to be manager and captain and that Kelly wanted the same positions. This is also silly and false. From the day that I was appointed captain...John Morrill did everything in his power to make my regime a success....If [he] was jealous then he had a peculiar way of showing it. He exerted himself in every conceivable manner to help me out. He did so many times, and I would indeed be ungrateful if I did not fully appreciate his worth, both as a man and as a ballplayer.

Despite the pressure that his heightened celebrity brought, Kelly responded in fine style, entertaining the crowds while hitting the ball well and running the bases with aplomb. Each day his arrival at the ballpark was accompanied by a growing legion of Kelly fans, people who admired his every heroic footstep. He could even deal with the hecklers, who would get on him about his new wealth. "I'm eating strawberries and ice cream off the salary I earn performing for suckers like you," he answered back one day. But the fan had the last word: "Yes, and the bartenders get yours, all of it!"

In time, his predictable daily arrival schedule led to schoolchildren gathering on the Boston streets for a chance to see him. And soon came the cries that would ring out in Boston: "Hey, Kel, how about an autograph!" "Hey, Mr. Kelly, can I have your autograph?" "King! King! Please sign this."

Patiently, Kelly would take a pencil and sign "M. J. Kelly." An American tradition was being born— the pursuit of the celebrity for the purpose of the autograph.

To this point, the art was not very developed. People who might own a Washington or a Jefferson or a Lincoln knew it was something to cherish. It was not uncommon for a boxer to sign some autographs as he entered or departed a boxing venue. But presidents did not pause to sign autographs and boxers, well, they had no routine to follow, except on days of their bouts. It was an unpredictable science.

Ballplayers, however, came and went almost every day to their ballpark. There was a pattern. One knew they could spot them at a given time. And, in time, it occurred to young fans that a Kelly autograph might be a nice thing to have.

New York autograph expert Charles Hamilton confirms that the pursuit of Kelly for purposes of a pencil-drawn signature, coming as it did around 1887, may indeed have been the start of the "hey, can I have your autograph" phenomenon. There are not many surviving Kelly signatures today, pencil scrawlings not having a very long life. But it was the first of a number of off-the-field contributions of Kelly to the American culture, most of which began with his sale to Boston.

Another was a contribution from the art world. A Frank O. Small painting of Kelly sliding into second (head first, not his famed hook slide) before a cheering crowd, was reproduced and made available to all of the Irish saloons in Boston. In no time, this painting was up on the wall behind the bar, replacing the more patriotic theme of Custer's Last Stand. Good-bye General Custer, hello King Kelly. For the Boston-born, Paris-educated Small, 28, it was a quick jump to fame, courtesy of the identification with his subject.

What little there might be in the way of product endorsements trickled into Kel. Having won the '86 batting title, his model bat was among those made available and advertised by Spalding Sporting Goods. A sled manufacturer produced a "Slide, Kelly, Slide" model, although whether Mike realized any financial gain is questionable. A Kelly shoe polish bore a baseball motif, but not Mike's likeness. He appeared on the few little trading cards produced at the time. The King was obviously too early for Coca-Cola, Wheaties, Lite beer, or Nike.

In early April of '87, prior to the opening of the season, Boston played four exhibition games at "Barnie's Grounds" (named after manager Billy Barnie) in Baltimore. Who was out there in right field to congratulate Kel on his riches—none other than Blondie Purcell, now with the Baltimores. While Kelly was reaching fame and fortune, Blondie was moving from team to team, playing for Syracuse, Cincinnati, Cleveland, Buffalo, Philadelphia (AA and NL), Boston, and now Baltimore. He was a journeyman among journeymen in the 19th century and how happy he must have been to see his ol' pal strutting onto the field that fine April day in '87, so far removed from the sandlots of Paterson. Kel was now a national hero.

More than 10,000 fans packed the stands each day beginning April 8, to see the first "official" appearances of Kelly in competition, wearing his new Boston uniform.

Barnie hired a local umpire for the first game, who "robbed the Bostons on every possible occasion." It got so that Kel, who had dropped a few easy flies in this preseason tune-up, got into an argument, and then insisted on a new umpire for the second day. (For the record, Boston won that first game 11-10.) After all these years, these were his first days as a captain. Cap Kelly, if you please!

Boston won two of the four games and the newspapers were more kindly to Mike than the first game would indicate. "Boston would have won all four, despite the umpires, had the balance of the team shown the nerve that Kelly did," one said. It was not a bad forecast for the upcoming season.

After two more preseason tune-ups against the American Association's Brooklyn entry on the 13th and 14th (Kelly's first "home" appearances in Boston), the Beaneaters opened the '87 season at Philadelphia on May 2, won two straight, went to New York, and then had their home opener on May 9 against the Athletics.

"I shall never forget the opening game of the season in Boston," he wrote. "It was the most memorable night in my life."

Boston dropped the game to Philadelphia, but afterwards, one John Graham of the local Elks Lodge happened on Kelly and invited him to the Boston Theatre, followed by a reception at the Elks Club.

After the theatre, the party, including many players from both teams, headed for the Elks Hall. What did Kelly find but a banquet prepared in his honor! He sat to the right of mayor O'Brien and when the Mayor spoke, he presented Kel with a gold watch, chain, charm, and pencil. Kelly described himself as speechless, and described the testimonial as "fit for a king."

He also enrolled as a member of the lodge, an important social connection for him, because men such as the mayor counted themselves among the membership. The lodge was also nice because it served as a place where a fellow could get a drink on a Sunday. And Graham became one of Kelly's greatest friends.

The first time Kelly faced his old teammates was on May 25 in Boston; the first time he returned to Chicago in a Boston uniform was June 24.

Boston had gotten off to a 19-8 start, just a game-and-a-half behind Detroit, with Chicago struggling in fifth place at 11-15. By May 25, for the first meeting, Boston had slipped a bit, to 29-18, while Chicago was coming on at 25-19. But the standings hardly mattered. It was a grand reunion for those still left on Chicago from the glory days, seeing their old loveable pal Kel, now "rich beyond all dreams."

Well, not exactly. "Contrary to the general understanding," wrote Mike,

> I am not a millionaire. There are a great many people who think I am, but such is not the case. I shall never retire from the diamond for the purpose of living on the fortune which I have saved. If I did, I am afraid that I wouldn't have very long to live.
>
> There are two classes of people whose wealth is always exaggerated by the great public. They are ball players and actors. There are a few rich ball players, and a few rich actors, but they are few and far between. They find so many different ways of spending money, that it is very hard for them to save very much.

Among the "different ways" Kel found to spend money of course, were at the faro table, at the race track, and in the saloons, where he preferred whiskey to beer and was always there to buy a round for the house. He liked to boast that "Mike Kelly will never go broke."

The highlight of the season had to be Mike's return to Chicago for the first time on June 24.

The Chicago newspapers were still beating up Spalding for the sale, playing to the sympathies of the saddened White Stockings faithful. The publicity however was having the effect of pushing attendance upward. Spalding himself told a tale of the give and take with the press:

> As showing the importance of taking advantage of opportunities presented for the gratuitous advertising of the game, I recall an incident following the sale of King Kelly to Boston. The newspapers of Chicago did not take kindly to this transaction. One paper—the Chicago *News*—was particularly severe in its criticism. The *News* strenuously urged, among other things, a reduction in the price of admission to games, claiming that if Chicago was to have cheap players it ought to have cheap admission.

> Frequent caricatures were printed, some of them occupying a half page, illustrating the slave pen of antebellum days, with the auction block, upon which, instead of the familiar forms of the unhappy slaves, abject ballplayers were displayed for sale to the highest bidder.

> Being at the time president of the Chicago Club, and having been instrumental in the sale of Kelly, I came in for much notoriety. While these daily "roasts" were being served out to me, I noticed that the attendance kept increasing. Gradually the controversy quieted down. Then one day on the street I met the prominent baseball writer "Harmony" White and asked him "What's the matter with the *News?* You haven't been giving me the usual amount of space of late."

> He replied that he was absolutely *out of ammunition.* I offered to furnish him fresh ammunition if he would only keep up the onslaught. His incredulous look indicated

that he was not impressed with my sincerity. I then explained to him that simply as a business proposition I could not afford to be neglected in his paper, for since he had let up in his attacks our attendance was dropping off.

"Well," said he, "if you feel that way about it, and will supply the ammunition, I will open up again...."

As a result of this casual conversation it was then and there agreed that he would send a trusted messenger to my office on two days of each week to secure the necessary ammunition. This plan was carried out to the end of that season, and, as a result, the Chicago club made more money that year than it had ever made during its history up to that time.

The Beaneaters arrived in Chicago from Indianapolis early in the morning following their all-night train journey. Mike, a little under the weather, spent the morning in his room at the Leland House, writing a rather humorous letter to a Boston newspaper about his road trip. If it was truly his own composition, and it likely was, it shows a great satirical wit, with clever references to the Atlantic Ocean and the Mayflower, and a bright style for a fourth-grade dropout, even if Columbus didn't land at Plymouth Rock.

Just before our second game in Indianapolis last week, I received a long letter from [A. Branson] Alcott, [a philosopher in Boston] urging me to attend the school of summer philosophy at Concord, next August, and to read a paper on that occasion. Of course my professional duties will not admit of my accepting the invitation, but as the only paper I ever read is the *Daily News,* almost anybody can take my place.

He further wrote that he was

charmed with life in Boston, and have been most cordially welcomed by the leading society circles, and in five months, I have become so thoroughly Bostonian that I can hardly realize that I had ever lived in the wild and woolly West.

You have no idea how different everything is there. Chicago people boast of their lake, of their Board of Trade Building, of their parks and of their refinement; but in each of those particulars, Boston can knock the socks clean off'n Chicago. We have a natural lake located just off Boston, that is, well, say ten times bigger than Lake Michigan, and it doesn't have to be dredged every three days to give the schooners enough water to sail in. Then there is Bunker Hill Monument; why it is three times higher than your Board of Trade steeple, and Boston Common was old enough to vote long before the buffaloes had got through making a stamping-ground of your Lincoln Park. As far as social advantages are concerned, Boston heads the league. It is the oldest city in America, having been founded in less than a fortnight after Christopher Columbus anchored the Maypole off Plymouth Rock. Everybody speaks all sorts of languages, and attends lectures, and reads poetry, and wears spectacles. I haven't been in the town more than two days before I got a craving for literature, and I couldn't get any peace until I had subscribed for the *Waverly Magazine.*

Did our Mike suddenly get "culture" or was he stretching the story for the benefit of his new fans, assuming that his old ones in Chicago would never see this letter in print?

By midday, a huge crowd gathered at the Leland and proceeded to celebrate Kel's return with a barbershop quartet improvising some special Kelly lyrics. Mike was unable to address the growing crowd, for a reason said to be "a charley horse."

At noon, the White Stockings, led by Anson, arrived at the hotel to escort their rivals to the ballpark. The parade of players was followed by a band and then the fans of Chicago, marching along. At the ballpark, Kelly received a floral tribute of hundreds of roses and carnations which spelled out "KEL."

Mike received other floral presentations, as well as a silk

jockey's cap and huge outpourings of love from the gathering crowd. A local businessman offered a silver service to be awarded to the winning captain of the day's game.

Chicago was enjoying a surprisingly fine season. They were not going to win the pennant, but most had thought they would collapse without Kelly and Gore. (This was not unlike the assumption that the Chicago Bulls would collapse without Michael Jordan a century later; instead, they made the playoffs). Chicago was in fact, playing quite well, with Billy Sunday the principal recipient of added playing time. Henry Chadwick would write in the 1888 *Spalding Guide,* "A lesson of the campaign is that one 'star' does not make a team; nor can the pennant be won by any costly outlay in securing the services of this, that, or the other 'greatest player in the country.' It is well managed and harmonious teams, not picked nines led by special stars, which win in the long run."

Chadwick also noted (and Spalding published these *Guides*) that Chicago's success in 1887 was largely due to the insistence of "strict temperance." He wrote, "Mr. Spalding's plucky and most successful experiment has conclusively shown that a baseball team run on temperance principles can successfully compete with teams stronger in other respects, but which are weakened by the toleration of drinking habits in their ranks."

Chicago defeated Boston that fine June day, Anson taking home the silver service. Kelly, limping from his charley horse, was thrown out at first on an almost sure hit to center. Did that ever give the fans something to hoot about! Suddenly, there was a genuine rivalry. The beloved Kel was in an enemy uniform and the fans found themselves applauding the heady play by the White Stockings, even if all in good fun. Kelly would later say that

> Boston always plays a better game against Chicago than against any other city [and] Chicago, even when broken up, will play a strong game with Boston. For one, I am very glad that there is such a strong rivalry between the two cities. It adds interest to the games and makes them as exciting to the men on the field as to the spectators.

Anson had to take great pleasure out of beating Boston nine

times in fifteen meetings that season. (The two also met in a pair of crowd-pleasing post-season exhibitions, with Boston winning both.) In fact, Chicago would finish at 71-50, a stoic third, only 5-1/2 games behind pennant-winning Detroit. Boston, without much of a supporting cast to Kelly, was 61-60, 5th place, and 10 games behind Chicago. They were holding their own, although clearly not pennant-bound, until a disastrous finish, which saw them lose 21 of their final 31 games.

A high point came on August 27, when Kelly enjoyed what would be the finest game of his career. He went 6-7, with a double, a home run, and six runs scored.

Five days later, on September 1, following three consecutive losses to Detroit, the Boston owners decided to remove the captaincy from Kel and restore it to Morrill. Clearly, the rivalry created between these two decent people was undermining the success of the team. And the Boston ownership would much rather reward their fans with a pennant than make Mike a happy captain. The end result would, no doubt, better justify their investment.

So Morrill got his old job back; there was no indication of any immediate controversy over the move, and the Beaneaters failed miserably in the closing month. Kelly made no public statements about the demotion and perhaps welcomed it. Somewhere, Anson was smiling.

The year 1887 is the odd year in baseball history in which it was decided that "walks counted as hits," and all batting averages were inflated. (Further, it took five walks for a base on balls; four strikes to whiff). The record showed Anson hitting .421 to win the batting title and Kelly in at .394, fourth in the league and tops on his team. When recalculated under "normal" conditions (as the record books of today show), it was Sam Thompson of Detroit who won the batting crown at .372, with Anson second at .347. Kelly came in at .322, second on Boston to Sam Wise's .334. (This was also the first year in which batters could no longer request a high or low pitch from pitchers.)

Kelly played 116 of the team's 121 games and stole 84 bases; the first year in which this was an officially recorded statistic. This was good for third in the league.

The promotion-minded publisher of the Boston *Globe,* General Charles H. Taylor, had offered a gold medal to the "champion base stealer" of the Boston Base Ball Club, and, of course, he reaped the publicity of making the presentation to Kelly at season's end. The medal was triple-tiered, reading "Champion" on top, with "Base Runner Boston B.B. Club" in the center, and an engraving of a man stealing a base, surrounded by "National League 1887," at the bottom. On the back, it said "Presented by the Boston *Globe* to Michael J. Kelly."

The medal was discovered about 20 years later at a New York jewelry store and given to Michael T. McGreevey, one of Boston's "royal rooters" of Kelly's era. The medal passed on to his granddaughter in 1943, who presented it back to the *Globe* with instructions that her grandfather wished it be sent to the Hall of Fame and Museum in Cooperstown. And that is where it resides today.

Kel was fourth in runs with 120 and second in doubles with 34. No one could blame Mike for the team's disappointing showing on the basis of his performance. What was heard in whispers was the bit of dissent and conflict caused by the Morrill-Kelly situation and how disruptive it might have been. Still, the team did improve by five victories from the year before. And given their talent and the diminishing skills of Hoss Radbourne, it seems unlikely they could have expected much more.

Kelly's reputation among the fans was intact. Indeed, he pulled off some mighty adventures in '87, as though to justify his pay.

Behind the plate, he would intimidate runners by dropping his mask on the plate to cause an obstruction before they began to slide. It was also reported that he kept a stock of birdshot in his mouth and would snap it between his teeth to imitate the sound of a foul tip. This trick allowed him to create the illusion of catching a foul in the days when such a play was considered an out. (The same tale says that this ploy ended when he accidentally began choking on his cache and coughed it up in front of the umpire.)

In the outfield, there was a tale of his keeping an extra baseball hidden in his pocket and, when the time was right, used it to camouflage a ball hit over the fence, pretending that he had instead caught up with it at the last moment. One day he actually got away with this, victimizing Detroit's Big Sam Thompson with the ploy.

Perhaps the most repeated of the Kelly stories was the "Kelly now catching" story.

According to the legend this occurred in a game in which he was on the bench with "Dimples" Tate doing the catching. It was the last of the ninth with two out and the bases loaded. (Naturally.)

The unnamed batter lifted a foul pop near the Boston bench. Kelly, seeing at once that it was out of Tate's reach, announced "Kelly now catching" in a loud voice, and caught the pop barehanded. Captains, you see, could make substitutions and the rule book never put restrictions on when a substitution might be made.

But it was his dash and daring on the bases that truly won the hearts of the Boston fans. "He was acknowledged to be the smartest, most resourceful player the game had known," wrote Boston sportswriter Walter Barnes in 1936. Wrote Hugh Fullerton of Chicago, "He was perhaps the most brilliant individualist the game ever knew." Sam Crane, in the New York *Evening Journal,* said he was the

> trickiest player who ever handled a baseball. There was nothing he would not attempt. Baseball rules were never made for Kel. He had his own way of interpreting them and it was in his own characteristic way that he made them conform to his ideas.

Fred Lieb (1888-1980), the longest living sportswriter from baseball's early days, citing his sports editor Jim Price, who knew and watched Kelly, wrote

> Kelly was of the flamboyant type, far keener mentally than old Cap. While Anson was born with an ability to hit, he reached his goals by dogged determination and persistence. Kelly had a hair-trigger brain, and was a genius in sizing up a situation and finding a weak spot in the enemy's armor. Some called him a dirty player, but Mike constantly was thinking up wiles to befuddle and entrap his slower-witted opponents. If the ethics sometimes were questionable, the game still was pretty rugged. While he was the brainiest catcher of his day,

his hold on the fans was more as an offensive player. Not quite as strong a hitter as Anse, Kelly was the better show at bat, and on the bases.

Mike had much the same hold on the fans of the '80's that Babe Ruth held in this century. To many, King Kelly and baseball were synonymous. His very nickname tells that story; he was baseball king of all he surveyed. Like Ruth, he burned the candle at both ends, and he could make headlines outside of the ball field. A handsome Irishman, with wavy black hair and a cavalry trooper's mustache, Kelly was all for wine, women, and song. Kelly gave Anse plenty of grey hair over his gay parties, much as Babe Ruth did to Miller Huggins four decades later.

As a catcher, Kelly often used wild, but fake pickoff throws to fool runners. He would intentionally throw the ball over the first baseman's head, having alerted his right fielder to charge in. The right fielder was positioned to throw the runner out at second.

"Mike Kelly was a direct contradiction of the old saying 'a good friend but a bitter enemy,' " recalled one observer.

Mike was a good friend but a poor enemy. His nature was too full of sunshine to harbor enmity. He was cast in a joyous mold. No occasion was too desperate, no subject too serious for him to "josh" about. When catching, it was the opposing batsmen who were the object of his good-natured railery. When playing right his delight was to get into an argument with the bleachers, and nothing pleased him better than to have two or three thousand people in an uproar and to be the recipient of their abuse.

His hook slides (he was credited with originating this play) and his lead on the hit and run, were feasts for the eyes. It wasn't long into his first season with Boston that a fan in the South End Grounds, yelled "slide, Kelly, slide" as Mike danced off first.
Another fan picked up the chant. And another. And soon, the

"slide, Kelly, slide" chant would fill the South End Grounds each time Kel reached first with second base empty. And thus was born a rallying cry which would come to take its place among the great expressions of baseball, a saying that would somehow make its way into the public consciousness even beyond ordinary baseball fans.

Although Kel had played superbly during the '87 season, the pressures of living up to his billing, coupled with the tensions with Morrill, must have made for an exhausting year. Still, when approached about a barnstorming trip to the West Coast in November, with the opportunity to bring Agnes along, he accepted.

The trip was scheduled to put four teams—New York, Chicago, St. Louis, and Philadelphia—in San Francisco for a 20-game schedule between November 19 and January 15. Mike was asked if he cared to play for the New York team. As the most famous player in the land, the tour was happy to take him in any uniform. His picture graced the cover of all the scorecards issued for the series, either alone or in the company of his "fellow" New York Giants.

His teammates gathered in Jersey City for what would be Mike's first trip to the West Coast since he was discovered by Anson seven years earlier.

John Ward was accompanied by his wife, the well-known actress Helen Dauvray (whose sister was married to Tim Keefe). Also on the trip were Buck Ewing, Roger Connor, Danny Richardson, Jerry Denny, Mike Tiernan, and Big Bill Brown, a San Francisco native who caught for the New Yorkers.

The team left Jersey City on October 25, while the world championship series between Detroit and St. Louis was still in progress. (It ended the following day, in the 15th game, Detroit winning 10 times.)

On the 26th, the team stopped in Cincinnati where Ward presided over a meeting of the Brotherhood; apparently just a general update on the business of the budding union.

From there the team continued south towards New Orleans ("at the rate of fifty miles an hour," wrote Kel, "...enough to make a fellow's hair stand on end.") The team played some exhibitions and then a few of the players, including Kelly and Ewing, broke away to accept an invitation to go quail hunting in Mississippi, while the other players went to Houston.

Kelly and Ewing killed three quail with 74 shots, then met their mates in Houston, where Kelly tried bronco riding for the first time.

"When I was a boy," said Kel, "it was the dream of my life to ride a fiery mustang on the broad prairies. I got all that I want, thank you."

On went the troupe to San Antonio and a visit to the Alamo, and then over the Rio Grande, which Kelly assumed was a great river, but which he found to be transverable in two jumps.

"We saw a good many Indians. They were lazy, peaceable, and dirty. They didn't wear any scalps at their belts, therefore they were not objects of special interest."

On they went to Los Angeles, and finally, in time for Thanksgiving, San Francisco.

New York played against local semipro and amateur teams at the California League Grounds. They played ten games, won most of them, and then Mike and Agnes journeyed home to Hyde Park, arriving in late January for a few weeks rest before the '88 season would be upon them.

In March, Kelly was approached about preparing a book on his life. He agreed to travel to Boston to discuss it with the publisher and left for New York City to get a Boston-bound train on Sunday, March 11, accompanied by his dog Nellie. He checked into the Hoffman House as a light snow began to fall.

By nightfall, it had turned into a blizzard; it would become known as the Blizzard of '88, still the biggest ever known to the northeast United States. With drifts reaching fifteen feet, Kel was marooned in the hotel for four days, leaving only to "rescue Nellie from a snow drift."

Stranded as he was, he happened upon one Charles W. Thomas, theatrical booking agent of Hoyt and Thomas, along with an employee, Johnny Ruddy.

Kelly began to talk of his long-standing interest in the stage and told the "hanging" story of he and Jimmy McCormick performing in Mac's basement back in Paterson. He also told of an offer from Charlie Reed, a Boston friend, who had offered him a part in "A Rag Baby" at the Park Theater in Boston.

Ruddy heard the story and encouraged Kelly to take the part.

Tales of the King

Kelly did have an innate sense that hell-raising was a short cut to a player's extinction and early grave. Once, the Beaneaters were playing an exhibition game with a team of collegians that represented the resort town of Cape May, New Jersey, George Reese, ace pitcher for the University of Pennsylvania and later a surgeon, was given an especially attractive offer to sign a Boston contract after the exhibition.

One of the other collegians wrote his memories of what followed: "Dr. Reese related the enlightening conversation he had with King Kelly after the contest. 'After the game, I went to see Kelly in the clubhouse, where we all were dressing. I was always trying to learn new things in baseball, and was particularly anxious to have Kelly explain a smart play which he and the Boston club worked on me. We got around to the subject of the Boston club's offer, and Kelly seemed to know I was a medical student at Penn. 'I'm not an educated man; I can't do much more than sign my name,' he told me, 'so I became a ballplayer. But you've got a good education, and are on your way to becoming a doctor. Stick to that and if you're as good a doctor as you are a pitcher, you'll make a mighty fine doctor.' Then, putting his arm around my neck, he said, 'And I want you to promise me you'll never take a drink.'

"I know King Kelly had a reputation for being a good two-fisted drinker, but that marvelous piece of advice from the greatest figure then in baseball made a tremendous impression on me. I took his advice, stuck to medicine and surgery, and always followed his instructions on drinking."

It didn't take much coaxing. Kelly was a born ham. When telegraph service was restored, he wired Reed and agreed to accept the part of "Dusty Bob."

Kel finally made it to Boston for a week's engagement. He slept through the first rehearsal.

But at last, the Park Theater was packed with Kel's friends for opening night. When Mike went on stage and delivered his first line, "Where is this 'Old Sport'?" he received "the greatest reception of my life. The applause and cheers lasted nearly a minute."

Describing the feelings of stage fright, Kel wrote "I would rather face ten thousand angry baseball enthusiasts on the diamond field, than go before a friendly audience in a theatre."

Still, his stage debut was a hit.

"Glad it was a success; glad that I lived through it," he wrote.

One reviewer was not so kind. "There was a lot less applause when he finished than when he started," he wrote. Mike would continue to appear on stage when the opportunities presented themselves. "Casey at the Bat" would be published in 1888, and was an immediate hit on the stage. It gave Kelly an act. He would recite it, but make it "Kelly at the Bat," to the delight of his audiences.

Boston II

Play Ball: Stories of the Ball Field, by Mike Kelly of the Boston Base Ball Club, was written in the few weeks between Mike's return from San Francisco and the start of the '88 season.

It was the first autobiography written by a baseball player, and, in many ways, it served as a prototype for the "tell no evil" life stories which followed for the next 70 years. In truth, not until Ty Cobb and Rogers Hornsby wrote their autobiographies with an edge of bitterness in the early 1960s, did biographies stray from the formula in the Kelly book.

Priced at 25 cents, the soft-cover book was published by the Boston publisher of Emery and Hughes of 146 Oliver Street. A handsome portrait of Mike in suit and tie adorned the cover. Despite the title on the cover, the title page read differently: *Play Ball: Stories of the Diamond Field.* A secondary title page, with an illustration of Mike in his Boston uniform, said it was "By 'The King of the Diamond,' Mike Kelly." It was dedicated to "the thousands of American people who annually grow excited and cheer on their favorite players to victory: to the ball players of America: and to the small boy who does so much to uphold the game."

There is a preface, which starts "...when Mr. Kelly requested me to write a preface to his little book..." but it is strangely unsigned; a publisher's glitch.

Was the author of the preface the ghostwriter as well? We cannot tell. Certainly there was a ghost, but just as certainly, Mike's contribution is obvious. There was no way in which the book could have been prepared without a great deal of personal cooperation.

Baseball historian John Thorn thinks it is a good bet that the

co-author was Jacob Charles "Jake" Morse of the Boston *Herald*.
Morse was a steady presence on the Boston baseball scene and,
in this same year, 1888, authored *Sphere and Ash*, subtitled
"History of Base Ball. Notable Record by Primitive Clubs. Contests for Supremacy in the Sixties. Remarkable Tours of the
Early Organizations. Games Conspicuous for Extra Innings.
Complete Review of All Championship Series." It was actually
a paperback edition of articles on the game's history he had been
writing for the *Herald*.

One might wonder if Morse could prepare two books in the
same year and whether he might have a different publisher for
each (J. F. Spofford & Co., right in the Herald Building, published *Sphere and Ash*), but no better guess is available. And as he
seemed to have been writing these essays in the *Herald* right
along, the task of producing two books in one year might not
have been so difficult.

The book is indeed autobiographical. We learn of Kelly's
youth, his parents, their deaths, his work in the Paterson mill,
his friendship with Jimmy McCormick, his first games of ball,
his signing with Cincinnati, his discovery by Anson, his great
glories with Chicago, and his sale to Boston. The book takes us
up to the start of the '88 season.

In addition there are lessons in training, advice to youngsters,
tributes to patriotism, and the general feel-good do-good deeds
found in books printed for young boys in the Horatio Alger
tradition. For such a renowned rascal to produce such strong
and good sense advice to young readers is both noble and
contrived, and that portion is likely the work of the ghostwriter.
But Kel gets in his warning to parents as well, advising them to
permit their boys to pursue their dreams of baseball if they
choose to.

As a resource for future historians, the book is important, but
lacking in so many of the basics one would hope for from a
biographer. Scant attention is paid to his wife—her name is
never mentioned—and the names of his parents are also omit-
ted. Few copies of the book exist today, but it remains another
important "first" in Kelly's growing list of contributions to the
culture of baseball.

There was to be more big news for the Boston fans for 1888.
Messrs. Soden, Conant, and Billings dug deep into their pockets

once again, and purchased John Clarkson for another $10,000 from Chicago. Boston now had the "$20,000 Battery" in Clarkson and Kelly, two former White Stocking teammates. Clarkson, born across the Charles River, was the best pitcher in the game, and while Spalding was no doubt pleased to pocket another huge payment, fans wondered why he was continuing to dismantle his proud club. They certainly hadn't been hearing what Evers later did.

There had been an intermediate transaction between Kelly and Clarkson, in the American Association, which affirmed the new going price for players and again set the stage for the Clarkson deal. Chris Von Der Ahe of St. Louis sold his star pitcher, Bob Caruthers, to Brooklyn for $8,250. Brooklyn also paid Caruthers a bonus of $1,500 and a salary of $4,000, and along with $500 in "costs," the sum of $14,250 put the Association in Kelly's league, so to speak.

Anson had also praised Clarkson's abilities, but, as he did with Kelly, he also had another point of view for his star. He claimed that Clarkson "takes a lot of encouragement to keep going. He won't pitch if scolded, but if praised he'll pitch three days in a row." What Anson was really saying was that Clarkson had a frightening temper and was thought to be uncontrollable when crossed.

Clarkson, 26, was coming off a 38-21 season with 237 strikeouts in 523 innings, leading the league in wins, games starts, complete games, innings, hits, and strikeouts. The move greatly improved Boston's chances to contend.

Another treat for the fans was an improvement of the South End Grounds, already the prettiest park in the country. At the end of the '87 season, it was leveled. By opening day of '88, May 25th, a Grand Pavilion appeared behind home plate, and after an opening of some six feet sat a second level, featuring six medieval looking spires made of tin, adorned with pennants. Square columns, adorned by tulip-shaped tops, supported the upper deck. It was magnificent; a place to behold for all Bostonians, if only of curiosity. One needn't be a baseball crank to spend a lovely day at the intersections of Walpole, Columbus, and Tremont Streets.

In 1888, the National League stayed intact with its eight teams and three strikes once again setting down a batter. There

were now just seven players left in the League from its first
campaign of 1876: Anson, O'Rourke, Deacon White, Paul Hines,
John Burdock, Morrill, and Sutton. Kelly was in the second
group—those entering their 11th season.

Ol' Hoss Radbourne was fading; Clarkson would take over as
Boston's ace, and Hoss would win only seven games in '88. Kelly
would do more catching in '88 than ever before: 76 games, as
opposed to only 34 in the outfield. The fans would see the
Clarkson-Kelly "$20,000 Battery" often.

Morrill would serve as both captain and manager for the
season and if that upset Kelly, again, he was quiet. In truth,
Kelly was now becoming more a celebrity than a common baseball player. So long as he had the plaudits of the fans and the
friendship of the players, he was happy. If the press occasionally
scolded him, he could serve it back, just as players do today.

A *Sporting Life* correspondent, who wrote under the pen name
"Mugwump," reported that

> The effect Kelly's presence will have on the Boston nine
> is very pleasant to contemplate. We have long needed
> such a man. There are not a great many like them in the
> business but one man like Kelly on a team is of inesti-
> mable value. His style of playing ball is catching. Put
> him on a team and the other men cannot help trying to
> play as he does. His good nature and even temper helps
> him in trying times, and the fact the he never gets
> rattled will hold the boys together.

Kelly seemed happy to talk to "Mugwump," who quoted him
as saying "interviews which have been going all over the country
are big fakes....Now that's a nice business, ain't it, writing
interviews with me when I haven't said a word?"

Once Kelly, armed with a horsewhip, searched the Fifth
Avenue Hotel looking for a Boston *Herald* reporter who had
written that Kelly was in a dispute with his teammates over a
bill for expenses in a benefit show. Some writers tried to present
Kelly as more than he was, one even writing that he had been
"educated for the priesthood at Georgetown College."

By and large, his attitude to the press was "as long as they
spell my name right." But if they got on him for his drinking, he

got defensive. "See what they say about the old man. I don't observe any reference to...my colleagues. I am the 'only player.' Why don't some of you dubs break a window and get yourselves talked about?"

Boston jumped off to a spectacular start in '88, winning their first nine games to jump well ahead of the pack. But they were only 28-41 over the next three months, including a 5-17 record in August, and were again fading from the chase. The season turned out to be a battle between the New York Giants and the Chicago White Stockings, much to the delight of all who felt pennants could not be purchased. Devoid of both Kelly and Clarkson, Anson's boys were fighting for first and barely noticing the Beaneaters.

Wrote Chadwick,

> ...while the Boston club had invested, at great financial cost, in securing the services of noted star players, the Chicago club, though weakened by the release of players from their team who had done yeoman service in their ranks for years, were yet able to excel the picked team of star players of the Boston club, simply by superiority in handling those they had left to them.

The Chicago-Boston rivalry still thrived, large crowds attending those games in both cities. One day Kelly was on first, with a short lead. Anson, playing first as always, took a few steps off the base in Kel's direction, and signaled to his pitcher for a quick pickoff throw. As both moved towards their left to return to first, Kelly stuck his finger in Anson's belt loop and distracted him from receiving the throw. Kel made it all the way to third, duplicating a trick which had earlier been played on him.

Anson, ever the no-nonsense captain, protested strongly to the umpire, but to no avail.

"Then I'll see to it that no other player is going to take advantage of blind umpiring," he said, and had all the outside belt loops removed from the White Stockings uniforms.

The season ended with New York winning its first National League pennant, finishing comfortably ahead of second place Chicago. The White Stockings of course, were hailed for their fine year—in which Anson batted .344 to win the batting title and Jimmy Ryan, who had more or less replaced Kelly in the Chicago outfield, led the league with 16 home runs.

Boston finished fourth with a 70-64 record, 15-1/2 games out of first and a little improved over 1887. Clarkson won 33 games and led the league in innings pitched, and Kelly was the team's leading batter at .318. His work behind the plate was spotty; the record book shows 54 passed balls and 77 errors in 74 games as a catcher; with a .796 fielding average. While gloves were still primitive and official scoring different than we know it today, Detroit catcher Charlie Bennett caught 72 games and had 14 passed balls and 18 errors, by way of comparison.

Kelly was third in the league in batting and fourth in slugging percentage. He stole 56 bases, sixth in the league.

Back in 1874, Spalding (then with Boston) and Anson (then with Philadelphia) had been part of a troup of two dozen players who had ventured to England for a series of exhibition games to demonstrate the game of baseball to a fairly disinterested audience of Britons. They played in Liverpool, Manchester, London, and even Dublin, but did little to advance baseball internationally.

With the game more mature now, the two Chicago mainstays decided to embark on a post-season trip to Australia and New Zealand, bringing with them some of America's best players. If nothing else, it would be a great holiday for the men and their wives.

Kelly was invited to go along. No doubt there was some thought given to whether his manners on the international scene would present baseball in its finest light. But he was the most famous player in the country and it would seem strange to leave him off.

The party was to be representative of two teams: Chicago, with Anson, Pfeffer, Burns, Williamson, Ryan et al; and the "All America Team" with John Montgomery Ward, Ned Hanlon, Herman Long, Kelly, and others. What a great adventure it figured to be.

The party left Union Station in Chicago on October 20. Once again the World Championship Series, this time between New York and St. Louis, was in progress. (It would end October 27 and Ward, of the Giants, would "catch up.") In the meantime, working their way west for their Pacific departure, the teams would play exhibitions in St. Paul, Minneapolis, Cedar Rapids, Des Moines, Omaha, Hastings, Denver, Colorado Springs, Salt Lake City, Los Angeles and San Francisco.

The Kellys, Mike and Agnes, were to meet the party in Denver on the 27th. Silver Flint was recruited to do the catching for the All Americans until then.

Came the 27th and Denver—no Kelly. Wrote Anson, "as Kelly's name was on the score card it was some time before the crowd discovered that it was 'Old Silver' and not the 'Ten Thousand Dollar Beauty' that was doing the catching."

Mike never did make it. The party left San Francisco on November 18. They went to Hawaii, then Australia, and New Zealand, and decided that they would continue their journey westward rather than return directly home. And the Spalding-Anson world tour of '88-'89 wound up playing baseball in Ceylon, and then Cairo, with time out to have the players photographed at the Sphinx. On to Europe they went, playing exhibitions in Naples, Rome, Florence, and Paris. Such a wonderful time was had by all that Anson devoted 143 pages of his 339-page autobiography to the journey, which concluded with a grand welcome home in New York harbor on April 6, 1889, barely in time for the '89 season.

Where was Kel? Although he had signed a contract to go on the tour, he wired that "business interests" in New York made it impossible for him to leave. Anson gave him not another word after indicating that he failed to show in Denver. Perhaps he was just as happy. Neither does Spalding make mention of the absent Mike in his account of the trip, although Kel's picture appeared on the poster advertising the tour.

Certainly, Kelly missed a wonderful opportunity. The *Spalding Guide* of 1890 called the trip "the greatest and most important event known in the thirty odd years of base ball history." (Of course, it also said that "Before the decade of the nineties ends, base ball will have become an established field game in England." If he meant the *nineteen* nineties, we're still waiting.)

Agnes must have been more than a little put out; the following winter, Mike took her on a European vacation.

What did Kelly have in store for American culture in '89? Nothing less than a silly song called "Slide, Kelly, Slide," music and lyrics by John W. Kelly, (no relation) for Miss Maggie Cline, a vaudeville and dance hall star, who would perform it on stage. It was published by Frank Harding with an 1889 copyright.

It has little to do with Kel, as one reads through the lyrics, but as a little baseball ditty, its title got attention.

I played a game of baseball, I belong to Casey's Nine!
The crowd was feeling jolly, the weather it was fine;
When the omnibuses landed That day upon the ground.
The game was quickly started, They sent me to the bat:
"I made two strikes" says Casey, "What are you striking at?"
I made the third, the catcher muff'd, and to the ground it fell;
Then I ran like a devil to first base, when the gang began to
      yell;
(chorus)
Slide, Kelly, slide! Your running's a disgrace!
Slide, Kelly, slide! Stay there—hold your base!
If someone doesn't steal yer
And your batting doesn't fail yer
They'll take you to Australia!
Slide, Kelly, slide!

'Twas in the 2nd inning, they called me in, I think
To take the catcher's place, while he went to get a drink;
But something was the matter, sure I couldn't see the ball;
And the second one that came in, broke my muzzle, nose and
      all...
The crowd up in the Grand Stand! They yelled with all their
      might
I ran towards the Club House, I thought there was a fight.
'Twas the most unpleasant feeling, I ever felt before;
I knew they had me rattled, When the gang began to roar;
(chorus)
They sent me out to centerfield, I didn't want to go;
The way my nose was swelling up, I must have been a show!
They said on me depended vict'ry or defeat,
If a blind man was to look at us, he'd know we were beat

64 to nothing! was the score when we got done,

And ev'ry body there but me said they had lots of fun

The news got home ahead of me, they heard I was knock'd
  out;

The neighbors carried me in the house and then began to
  shout

(chorus)

The song made Miss Maggie Cline a star, and of course, added much to the growing legend of King Kelly. As popular as the song was, it was limited to recitals, until modern technology caught up with it.

Thomas Alva Edison had patented his phonograph in 1877, but not until 1887 had the first wax cylinder been developed and only in 1889 were the first commercial records sold. They were largely classical, Italian opera, religious, or patriotic.

On August 3, 1891, George J. Gaskin, one of the leading pioneer recording artists in America, recorded twenty songs at the United States Phonograph Company on Orange Street in Newark, New Jersey, "Slide, Kelly, Slide" was both the ninth, and the twentieth. He sang it onto five wax cylinders. There were no "masters" used to mass produce records; the technology permitted five originals to be recorded at a time and immediately shipped for sale. If you wanted 1,000 copies, the artist would have to sing the song 200 times. So ten copies were recorded that day.

Gaskin would have been selected over Maggie Cline because the recording capabilities of the time were not considered strong enough for the female voice. Not until 1893 did women begin to record.

Gaskin was accompanied by pianist Edward Issler. By January 9, 1892, the recording had become the nation's first "pop vocal hit," that is, a song that did not fit under classical, opera, religious, or patriotic labels. There is no record of how many times Gaskin recorded the song, nor of how many copies exist today. (It continued to be recorded by other artists into the 1920s after the 78-rpm flat vinyl record replaced the cylinders.) And the song took its place among American pop culture history at a point where music and baseball converged.

Disappointed over two lackluster seasons, Conant and Billings, and to a lesser degree Soden, were becoming disillusioned
with John Morrill. Said Billings, "Morrill is too sensitive, and in
losing does not play the game of which he is capable."

Still, he signed to manage the team for 1889 in March. Said
Morrill, "I'm perfectly satisfied. I appreciate the many kind
words spoken in my behalf by the baseball public."

But came Fast Day, and the annual exhibition between the
Beaneaters and a picked team of amateurs, Morrill was asked
to manage the picked team and Kelly the Bostons. Morrill
refused. It was his final act for Boston after 13 seasons. The next
day he and Sam Wise were sold to Washington.

Said Soden,

> The directors saw yesterday that the patrons of the
> game were divided between Morrill and Kelly. It came
> down to who should go. Morrill has many friends in this
> city and is a perfect gentleman. Kelly is a ballplayer. So
> it was for us to choose between the men, and we picked
> out Kelly as the one who could win the most games.

Tim Murnane, in the Boston *Globe,* was one of several who
took Morrill's side. "Some of the best known business men in the
city called at the *Globe* office last evening to condemn the action
of the Boston directors in allowing Mike Kelly to drive Honest
John Morrill out of his home."

James A. Hart, who had managed Milwaukee of the Western
Association in '88, was hired at once to manage Boston. Kelly
got his captaincy back.

The '89 Bostons were a new look team. Detroit was out,
Cleveland was in, and Boston picked up four Detroit stars for its
roster, the current incarnation of the so-called "Big Four"—second baseman Hardie Richardson, first baseman Dan Brouthers,
utility man Charlie Ganzel, and catcher Charlie Bennett. The
signing of Bennett would free Kelly for the outfield, where he
would play 113 games in 1889, as opposed to only 23 behind the
plate.

Bennett was a catcher who would truly help the team, delivering Kelly to the outfield after his poor defensive season of '88.
Charlie was a 12-year man, the last eight having been spent in

Detroit. He was never a star, but he could provide stability to a lineup.

Poor Charlie would remain with Boston through 1893. Then in January of '94, while on a hunting trip in Kansas with Clarkson, he slipped on the ice at a train platform and was run over by the departing railroad car. Clarkson frantically cradled his buddy and screamed for help. The accident cost him use of his legs, one cut off at the ankle, the other at the knee. He would live in a wheelchair, running a newsstand in Detroit for 33 years. The Tigers would name their new ballpark, the one in which Ty Cobb broke in, Bennett Park.

The accident took its toll on Clarkson as well. Many said he was never the same again. He pitched only one more season and was 8-8. He opened a cigar store in Bay City, Michigan, but behaved erratically and was eventually placed in an insane asylum. While visiting relatives in Boston, he died in 1909 at the age of 47. (A story appears occasionally portraying Clarkson as having gone mad and slashing the throat of his wife, but there does not appear to be any basis to the tale.)

As solid an addition as Bennett proved to be for Boston, it was Brouthers (pronounced BROO-thers) who was the steal of the winter. At 6'2 and 205 pounds, he stood above most of his contemporaries. He was 31 years old when he joined Boston. He had already won two National League batting titles while with Buffalo, had eight consecutive .300 seasons under his belt, and his lifetime average trailed only Anson's in league history. He would not disappoint in '89, leading the league once again with a .373 average and taking a good deal of the pressure off Kelly to provide the club's offense.

Richardson, the other big acquisition, was one of the best 19th century players who is not in the Hall of Fame. Not quite in Brouther's league statistically, he nevertheless hit .299 over 14 seasons. He was part of the "Big Four" with Brouthers in both Buffalo and Detroit. At 34, he might have been considered in decline as he moved to Boston, coming off an injury-riddled .289 season, but he would rebound to hit .304 for the Beaneaters in 132 games.

James Aristotle Hart, at 34, the new manager, did not enter the job with a particularly imposing resume. Never a major league player, he had managed Louisville of the American Asso-

ciation in 1885 and 1886 to sub-.500 seasons. By 1888 he could
be found managing the Milwaukee entry of the Western Association to another sub-.500 year. He was hardly a figure to
overshadow Kelly, but that seemed fine with him. He would
quietly manage from the Boston bench, while Kelly resumed his
on-field leadership role as captain. Perhaps this low-key approach would fare better than the Morrill-Kelly pairing.

Boston's preseason training period of '89 was again far from
the glamour Chicago was enjoying in the hot mineral baths of
Hot Springs, Arkansas. The Beaneaters training was in the
chilly April weather of Boston, where they would play an occasional game against amateur or college competition and train
quietly in a gymnasium.

A tale was told of one preseason game in '89, when the Bostons
faced a wild college pitcher, who hit seven players with pitches,
Kelly twice.

After the game, the brash hurler went to Kelly and asked
what he thought of his pitching performance. Kelly replied,
"Sport, you'd be the best man on earth to teach boxers how to
sidestep. I'm much obliged to you. You've made me shiftier on
my feet and quicker at ducking than John L. Sullivan!" (Sullivan
incidentally, Boston's other sports hero of the time, would fight
his last bare-knuckles championship bout in July of '89. No
anecdotal record exists of a Sullivan-Kelly encounter, such as
the day the Beatles met Elvis, but it is likely they shared a toast
at some point.)

The combination of the new players and the Kelly-Hart management seemed to turn things around for Boston. After two
disappointing years following the purchases of Kelly and Clarkson, resulting in noncontending teams, the Beaneaters found
themselves in the thick of a thrilling pennant race in '89. For
Kelly, it was his first race in three years, and it got his competitive juices going. No one knew more about the value of team play
and self-sacrifice than Kel. For all of his nocturnal highjinks and
poor habits, he remained one of least selfish players in the game,
much more concerned with team performance than with personal statistics. In short, he had the perfect credentials to lead
by example on the field, provided he arrive sober and able
bodied.

The season began on April 24 with Boston facing the Giants

in Jersey City. The Giants had been taken by surprise by the City of New York, which had decided to claim the Polo Grounds property in order to construct a new road at 111th Street in Manhattan. The Giants were forced to play their spring games at Jersey City and Staten Island sites while a new Polo Grounds was hastily constructed in its place. The new park opened on July 8.

Boston got off spectacularly again, winning 20 of its first 26 and holding first place through May, June, and July. Only in August did they begin to slip, while the Giants, in their new home, went 18-9. The tight race had its benefits; on August 31, a crowd of 14,364 jammed the new Polo Grounds to watch New York and Boston square off head-to-head for the final time. With the conclusion of the month, Boston was 63- 35, New York 62-38, two games back.

One team not figuring in the race at all was Washington— headed for a last-place finish. John Morrill, having been signed as player, captain, and manager, was released in July after breaking a finger. "He was no use to us," said the Washington president. "He did not produce."

Worth noting, however, was the last great moment of Morrill's career, his return to Boston on June 13. As he came to bat in the second inning, he received an ovation "that might have been heard a mile away," wrote Murnane, the *Globe* reporter who condemned his sale to Washington. "Cheers were given with a will, hats were thrown in the air. Then came a steady round of cheering for fully five minutes, while Mr. Morrill stood with bowed head at home plate."

Clarkson's pitching was carrying the season for Boston. He was en route to a 49-victory campaign, completing 68 of 72 starts, hurling 8 shutouts, 620 innings, and leading the league with 284 strikeouts. The 49 victories are the fourth highest single season total, trailing only Radbourne's 60 in 1884, Clarkson's own 53 in '85 with Chicago, and Guy Hecker's 52 in 1884.

Clarkson beat New York six out of seven decisions, and really beat up on Philadelphia, Pittsburgh, Cleveland, and Washington, with a combined 34-8 record against them. Oddly, his most trouble came from his old mates at Chicago, against whom he was but 5-4, and an unimpressive Indianapolis club who beat him six times in ten tries.

In September, New York began to chip away at the small Boston lead and took over first with a 79-42 record to Boston's 80-43, a .003 lead.

On September 30, before just 300 fans on a dark and rainy day in Cleveland (modern fans who put in their time in Municipal Stadium can relate to such a day), Boston trailed 3-2 when the umpire wanted to call the game. Captain Kelly talked him out of it. "We can see to play," he said. "I'll show you I can see the ball."

He doubled to ignite a four-run rally; Boston won 6-3 behind Clarkson's six-hitter. New York beat Pittsburgh to retain their small lead.

The next day Boston again defeated Cleveland, but this time Pittsburgh topped the Giants, and the Beaneaters were back on top. Clarkson was again the winner, and Kelly said that "If Clarkson should win the pennant, they ought to erect a monument to him in Boston."

On October 2 though, things fell apart.

King Kelly was unavailable to play.

Owing to "a jollification during last night with several theatrical friends," Kel was too hungover to put himself in the lineup. One of the friends was Al Johnson, his Cleveland drinking buddy. Pomer Sec was said to be the whiskey of choice that evening.

Johnson was one of the early "hanger-oners" with a little money who liked the company of famous players. He liked playing cards, drinking, basking in their limelight, and providing them with loose women and fast times. Once he loaned his apartment to Kelly and some teammates, and the men proceeded to drink the night away. Kelly and Williamson began a "hat smashing exhibition," stomping on every hat in the room. Only Pfeffer saved his by tossing it out the window.

This didn't bother Kel, who was so drunk, he was preparing to jump from the tenth floor window to retrieve the hat, only to be grabbed by Johnson and Gore and pulled back to safety. They said Kelly fainted when he sobered up and learned of the deed the next day.

Now, Mike sat on the bench, wearing an overcoat over his uniform. It was pathetic. Cleveland was a bad stop for many players, but Kelly was carrying much responsibility into the big game. Indeed, hundreds of Boston fans were poised at the Music Hall back home to get telegraphic batter-by-batter reports.

Shortly after the game began, Hardie Richardson was called out at home by rookie umpire John McQuaid. Kelly, argumentative if not entirely coherent, told the poor ump, "You're stealing the championship from us! You're bound to do the Bostons out of the championship!" Kelly was beside himself with anger and McQuaid, fearful of an ugly scene, summoned the ballpark police to remove him.

The Cleveland cops were up to the task. One actually held a billy club over Kel's head, until a Cleveland player intervened, and said, "Let him be; you'd think he was a murderer!"

According to game reports, the policeman replied, "We've heard of this chap and think he's a disgrace to the business." He was tossed out of the park.

Hart, ever the thinking manager, hastily purchased a ticket to permit Kelly back in, but the police would have none of it. The Beaneaters went down to defeat 7-1, as Ed Beatin, the Cleveland left-hander, held Boston to but four hits. Clarkson, pitching in his seventh consecutive game, had nothing. And Kelly, the captain and inspiration, was on the outside looking in as the game ended. In Pittsburgh, New York was winning 6-3 to pass Boston by three percentage points once again.

On October 3 in Pittsburgh, Clarkson was back out there, "intending to fight for the old rag as long as there was the slightest show to get it." Kelly was back in the lineup, but played without his usual smile, muffing a fly ball and being caught in a rundown between second and third. Both Boston and New York won, the latter defeating Cleveland.

On the 5th, after the Sunday off day, both teams won again, Boston eking out a 4-3 victory when Brouthers singled home Bennett in the ninth. One game remained: New York at Cleveland, Boston at Pittsburgh.

Back home in Boston, General Charles H. Taylor, publisher of the *Globe,* put up $1,000 for the Beaneaters if they would win the pennant. Hart and Clarkson, learning of the offer, turned around and wired Cleveland manager Tom Loftus: "WILL GIVE YOUR TEAM $1000 IF BOSTON WINS THE PENNANT; $500 TO THE BATTERY IN TODAY'S GAME, AND THE LIKE AMOUNT TO THE REST OF THE TEAM."

Sadly, the entire script failed to play out. New York handled Cleveland 5-3, while Pittsburgh beat Clarkson 6-1, and the Beaneaters finished a game out. Kelly had three hits and scored the Boston run, but it was too little, too late.

Instead of the thrill of a great season and an exciting pennant race, there was a gloom over Boston. Newspaper editorials put the blame on poor Hart, noting that he had allowed Kelly to "make an exhibition of himself in Cleveland." It was a low blow to Hart; Kelly, 31, was old enough and seasoned enough to have known better.

Hart defended his performance by noting that his team had faced all the best pitchers; the Giants faced "green amateurs." Hart had nothing bad to say about Kelly. In fact, said Hart,

> I have never in my experience, had control of a player who was easier to "get along with" than Kelly. Uppers in sleepers never caused a grumble; hotel rooms were always good enough; exhibition games could not come too often to suit him; in fact, all the little complaints of ball players, which a manager knows so well, we never heard from Kelly. His one great fault and against which he fought harder than the public will ever know was that he was a born "good fellow," and had friends by the hundreds in every town, large or small, that he visited, who were only too anxious to entertain him. He was so big hearted and so honest that it was a difficult task to discipline him in this, his one fault. He would always admit the truth, no matter in what light it placed him; and when the other players were equally as guilty as he, in his story he only was the culprit. No player can truthfully say that Kelly ever shielded himself at their expense; in fact, when players on the team got into trouble it was always to Kelly that they looked for help to extricate them.

Bennett blamed the umpiring. Kelly blamed league officials, stating that "We didn't win the pennant because we were out-played off the field, not on it."

He ought to have known the irony of his comments.

One last positive note was struck by the *Globe,* which paid the $1,000 anyway, "because they worked so hard for it. Defeat never scares the *Globe!*" Was the payoff worth it? More than 100 years later, with the story appearing here, the *Globe* still gets public relations benefit from it. A wise man was General Taylor.

Players League

While the '89 season was going on, there was a subplot unfolding. Labor trouble was in the air. Indications of this brewing tempest could be found in the 1889 Reach Base Ball Guide, published in April, which went on at great length about "The High Salary Evil."

> Every professional organization in the country has been suffering...from the evils arising from the payment of excessive salaries to players. This has reached such enormous proportions that it seriously threatened the existence of many of the professional organizations. It was an open secret that several clubs in the great organizations of the League and the American Association had reached the limit of endurance and some immediate relief must be had.

On November 21, 1889, that relief took the form of new salary classifications for all players ranging from $1,500 a year for Class E players, to $2,500 a year for Class A. In other words, salary caps were now both obligatory and assigned to all players of varying grades, based arbitrarily on "habits, earnestness and special qualifications." The reserve clause remained in force, even if someone thought they might get a better grade with a different organization.

Ward's Brotherhood, which dated back to 1885, was being forced into a position they did not at first seek. It was supposed to be a secret organization, knowing that reprisals could be attached to known members. It was, in fact, mostly a New York Giants organization, Ward having set it in motion while a Giant.

As the Giants traveled the league, Ward recruited new members. In May of 1886, the Detroit club formed a "chapter." A few days later, Pfeffer, Williamson, and Flint signed up from Chicago. On a later trip, Ward recruited Kelly and McCormick. By the end of that season, 107 players had joined up through their clubs.

Ward first took on the reserve clause in an August 1887 magazine article, in which he wrote, "Like a fugitive slave law, the reserve rule denies [a player] a harbor or a livelihood, and carries him back, bound and shackled, to the club from which he attempted to escape."

Following the 1887 season, the National League formally met with the Brotherhood. specifically Ward, Brouthers, and Ned Hanlon. While the league agreed to eliminate the salary cap "if the American Association went along," it never came to pass.

The classification scheme was invoked while Ward was traveling the globe with Spalding prior to the '89 season. Although Ward talked of a strike when he learned what had taken place, too many players were already signed for the season, and a strike, at least to Ward's thinking, required unsigned players or "free agents."

So on May 19, a grievance committee was formed from the Brotherhood to negotiate relief from the league. Nothing happened. In June, Ward and Spalding met alone, and Spalding merely announced that the matters could wait until after the season.

An angry sentiment was growing among the players over the lack of attention to their very real concerns. There was talk of a strike on July 4, knowing how that would hurt the big gates the owners counted on. It didn't happen.

On Sunday, July 14, an off day, delegates from the different teams went to New York to contemplate their next course of action. Brouthers represented Boston. The talk turned to the formation of a new league, and Ward indicated that there were people ready to step forward to finance it.

Charles Prince of Boston, for one, was identified as someone who would "even put in the capital without any return whatever out of love for the sport."

The group broke up, heading back to their respective Monday games, and kept their activity secret. But in early September,

The Sporting News spilled the news of a "widespread plot," and noted that everyone but Cap Anson was ready to jump the National League and begin a new "Players National League." This was the atmosphere as the regular season ended, with the World Series between New York and Brooklyn staged over the period of October 18-29 (New York winning, six games to three).

Five days after the series (in which Ward had batted .417 to help win the world championship), nearly 40 players returned to the Fifth Avenue Hotel in New York to further their talks of "seceding" from the National League. They issued a long manifesto, drafted by attorney Ward, denouncing the reserve clause, the inattention to grievances, and the fact that baseball had become, to their thinking, a business. "There was a time when the league stood for integrity and fair dealing; today it stands for dollars and cents." And a new league was born.

The league, the Players National League, would have teams in all the National League cities except Cincinnati. A 16-player senate would govern the league, two from each club. Gate receipts would be divided 50-50 between home and visitor, all contracts would be three-year deals, and only the board of directors of each club, which included players, could release a man. A profit-sharing plan was introduced from which salaries could be drawn. Prize money would go to all but the last-place club. There would be two umpires, dressed in white, foiling any chicanery on the bases by you-know-who.

The first man to step forward as an investor was Al Johnson of Cleveland, Kelly's shady benefactor. This was not a good sign.

The National League tried to fight back with public denouncements, but they couldn't hold the players. They published a list of the lavish salaries the bigger stars had drawn, Kelly's name being atop the list. The chart, which traced player's pay back to 1881, showed Kelly to have earned $23,150 over the previous nine seasons, as follows: 1881-$1,300; 1882-$1,400; 1883-$1,700; 1884-$2,000; 1885-$2,250; 1886-$2,500; 1887-$4,000; 1888-$4,000; and 1889-$4,000.

The chart did not explain what happened to the announced $5,000, even though it was to be $2,000 salary and $3,000 for promotional use of his picture. The chart also claimed that Buck Ewing made $5,000 in 1889, Brouthers $4,700, Keefe $4,500, and Ward $4,250, putting Kelly fifth, tied with Hardie Richardson.

Virtually everyone of note—more than 100 players—defied the reserve clause and defected, including a number of American Association players. Anson remained with the White Stockings, given his relationship with Spalding and his being on the verge of an ownership position. Clarkson remained with the Beaneaters; he was always hard to figure. As he had been a member of the union, he was considered an agreement violator, one who turned against his deal with the Brotherhood in remaining with Soden's team. Charlie Bennett and Charlie Ganzel were others who met that criteria. In all sixteen Brotherhood members declined to play in the new league.

The new Boston franchise included ex-Beaneaters Richardson, Nash, Brouthers, Quinn, Radbourne, Tom Brown, Bill Daley, Dickie Johnston, Kid Madden, and Kelly, who was appointed manager and captain, previous misgivings notwithstanding. Even John Morrill was given a new office job back in Boston and played a couple of games along the way. Office space was rented at 86 Washington Street.

Mike basked in the opportunity. "I'm one of the bosses now," he said, "and the triumvirate [Soden, Conant and Billings]— well, to be frank, they are my understudies. Next year we will be in command and the former presidents will have to drive horse cars for a living and borrow rain checks to see a game."

Nice talk for the men who had paid him $5,000 to bring him over from Chicago, who had deposed Morrill in his wake, and who had turned him into the "King" of baseball. But Mike was loyal to his brothers, and that called for antimanagement talk on any occasion. "No one would pay a nickel to see Soden play first, Conant second, and Billings third," noted Brouthers.

Kelly's responsibilities would now include some bookkeeping, for which he was ill suited. A sportswriter recalled running into him at the Bay Street House in Worcester where he was wrestling with a small account book and a big carpenter's pencil. "What's up, Mike?" asked the writer. "This bookkeeping's hell, me boy," he replied.

Hardly running scared, the National League waited for the Players League to release its schedule—and then scheduled competing home games on almost every date, pretty much dooming any chance for success for either league.

The Boston Reds, the little-used nickname for the Players League team, would play their games at the Congress Street Park with its inviting 250-foot foul pole in left field.

The season began on April 19. Both leagues struggled along financially. Artistically, Kelly was doing just fine. He had the best team in the league and was keeping a good pace ahead of Ward's Brooklyn team, Buck Ewing's New York team, and Charles Comiskey's Chicago team.

On June 25, Kelly arrived in Chicago to begin a four-game series. He received a message; an old friend wished to visit with him. The friend, Al Spalding, was going to play one more hand to see if he could break the Brotherhood. He was going to try to break Kelly, cause the biggest name in the league to defect back to the NL, and break the back of the Players League.

Kelly agreed to meet. Spalding told the story in his memoirs, 21 year later.

> We passed the usual conventional civilities, talked about health, the weather and kindred exciting topics, until at length I opened the ball with the question.
>
> "How are things going with the game, Mike?"
>
> "Oh, the game's gone to ——."
>
> "What? You don't mean to say that the managers are getting discouraged?"
>
> "Aw, the managers!"
>
> "Why, what's the matter?" incredulously.
>
> "Everything's the matter; everybody's disgusted; clubs all losing money; we made a foolish blunder when we went into it."
>
> I thought the time was ripe. Placing a check for $10,000

on the table, I asked, "Mike how would you like that check for $10,000 filled out payable to your order?"

"Would Mike Kelly like $10,000? I should smile."

"But that's not all, Mike. Here's a three years' contract, and I'm authorized to let you fill in the amount of salary yourself."

His face blanched. "What does this mean? Does it mean that I'm going to join the league? Quit the Brotherhood? Go back on the boys?"

"That's just what it means. It means that you go to Boston tonight."

"Well," said he, "I must have time to think about this."

"There is mighty little time, Mike. If you don't want the money, somebody else will get it. When can you let me know?'" [Mike was silent as Spalding awaited a reply.]

"What are you going to do, meanwhile? Consult a lawyer?"

"Lawyer?" said Kelly. "Naw; you're good enough lawyer for me," and saying that he would be back in an hour and a half, he left the room.

At the appointed time I was awaiting him—and he came, true to the appointment. I didn't see much of encouragement in his face. His jaw was set, and there was a bright sparkle to his eye that somehow seemed to augur ill for success of my mission.

"Well, Mike, where have you been?" I asked.

"I've been taking a walk," he answered. "I went 'way up town and back."

"What were you doing?"

"I was thinking."

"Have you decided what you're going to do?" I asked.

"Yes," he replied without hesitation. "I've decided not to accept."

"What?" I ejaculated. "You don't want the $10,000?"

"Aw, I want the $10,000 bad enough; but I've thought the matter all over, and I can't go back on the boys. And" he added, "neither would you."

Involuntarily I reached out my hand in congratulation of the great ball player in his loyalty. We talked for a little while, and then he borrowed $500 of me. I think it was little enough to pay for the anguish of that hour and a half, when he was deciding to give up thousands of dollars on the altar of sentiment in behalf of the Brotherhood.

It was a defining moment for Kelly. He could have taken the money, crossed his "brothers" and crippled the Players League. But money, as Anson said, always slipped through his fingers anyway. His friendships and the virtue of loyalty meant far too much.

The season went on with one eye on a pennant race, and one eye on the small gates. With two games in each city at once, 2,000 was a good crowd. As the players had a stake in the profits, they no doubt counted the house and talked about their concerns while on the bench. In a Players League game in Brooklyn, where Ward was the manager, 80 people showed up to watch visiting Buffalo. It was hard to put a good face on the situation.

The Players League used a more lively baseball, and on May 31, George Gore, Buck Ewing, and Roger Connor hit three consecutive home runs against Cincinnati. It may have been hoped that added offense would help the gate, but a number of teams were clearly in trouble. Cleveland, for one, would draw only 58,430 for the entire season, while their National League counterparts drew 47,478. That was the weakest showing, but

Brooklyn and Buffalo of the Players League also failed to reach 100,000, and National League clubs in Pittsburgh and New York also failed to reach six figures.

Boston was the most successful of the PL teams, drawing 197,346. Kelly could bring them out. The Beaneaters drew 147,539, second best in the National League to Philadelphia's 186,002. The bottom line was that the Players League outdrew the National League 980,611 to 813,678, and it is likely the figures were inflated wherever possible. It was a disaster all around.

On the field, Harry Stovey joined Kelly's team, and on July 23 hit his 100th career home run, the first man to achieve that milestone in major league history. Stovey also ran crazy on the bases, stealing 136 of them in a 118-game season. Boston was playing well and Kelly was looking good as a manager. Decades later Jacob Ruppert would say that he didn't give Babe Ruth a managerial opportunity because "he can hardly manage himself." Obviously, Ruppert did not have an eye on history when he made the statement. As to Kelly managing his underlings, he once handed one of his charges some money and ordered him to get drunk. "When sober," said Mike, "you're the rottenest ballplayer I ever saw."

Despite the stresses of the Brotherhood war, the fans still loved their King.

They even gave him a house.

On August 15, a front page story in the Hingham (Massachusetts) *Journal* proclaimed,

> Mr. and Mrs. M.J. Kelly took possession of their new home on Main Street last Tuesday evening. The formal presentation and delivery of the deed of the house and its surroundings took place at the Cushing House where the company had gathered, they having arrived on the 6:19 train from Boston....After the ceremonies at the hotel, barges were taken and the company proceeded to the house, where Mr. and Mrs. Kelly greeted them on the piazza, they having preceded their guests in their own conveyance. The house was illuminated from top to toe, and each apartment was visited in turn and admired

by the visitors. The Boston parties left for home on the
9:50 train....

A few months later, the Kellys received a coach and a match-
ing pair of white horses, so that he might travel in comfort to
the railroad station. (Sometimes, he took the commuter boat
north to Boston, "after a long night of drinking and gambling at
the Rose Standish House on Crow Point.")

Not only did Kel cut a dashing figure, emerging from his new
home, escorted by carriage or boat by loyal admirers en route to
work, but around this time he acquired a pet monkey, which
became part of his entourage. Kel could be seen walking the
streets in his fashionable attire, the monkey on his shoulders or
at his side.

On September 14, Connie Mack was made acting captain in
Buffalo, effectively marking the start of his long managerial
career. Kelly managed against him on September 29, 30, and
October 1. When Mack concluded his managing career 60 years
later, his opposing managers included Casey Stengel, Lou
Boudreau, Joe McCarthy, Bucky Harris and Red Rolfe, and on
the playing field could be found such men as Yogi Berra, Whitey
Ford, Nellie Fox, Ted Williams, Joe DiMaggio and Bob Feller.
Would they know that they shared a common opponent with
King Kelly?

The season ground to a halt on October 4, with Boston 81-48,
6-1/2 games ahead of Brooklyn. They beat Brooklyn 11 times in
18 meetings to help insure the easy title, which was Kelly's first
since his White Stocking days. Not until October 17 was it
officially determined by the NL and AA bosses that the Players
League would not be part of any post-season championships.
The last Players League games were three post-season exhibitions between Boston and New York called fundraisers for 1891.
They were poorly attended. Mike had arranged for them when
the funeral of Agnes's mother brought him back to Paterson.

Near the end of the season, the Players League got a big
psychological boost when the owner of the Cincinnati Nationals
sold his team to a group of Players League backers, including
Julian B. Hart, the Boston principal. Said Ward, desperate for
a good sign, "It will not only bring into our league one of the best

ball teams in the country, but it will give us an ideal circuit."
Cincinnati had been the lone NL city without a PL franchise.

Ward invited National League magnates to a "peace conference" on October 3, feeling he was in the driver's seat. Six days
later, the National League met and a stockholder from Columbus of the AA began to assemble the makings of a peace treaty.
It called for consolidating the three leagues into two, even
though it left competing teams in a number of cities.

Spalding, furious over the Cincinnati sale, took an aggressive
position to salvage his league. He demanded "unconditional
surrender" by the Players League, and to his surprise, the
wounded enemy took it. The process of reworking the leagues
and taking back the Brotherhood players was ready to begin.

There were holdouts among the Brotherhood, and not a small
degree of anger by many of them. But by November 1, when
Ward admitted that consolidation seemed inevitable, the movement was effectively broken. By Thanksgiving, the white flag
was flying over the Players League office in Chicago; they had
been evicted for nonpayment of rent. It was over. A wake was
held in January at Nick Engel's Home Plate Restaurant in
Manhattan. "Pass the wine around," said Ward. "The league is
dead. Long live the league!"

Not a lot of attention was paid to the pennant races and
individual statistics during such a turbulent season, but it would
mark Kelly's final .300 campaign. He played 89 games, as usual
well divided: 56 at catcher (wearing a new and larger catcher's
mitt), 27 at short, 4 at first, 2 at third, 1 pitching, and only 6 in
the outfield. He batted .326, third on his team and 18th in the
league. He was not among the league leaders in any category,
and at 33, was showing signs of age. Kel was still the toast of
the town, but the fans too had been pounded by the wars, and
maybe everyone needed a breather.

With the end of the Brotherhood war of 1890 came the end of
Spalding's presidency in Chicago. He retired after buying out
the assets of his PL counterpart and turned over the presidency
to Boston manager James A. Hart.

And Kelly was facing the prospect of leaving Boston.

Cincinnati II

Where should King Kelly wind up following the break-up of the Players League, but Cincinnati, Ohio, where his major league career had begun, 13 years before. It was after all, a time to start over.

Boston did not place him on its reserve list for '91. Had they seen his deterioration during the 1890 season? His weight gain? Had they resented his unkind remarks, even in the heat of the Brotherhood war, after they had been so generous and forgiving with him? Had they remembered his inability to take the field at the end of the '89 season? Had they taken measure of the situation and counted their pennants under Kelly—zero—and decided to regroup?

The team was not asleep during the war. They were starting to put together a champion-caliber contingent with the likes of Tommy Tucker, Herman Long, Bobby Lowe, Joe Kelley, and the promising Kid Nichols, who would pitch his way into the Hall of Fame. Billy Nash was the new captain, signing a three-year contract worth $7,500. Frank Selee was the new manager and would prove to be a good one.

Boston also fielded an American Association team, with Charles Prince as president, once again taking on Soden and company. Arthur Irwin, a Boston native fresh from the Players League, was the manager, and Hugh Duffy, a terrific outfielder, was the captain. From the Players League, they also signed Brouthers, Richardson, Daley, Buffinton, and even a young pitcher named Clark Griffith, who would one day own the Washington Senators.

But neither of the Boston teams signed Kelly. And while

Mike's fame in that city was as grand as ever, he had to seek employment elsewhere.

He chose the motliest franchise in all the major leagues, the Cincinnatis of the second-class American Association. But they made him manager and captain, and he had a warm spot for the Queen City, so he and Agnes packed their bags and headed west. His salary was to be $1,750.

The Hingham *Journal* was not very forgiving, Kelly having just received the house at 507 Main Street a year before. "Mr. Kelly, like every other man who professionally follows base ball, is in it for the money," they wrote. "And as much can be said concerning the principle which tempts a man by a big money consideration to jump a contract as there can be of a man who is influenced by it."

But of course, Kelly was not jumping a contract—there was no contract. He was going where the work was.

Could there ever have been a more sorry site than the pitiful ballpark in the forlorn "suburb" of Pendleton, Ohio? It was a stretch to call this the Cincinnati team, for a trip to Pendleton could almost be viewed as an overnight excursion. East End Park seemed so far from the big leagues that the team was not even called "Cincinnati" by its few fans. It was known as "Kelly's Killers."

East End Park, or Pendleton Park, was put together on the banks of the Ohio River and, except for a beer garden across the street, the neighborhood wasn't much to speak of.

A beer garden? Kelly as manager? A bad combination. The man who selected Kelly was the bombastic dynamo of the American Association, Chris Von Der Ahe, 40. German born, he was a founder of the Association and owner of the champion St. Louis Browns teams that had played so well against Kelly's White Stockings in '85 and '86. Ever promotion minded, he figured the Cincinnatis could use any help they could find against the better-financed Reds of the National League. Kelly had not played in Cincinnati, save for exhibitions, since the National League had left the city eleven years earlier. Mike had not been a star when he left the Red Stockings after the 1879 season, but he was now well known all over the country and his "homecoming" would be a big story.

Before the season opener in St. Louis, Kelly promised that

"We all have bets of hats that we will not take a drink during the season. It is not an extravagant bet, but I think, nevertheless, that our boys will remain straight, as they are a well-behaved lot of fellows."

In the opener, Kelly got into an argument with the umpire, Bill Gleason, after six consecutive St. Louis batters walked. He got himself thrown out of his debut game. Departing the field, he told the fans within earshot that the game's outcome was a "sure thing" and that he wouldn't go against it. The following inning he decided to return to the field and was of course, refused by Gleason.

With the score 7-7 in the ninth and the sky rapidly nearing darkness, Kelly ordered his players to permit every St. Louis batter to reach safely. The strategy was to bring about too much darkness to continue, forcing a suspended game. (Cincinnati was last up.) With the crowd booing and directing anger towards Gleason, who had allowed Kelly to take control of the contest from the bench, the umpire forfeited the game to St. Louis. It was a disgraceful beginning.

A few days later in Louisville (the team had yet to play its home opener), Kelly was returning to his hotel at 3:00 A.M. when he spotted two of his players, veteran Ed "Cannonball" Crane and young "Kid" McGill tossing firecrackers at a lamppost. When a resident tried to intervene and quiet things down, he was the recipient of a "flying trash can."

Crane and McGill went off to jail. Kelly bailed them out in the morning, but found them off for another night on the town later that same day. Trying to act with a measure of responsibility, Kel put his hand on McGill's shoulder to lead him back to the hotel. Crane, who five years later would be dead through his own ingesting of poison, immediately socked Kelly in the back, to which Kelly responded with a right to the eye. Crane missed the home opener with a black eye and he and Kelly didn't speak for days.

On May 6, Kelly's Killers arrived in Boston for Mike's first return. The game was at the Congress Street Grounds, where he had played with the Players League the year before. He hadn't been gone all that long, but coverage in the *Globe* gives a pretty good idea of how he was received.

King Kelly appeared on the Congress St. grounds yesterday for the first time in his Cincinnati uniform, and for nearly two hours he kept the crowd in good humor and struggled for victory unavailingly.

The Only Mike seemed much at home on a Boston diamond, and after he had limbered up a little in practice, he shouldered his bat and started for his old seat on the Boston bench, but in a moment recalled the fact he was no longer a member of the champions, and sorrowfully turned and made his way to the visitor's bench.

The day was cold and anything but conducive to a good attendance, but still the fame of Kelly and his champion killers was enough to make over 3,000 people journey to Congress St. to greet him on his return to the scene of his triumphs of last year.

Before the game the two teams paraded the streets headed by the National Guard band, and evoked much enthusiasm on their way.

Kelly came into the grounds riding in a hired barouche. He went out in his own turnout, a natty Kimball wagon driven by a prancing dapple gray.

The rig was complete with russet leather harness, fine robes and whip, and was the gift of some of Kelly's Boston friends who appreciate the manly stand the "king" has taken all through the base ball war.

Kelly has a strong team, and all of his men in the game, with the exception of Canavan, have played championship ball before Boston spectators.

It was in the first inning that Kelly was given the horse and carriage. He was the third man at the bat, and as he stepped to the rubber, the band struck up "Hail to the Chief" and then all eyes were centered upon a team of horses coming through the left field gate. Play was stopped and the team was driven up to the plate. The whole rig was complete. The horse is a young, well built beauty indeed.

The wagon is two-seated with top. It is built throughout of light wood and is finished in the natural color. The driver circled about and drove up in front of the stand and the players of the two teams gathered about, while Thomas J. Barry, Esq., the well known lawyer, presented Michael with the whole outfit. Briefly and in well-chosen words, Mr. Barry said that he was glad in behalf of Kelly's friends to welcome him back to the scene of his past base ball triumphs. His time on the diamond had been an honorable one, and what he had done for the national game deserved recognition. His friends took this opportunity to express their appreciation of his good work and the sacrifices he had made to further the welfare of the American Association this year and the players' league last season.

Kelly said he wished to thank his friends through their spokesman, and he thought about the best way to signify his appreciation of the gift was to play ball, which he proposed doing.

A magnificent floral horseshoe, six feet high, was the tribute of the Elks to their fellow member.

The band played "He's a jolly good fellow," the sleek pony pranced around the diamond again, and Kelly went back to bat and got his base on balls.

The presentation was witnessed by a large number of Boston Elks, the Social Club of Hingham, and a delegation of Kelly's friends from Paterson, N.J.

The Boston and Cincinnati teams have been invited to attend the performance of 'A Night's Frolic' at the Park Theatre tonight.

President Prince, Secretary Hart, John Graham, Tom
Hardy these are some of Kel's well wishers.

Indeed, President Prince and Secretary Hart had to be impressed by Kel's continuing drawing power in the city in which
he could do no wrong.

Boston won, 2-1. Kelly, who caught, was 0-2 with two walks.
Boston was in first, 15-6, Cincinnati sixth, 10-15 after the game.

Back at home, Kel's antics did not go over as well as they did
in Boston. He took to swimming back and forth across the Ohio
River two or three times before games. One night, after downing
a few whiskeys after a loss, he nearly drowned himself by
removing his clothing and overdoing the swimming exercise in
the dark of night.

Kelly's Killers became best known for playing ball on Sunday,
a practice strictly prohibited and rigidly enforced in Pendleton.
Each Sunday they would play, and each Sunday evening, would
find themselves in the local lockup, paying a fine or spending
the night in jail. They would repeat the practice each Sunday
the team was at home. It became a joke to them. It is, as far as
can be determined, the only times Kelly may have been impris-
oned.

Kelly was also making a joke of his roster, allowing anyone to
pitch, or in fact play any position. It was still an era of two
starters, with perhaps a third "change" pitcher, yet Kelly used
eleven different pitchers. Sometimes, in the middle of an inning,
some outfielder might run in and ask for his turn, and simply
take over.

Kelly used seven "one-game wonders" during the season,
perhaps young men he met at the beer garden the night before.

The lack of seriousness in their play was reflected in some of
their scores. They beat Philadelphia 21-16. They lost to the
Browns 20-12. They beat Washington 17-2. They lost to Boston
20-5.

The attendance was horrid, and the team was running out of
money. By August, they were broke and the team simply folded.
It was a precursor to what would follow in two months—the
dissolution of the entire American Association after ten years of
operation.

Kelly had played in 82 games for his Killers and had batted

.297. The Association decided to move the franchise to Milwaukee for the final weeks of the season, but Kelly was offered his release if he chose not to go. He asked for the release.

His five zany months in Cincinnati were history.

Boston III

And so where did he go from Cincinnati?

As noted, the directors of the American Association's Boston franchise, having seen his drawing power in May, and noting his .297 average, decided to take a chance and bring the hero back. On August 17, they signed him and made him captain. He was "going home."

One would almost think that the excitement could not be rekindled yet again, but newspapers followed his journey east and 10,000 faithful in the city of Boston prepared to welcome its hero yet again.

This was only the start of a bizarre week for baseball and for M. J. Kelly.

Mike suited up in his new Boston flannels and took the field against Baltimore to a tremendous ovation. So thrilled were the fans to have him back that the carriage which had been provided back in May was now carried by able-bodied men, unhitching the horse and hoisting the beloved Kel like a traveling sultan.

The Boston Reds were the class of the Association in '91. They were en route to a 93-42, first-place finish, led by Brouthers .350 and Duffy's .336.

Kelly played a game against Baltimore and three against Philadelphia, collecting four hits in 15 at bats. But no sooner had the fans begun to accept him back in a Boston uniform when, in an act which would ignite an overt war between the rival leagues, he accepted a better offer from the Beaneaters, which included a trip to Europe for him and Agnes. Kelly returned to his old National League team after just eight days with the Association team.

The two leagues had met in Washington in midseason to try

to sort out a new peace agreement following the disorder brought about by the Players League demise. When the committee representing the Association received a telegram notifying them of Kelly's broken contract and his jump to the National League, all negotiations were suddenly halted.

The committee hastily informed their counterparts from the National League that all friendly negotiations were now "off" until Kelly was returned to the Association. The NL's committee merely said it was powerless to return Kelly, as the entire league would have to agree to it. The Association then broke off all discussions and decided to fight back by raiding National League players.

Kelly, happy to be on familiar turf at the South End Grounds, rejoined his old mates after nearly two years in rival uniforms. Like the Association Bostons, these men were also in first place and driving towards a pennant. Clarkson was still the leading pitcher, although as one who had broken his promise to the Brotherhood, no longer especially popular. Quinn, Nash, Bennett, and Ganzel remained from the old days, and the new fellows were talented and hungry. Selee, the manager, may not have been especially excited about welcoming Kelly, but he was not about to let this disturb his pennant drive.

Kelly wound up playing in only 16 games in the final six weeks of the season, batting .231 while controversy reigned about him in league offices. But perhaps his presence had the effect of a magic potion: his club rolled off 18 straight victories after his arrival, still a franchise record, covering Boston, Milwaukee and Atlanta, more than a century later. And there he was, at season's end, a member of the 1891 National League champions, his seventh championship club.

Arthur Irwin challenged Frank Selee to a world championship when the season ended, but Selee declined, and no post-season games were played. An all-Boston post-season would have been thrilling for the great fans who had weathered the baseball wars better than most. But more serious matters were confronting baseball. The American Association was dying.

They raided some players before they passed away. They got Fred Pfeffer for $7,000 and Amos Rusie, the fine young Giants pitcher, for $6,000. Philadelphia lured Connor and Richardson.

The National League answered back. Brooklyn stole Brouth-

ers away from Boston; Philadelphia grabbed Comiskey. The new
high salaries scared people on both sides and another peace
conference was called. On December 15, they met in Indianapolis and drafted a constitution for a new, consolidated and expanded league of 12 teams, the National League absorbing
Baltimore, St. Louis, Louisville, and Washington. It was thought
that the league would be called "The National League and
American Association of Base Ball Clubs."

It didn't catch on. It would be, then and forever, the National
League, winning at last after two tumultuous seasons which saw
the deaths of the Players League and the American Association,
and with them, many professional jobs.

Mike and Agnes took off for their long overdue trip to Europe
as the battlefields came to rest. They were accompanied by
Agnes' father. Mike loved the European style in which everyone
called him "sir." But he couldn't get the hang of British money
or the exchange rate. He thought he was tipping sixpence and
shillings, but he was in fact tipping the bootblacks "half-sover-
eigns."

"I got home at 6:00 A.M. with as fine a jag as you could get in
any country in the world," he reported. "This is a pretty good
town. The girl likes it too, and his nobs says it ain't bad for an
old country." It is possible that Europe was not so taken by a
visiting American baseball player until Lenny Dykstra of the
Philadelphia Phillies dazzled the French with his tobacco-chewing manners at elegant restaurants following the 1993 season.

The off-season offered some sad notes for Kel; his old Chicago
teammate Larry Corcoron died on October 14, 1891 of Bright's
Disease at age 32. Catching partner Silver Flint died of consumption (tuberculosis) on January 14 at 31. By all terms, Kelly
was still a young man of 34, except perhaps by athletic terms.
But he had abused his body with alcohol for nearly 20 years. He
was no longer swift; in fact, he was flabby. *The Reach Guide*
noted that his arm had grown weaker each year during the last
decade. His popularity was as high as it had ever been; his
on-field performance meant little in that league. "Slide, Kelly,
Slide" was playing on everyone's Edison phonograph. But he was
marking time in the big leagues.

New pitchers were having their ways with Kel quite easily.
An example would be the Hoosier Thunderbolt, Amos Rusie of

the Giants, who had arrived in New York in 1890 to play in the National League and who had led in strikeouts in his first two years there with 341 and 337 respectively. He had 62 victories in his first two seasons with the Giants and would win another 101 in the next three. Men with lively arms like that were beginning to usher in a new fastball era—an era in which new younger hitters would have to emerge to conquer the changing game. Cleveland had a 25-year old pitcher named Denton Young, entering his second full season. They said he could throw the ball like a cyclone.

In 1892, a pair of 5' 7" outfielders arrived in Boston, the "Heavenly Twins," Tom McCarthy and Hugh Duffy. Both were headed for the Hall of Fame.

McCarthy, 28, had been with the Browns in the American Association for the previous four years, and had even managed the club at age 26. He had batted .350 and .310 in the previous two seasons.

Duffy, 25, from Cranston, Rhode Island, was captain of the Association's Boston team in '91 after three years in Chicago: two with the National League, one with the Players League. He had batted .336 in 1891.

The Heavenly Twins joined Bobby Lowe in the outfield, with the infield composed of Tommy Tucker at first, Joe Quinn at second, Herman Long at short, and Billy Nash at third. Kid Nichols, Happy Jack Stivetts and Harry Staley were the main pitchers, with Clarkson filling in as the fourth starter. Kelly, his arm wearying, had become a weak link at catcher, where he played 72 of his 78 games. The other catchers were Ganzel and Bennett, who caught 51 and 35 respectively.

Selee took his team south for the first time for spring training, running two practices a day, imposing an 11:30 curfew, banning drinking and limiting smoking, telling his charges to "let up a little on the weed."

The National League season of '92, lacking a competing league, would be a "split season," with the winners of the first and second halves meeting in a post-season championship. With 12 teams in the circuit, it made sense, as it gave even the hopeless tailenders a fresh start in mid-summer.

Boston did well and could relax on their way to the first half title. They won 11 of their first 13 and by the end of May were

4- 1/2 games ahead of Chicago, well positioned to clinch the first-half title before the half ended on July 13.

One historically interesting game took place on May 6 at Cincinnati. Boston and Cincy were deadlocked after 14 innings, when umpire Jack Sheriden called the game—on account of sun! The setting sun was squarely in the batter's eyes, and all agreed there was a clear and present danger. More than any other recorded game, that one influenced the decision to always construct diamonds with the sun setting behind home. That put all pitchers facing west, their left arms on the south, hence, the term "southpaws."

Two days before the end of the first half, the title clinched, Mike had a treat for his old fans in Chicago. On July 11th, Selee permitted Kelly to undertake a theatrical farce on the field to the grand amusement of the crowds.

A year before, showing good humor over his advancing years, "Pop" Anson had played a game in Chicago wearing what was described as "Santa Claus whiskers."

Now, with Boston coming to town, Anson advertised the use of a young lineup made up largely of rookies. The White Stockings were being called the Colts because of their youth. Kelly, always up for a laugh, decided to dress his team as old men to mock the Anson lineup. Eddie Foy the early stage star, and a friend of Kel's, helped with makeup, and a local costume man provided the outfits. Reported the Boston *Globe,* "Mike Kelly was made up as an English dude. Hugh Duffy wore Red Galway sluggers and a red nose. Tommy McCarthy was made up as the only fireman. Jack Stivetts had a heavy beard, also a red nose. Kid Nichols wore Danite whiskers. Joe Quinn sported a handsome pair of whiskers, of the reddish hue, a white necktie and a blue cap, looking very Fourth of July. Tom Tucker wore a full beard. Herman Long was made up as the three ball merchant Frank Bush. Bobby Lowe wore black whiskers, a red nose and one black eye. Charley Bennett wore gray whiskers."

All the players except Nichols and Bennett, the battery, played in their costumes, and Boston won 3-2.

The second half the season went not as smoothly, with Boston losing the first game of the half 20-3 to St. Louis, and finding themselves tied for fifth in short order. A local scribe said the team was "too exhilarated" from its first-half success.

Meanwhile, attendance was not keeping up with the salary levels Boston had reached. Season attendance would be only 123,898, even with no competition. Players were asked to take pay cuts. Boston, in fact, began to set an example for the rest of the league by dumping higher salaried players in favor of younger ones. When Clarkson complained about his cut, he was released and signed with Cleveland. Also released was Harry Stovey, who had batted only .164 in 38 games in the outfield.

And so too, unthinkably, was Kel.

It only lasted a few days before he was re-signed, Boston saving a few bucks in the process. The re-signing, on July 21, was accompanied by the big news that Kel was to be made captain again.

The team recovered from its poor play in August, with Stivetts no-hitting Brooklyn 11-0 on the 6th, the first no-hitter in Boston history. A strong finish (28-9) brought them to within three wins of a second half title as well.

But by the end of the season, it was Cleveland that had topped the league for the second half, setting up a post-season championship between Boston and Cleveland. Boston, with a better overall record, (a fantastic 102-38), was awarded its second straight pennant, Kelly's eighth.

The team was 25-10 in one-run games and had 14 shutouts. It was coming together as a new dynasty, but Kelly was not a major factor. His season average was an embarrassing .189.

His final days with Boston would not be proud ones.

The first three games of a best-of-nine series would be played in League Park in Cleveland beginning October 17. This was the same League Park that would be home to the Indians until 1946; the park where Joe DiMaggio hit safely in his 56th straight game; the park where Bob Feller broke in.

Stivetts would pitch the opener for Boston and Cy Young, 36-12 with nine shutouts in the regular season, would go for Cleveland.

The game began at 3:00 P.M. before 6,000 fans in the grandstand and hundreds more roped off in the deep outfield. Kelly, who had shared the catching chores all season, was behind the plate.

In the fourth inning, he struck out with a man on third in a scoreless game. On it went, 0-0, into the ninth, when Jesse

Burkett nearly scored on a force-out at first. But Kelly made a hard tag at the plate for a big double play. In the last of the ninth, Stivetts led off and hit a high pop over home plate. Chief Zimmer, the Spiders' catcher, circled under it. From the bench, Kelly shouted "Virtue, Virtue!" calling for first baseman Jacob Virtue to make the play. His actions caused a collision, although Zimmer held on for the out. Patsy Tebeau, the Cleveland manager, raced onto the field and demanded that Kelly be tossed out for the action. It was actually a typical Kelly moment. But the game was moving past its early days, when such plays were more the norm. In major league baseball of 1892, it wasn't well received.

The press would call it a horrible example of sportsmanship and even suggested that the King had bet heavily on Boston to win. The game wound up 0-0 in 11 innings, when darkness prevailed. Kelly went 0-4.

Kelly was behind the plate again the next day, again hitting cleanup, and facing none other than old teammate John Clarkson, who had begun the year with Boston. In perfect fall weather, 7,000 turned out. Harry Staley pitched for Boston.

In the first, Herman Long led off with a single, and took third on a base hit by McCarthy. With Kelly batting, McCarthy broke for second. As Zimmer began to throw down, Kel knocked the ball out of his hand with his bat, and was called out for interference. Tebeau was exasperated with Kelly's antics.

Boston won the game, 4-3. Kelly went 0-4 again, for an 0-8 in the first two.

He had played his last game in a Boston uniform.

Ganzel caught game three, Bennett game four, Ganzel five, and Bennett six. Boston won them all for a clean 5-0 sweep (with one tie), and could claim the world title.

The celebration in Boston must have been a little bittersweet for Michael Joseph Kelly. To have watched four straight championship games from the bench could not have been easy for the King. Maybe the game was passing him by. Maybe his skills were fading. Maybe he had to face his future long and hard.

New York

Quietly, during the winter of 1892-93, Mike Kelly drifted away from Boston baseball forever. He decided that his future was on the stage. No longer would he grace the baseball diamonds of America; the nation would now see the great King Kelly in song and dance and comedy and recital—if they cared enough to buy a ticket for the vaudeville theatre.

It had always been his ambition. Extroverted, dashing, and filled with self-confidence, he possessed all that seemed necessary for a career on the stage, except perhaps for talent.

And thus the 1893 major league baseball season began without King Kelly, the first since 1877. Mike took some engagements with "O'Dowd's Neighbors" and followed the fates and fortunes of his old pals in the daily sporting press.

The New York Giants were regrouping in '93, bringing Monte Ward back from three years in rival Brooklyn, to manage, captain, and play second. Ward, it was said, got a bigger deal than Kelly got in '87, with New York agreeing to pay Brooklyn five percent of their gross receipts for the season, which, estimates had it, would top the celebrated $10,000. (It didn't.)

The Giants did not get off as well as they had hoped and, by mid-May, Ward decided he might lure Kelly back onto the playing field for one more go. They had been "Brothers" in the Players League war, and although never teammates, mutual admirers. Ward too had published a book in '88 (not an autobiography), making them both men of letters. Ward, of course, had a Columbia law degree; Kelly was pretty good at signing his autograph.

On May 25, Kelly agreed to sign with the Giants. Wrote the *New York Times:*

With Michael J. Kelly, the erstwhile actor, poet, philosopher, composer and baseball player, the stage is a thing of the past. Kelly's histrionic ambitions have been shattered, and in the future he will confine himself to work on the baseball diamond. One-night stands, poor receipts, irritating hotels, unappreciative audiences, and other nightmares incidental to the life of a variety actor have caused the great ball player to go back to his first love.

Kelly made his first appearance as a member of the New York club on the Polo Grounds yesterday in a game against Philadelphia. To say that he was warmly welcomed is using a mild term. Six thousand persons were on the grounds and Treasurer Talcott is authority for the statement that three-quarters of that number came to see the king of the diamond. And he was correct. Faces that have not been seen on a ball ground since the disastrous fight between capital and muscle were noticeable in the throng that assembled to welcome Kelly's advent into the ranks of the Giants.

When the great player walked onto the field it was the signal for an outburst of applause. He smiled, waved his hands at friends whom he noticed in the crowd, and began to practice with the boys. All eyes, of course, were centered on the new player, and comments were made on his work. As the gong sounded for the game to begin, the catcher got his mask, pad, and big glove and was once more in harness. At that moment, a spectator shouted, "Good house to-night!" and Kelly smiled.

"Say Kel, just one moment," said another. "Give us a verse of Casey at the Bat."

"Let's have 'Daddy Wouldn't Buy Me A Bow Wow.'"

"Slide, Kelly, Slide."

"The Day I Played Baseball."

"Just A Few Footsteps in the Sand."

"Now Won't You Be Good."

Kelly waited until the crowd got through, and then gave pitcher Mark Baldwin the signal to begin work. At first he was a trifle shy, but he soon warmed up to his task, and was right in the game after an inning or two. The catcher coached players every time a ball was hit, and imparted life to the play of the team. In the sixth inning, Kelly made his first hit of the season, sending in a run that gave New York the lead. As usual, he played several neat tricks that told heavily in favor of his club. The king took to the game like a fish to water. He pranced about the field like a schoolboy, and yelled at the players of his club, the umpire, and the opposing team whenever an opportunity presented itself. At one stage he ran over to the water pail, took a big dipperful, and swallowed it.

"Oh Kel," yelled a friend, "taking to ice water now! I've got a big cold bottle on ice!"

"Keep it until next October," replied Kelly, with a smile, "and I'll break it with you. I'm a cold-water guy this summer; make no mistake."

After the grand entrance, things began to go wrong. He didn't play especially well. Ward used him on May 25, 26, 27, 29, 30 and June 1, obviously preparing to get a lot of action from him. On the 27th, it was written that "Kelly handled Rusie's curves in a most refreshing fashion. The 'King,' with his few days practice, is in fairly good shape and from the present outlook, in a few days he will be able to play as well as he ever did."

But a reporter on June 1 noted that "Kelly is sore and stiff and cannot do himself justice."

Three days later, it was reported that "The King is rapidly getting into shape and will be able to play in a short while."

He played on June 16, but on the 19th, it was reported that Kelly, overcome by heat, left early and was not available for the game. Hmmmm....

New York City should have been a great stop for Kel. He arrived with a Japanese valet, and his pet monkey sat upon his shoulder. A New Yorker at heart from his years in suburban Paterson, New Jersey, his birth in upstate Troy, and his winters in Hyde Park, he had always loved the spotlight of the nation's biggest city and always dreamed of playing there. He and Honest John had their Sixth Avenue saloon there, "The Two Kels," Mrs. Kelly was a Paterson native, and plenty of his friends could attend the games. But it was not a great season for the once proud King. The pitching plate was moved back to 60' 6", largely due to the success Amos Rusie was enjoying in New York with his blazing fastballs. Now Mike would be asked to catch them, while also hitting against fresh young arms from a new distance. It was a tall order.

He was also apparently, drinking heavily again. Ward ordered Kelly into the Turkish baths each morning to dry him out by game time. One day, when he was supposed to be at the Turkish Baths, he instead attended a clambake of the "Brower House Ball Club," and then went on to the races at Morris Park. Ward had no choice but to suspend him.

Although the suspension was brief, it was widely discussed, and the subject of numerous editorials and sports cartoons.

Mike rode the bench the rest of the season, playing only ten more games after those first couple of weeks, 16 in all. His appearances were about a week apart; June 30, July 3, July 4, July 8, July 19, July 22, August 4, August 9. His final game in Chicago was on June 30 before just 600 fans. He caught and batted sixth against Anson's "Colts," in a 9-5 loss.

On July 8, the New York *Times* noted that "Ex-King Kelly was behind the bat for the Giants but played a listless game." He made two errors and had a passed ball.

After a bad road trip, the Giants returned to the Polo Grounds on July 17, and the players entered the field in a good mood. "Kelly whistled a few bars of 'Daddy Wouldn't Buy Me A Bow Wow,' as other members of the team looked on in astonishment." Kel coached at first base that day, trying to steal the catcher's signs.

He stole his last base on July 19 against Boston, but was by now the team's number four catcher, behind Parke Wilson, Jocko Milligan, and Jack Doyle. The *Times* thought he might be improving, writing, "King Kelly is in form now—his work yesterday was greatly admired."

On the 21st, he was credited with "tipping" rookie pitcher Les German through the game with signs, as New York beat Boston 4-3. The next day he played his final game in Boston, catching Baldwin, and going hitless in a 13-8 loss.

On June 25, eight Giants were invited to the Pelhamville Gun Club for a sweepstake pigeon shoot, but Kel was not on the list. He was starting to feel like the odd man out.

He collected the final 17 hits of his career over the long season. He made an ungodly 22 errors in his few appearances and at least one passed ball in every game, for a .778 fielding average. The last time his name appeared in a major league box score was on September 2, a pleasant afternoon at the Polo Grounds. The Giants played Louisville, who featured ol' Fred Pfeffer at second base.

In a sloppy, high-scoring contest before 5,000 fans, the Giants ran up a 15-3 lead after four innings, at which point Ward told Kelly to relieve Wilson behind the plate. He hadn't played in weeks.

Kelly donned his catching gear and took the pitches of right-hander Charlie Petty, and later, of Mark Baldwin, who had, eight years earlier, been one of those two odd call-ups Anson engaged in the '86 World Series, without having previously played a major league game.

Kelly recorded two putouts in the game, off a pair of Baldwin strikeouts. He had an assist and two passed balls. At the plate, he hit a single, the last of his 1,813 hits, and scored his 1,357th and final run. His lifetime average was .308. The Giants won 23-14, despite commiting eight errors.

The schedule ran through the end of the month, but Kelly played no more. At season's end (the Giants having finished fifth), after a few exhibitions games with Brooklyn, he was quietly, and unsurprisingly, released. The nation was in a financial depression (600 banks had closed), and Kel was out of work, and nearly broke.

Mike spent the winter once again booking vaudeville appearances, where no one could tell if there was concern over his career. He was lively and full of confidence on the stage, reciting "Kelly at the Bat" to the applause of his fans. He was far more a celebrity than a man to be measured by his statistics; most in the audience probably didn't even know he'd been with the Giants during the year past.

Allentown and Yonkers

Mike's many friendships around the country would surely pay off for him come spring. One did, but it was not a major league opportunity, and it didn't come until March, a few days after Mike learned of the death of Ned Williamson—dropsey of the stomach at age 36. The old White Stockings were dying young.

The owner of the Allentown club of the Pennsylvania State League, was none other than Al Johnson, the old Brotherhood benefactor, and lender of rooms in Cleveland for hat-smashing parties. Johnson offered him a player-manager-captain job. Looking at no other offers, Kelly took it.

Allentown was not at the top of the minor league pecking order; the Eastern League, the Western League, and the Southern League were considered stronger. At Allentown, Mike's road trips would be short hops across the state: Altoona, Danville, Easton, Harrisburg, Johnstown, Scranton and York. He would move his pregnant Agnes with him to Allentown and assume his new duties. They took a little cottage just a few hundred yards from the ball park.

Yes, Agnes and Mike were to become parents for the first time. At 36, it was late in Mike's life to have a first child, but perhaps it would provide a reason for a more stable family life now that his baseball career was winding down.

From afar, Mike heard of the events in the major leagues in which he was a nonparticipant for the first time since 1878. Remarkably, four National League ballparks suffered heavy fire damage during the year, including the South End Grands in Boston. The structure caught fire during the third inning of a game on May 14 and was totally destroyed.

Chicago was a very different city than Mike had first discov-

---

Tales of the King

Mike still was up to his old tricks. One day Browning was on first and Kel was at bat. A fellow named Sprague was pitching for Harrisburg.

On the first pitch, Kelly stepped in front of the plate and made a wide sweep with his bat even before the ball left Sprague's hand. This disarmed the catcher, Swink, who dropped the ball as Browning easily stole second. Kelly danced gleefully on home plate.

One day while catching against Harrisburg, Eddie Sales came to bat with two Harrisburg runners on. With the sun setting behind home plate, Kel held his glove high so as to create a large shadow, while seemingly calling for a high pitch.

Instead, as planned, the pitch was low, as Sales struck out.

---

ered in 1880. Hoards of national and international visitors to the World Columbian Exposition of 1893, with its great Ferris Wheel, brought a new worldly promience to Mike's old stomping grounds. On August 5 (with Anson at bat), a man yelled "fire" from the grandstand of South Side Park, and following a stampede by the crowd, half the grandstand and all of the bleachers were destroyed.

Fire also claimed the ballpark in Philadelphia the very next day.

In little Allentown, Mike made the best of a bad situation. He recruited some ex-big leaguers like Jocko Milligan and Jack Coleman, who had been with the Giants the year before, Sam Wise, his old Boston teammate, Matt Kilroy, Joe Mulvey, and George Wood. He almost got Pud Galvin but the deal fell through. His big signing was Pete Browning, "The Gladiator," a three-time batting champ.

Kelly did all that he could to rouse interest in the team before the season, and that was plenty. "Nothing but the championship will suit me," he boasted, "and I propose we win it. I will play in every game."

Agnes too was a help as the First Lady of the team. She was a frequent occupant of the grandstand and watched Mike with "eyes kindling with pride and devotion. She knows all the points of the game," wrote *Sporting Life.* She also predicted a championship. One newspaper described her as "a very pleasant, quiet lady, who made friends with everybody."

The club, known as the "Terrors," was losing money. Mike installed himself as the first baseman, and occasionally as catcher. True to his word, he did play virtually every game.

Mike had to finish a theatre engagement at the National in Philadelphia, where he was performing with "O'Dowd's Neighbors," and he arrived in Allentown with his theatrical manager, Charles Hudson. Just before the season opened, as a publicity stunt, he visited a mill in Allentown which was run by the son of his old Paterson boss, John Ryle. Mike sat for a time and ran a loom with his old skill. Today, that would be called a "photo op."

He arranged for a preseason exhibition with Boston and drew the biggest crowd ever to the Lehigh Valley, about 5,000.

Before the game, Kel opened telegrams of good wishes from many friends, including Fred Pfeffer, Tim Murnane, Jake Morse, Horace Fogel, and Patsy Tebeau. On hand to wish him well were other baseball notables. He received a letter from a Boston fan, who said that while it was impossible for him to be in Allentown, he would pay a "great amount of money" for the ball which would receive the first "whack" from his bat. Another letter writer, from New York, wanted the bat with which he made his first hit. (Neither request was honored.)

At 2:00 P.M., the Boston and Allentown teams arrived at the park to great festivities, and Boston won the game 5-4, with Mike getting a hit and stealing a base. The crowd got their money's worth. The Allentown players looked splendid in their white uniforms with blue trim. "Interest here is aroused to the highest pitch," wrote the local press. "The arrival of Kelly has set the enthusiasts wild."

The regular season began at Easton on May 2 with a 9-0 victory, in which Kel played first and went 1-5. The next day, he received a large floral tribute for the home opener, won by Allentown 19-1, with Mike going 0-4.

Things were not going well, however, at the league offices. On May 17, Kel attended a league meeting in Harrisburg, and after making a motion to throw the press out of the room, listened to the political woes of the league officials. He then moved to disband the league, a tactic which never went to a vote. But by June 1, Easton had withdrawn from the league, leaving only seven teams. Some weeks later, Scranton was forced to withdraw. It was not a healthy situation.

In July, little baby Kelly was born in Allentown. There is no written record of the baby's birth, as birth certificates were not required at the time. Whether the child was male or female, or what its name was, is lost to us over time. No birth or baptismal certificate exists today at any of the Catholic churches in the Allentown area or back home in Paterson.

Allentown finished second to Harrisburg in the first half of the season and at 31-20 was five games out.

Not long after the second half began, Kelly released Browning to the raised eyebrows of the fans. Browning had been doing well and winning fans. For the first time, Kel's popularity suffered.

Still, he gave the fans a great time at the park. Once with the bases loaded, he raised his cap and got the crowd wild when he announced in a loud voice, "A thousand dollars to a nickel I clear the bases."

He struck out.

"I made a mistake," he yelled, as he assumed his position.

The team was 21-9 in the second half, second place again, when they were themselves forced to drop out of the league on August 6. Johnson immediately moved to transfer Kelly and several of his other players to Yonkers, New York, of the Eastern League. The move crippled the Pennsylvania State League, but Allentown was practically broke.

Kel left Agnes and the baby in Allentown and moved to Yonkers, just north of the New York City line, where he managed to schedule a few of the remaining games in the Polo Grounds when the Giants were away.

In Allentown, he had his followers, but the unpleasant departure, not his fault, caused some to turn on him. One headline said, "Kelly's Absence Not Felt; Allentown Talking Much of Plans for Next Season," and took note of the fact that Kelly had pledged to put some of his own money into the maintenance of the field, but was in fact, broke. It was his "dirty little secret."

"The joke of the matter," wrote *Sporting Life*, "is that Kelly was dead broke from the time he came here and probably the

---

Tales of the King

John McGraw, who played against Kelly in 1891, 1892, and 1893, said "The greatest play from the standpoint of quick thinking that I have ever seen was one made by King Kelly.... Kelly was catching in a close game. In the ninth inning his team led by a run when the other side stepped to bat. Two men were easily retired easily. Then a base on balls and an error put the tying run on second and the winning run on first.

"The next batter shot a hot single to right and the man on second tore for the plate. The outfielder's throw came in true enough but to Kelly's left, on his gloved hand. As the ball was in the air Mike saw that he had to take it with his left hand. If he used two hands he would miss the runner. Yet taking the ball with the glove and swinging into the sliding man, he ran the chance of dropping the throw.

"Kelly figured this out quicker than it takes me to tell it. He flung off his glove, caught the bounding ball with his bared left hand and touched the runner out.

"I've seen many great plays in my twenty-seven years in baseball. This one has always stood out as the headiest play of them all."

---

present and the idea of his expending $2600 on the grounds and using his money to beautify the place was a whopper, as to excite the sensibilities."

Mike ran out the season in Yonkers. Not everyone was amused by what they were seeing. In Syracuse, he was seen as an aging joke.

"We have in contrast," they said in the local press there, "a team run by the notorious Mike Kelly. The spectacle this fellow has made of himself here in Syracuse was enough to bring the blush of shame to every lover of the national game. Is it not time that such loafers as this Kelly be drummed out of base ball? Is the game elevated by his presence? Providing the Eastern League is inflicted by him next season, his reception here will not be flattering."

Unknowingly, Mike played his last professional game on

September 14 in Erie, Pennsylvania, playing first, batting third, and going 2-5 in an 8-3 Yonkers victory. The next day, the final game of the season was played in Erie. "Kelly did not play," reported the press, "but was on hand to insist on playing long enough to secure the guarantee. He also danced a jig to amuse the crowd while waiting for the shower to pass over."

Mike played 75 games and batted .305 in '94. Said Anson, from afar, "Whiskey had become at this time his master, and he made a failure of the managerial business. Not being able to control himself it is hardly to be wondered at that he failed when it came to the business of controlling others."

Agnes and the baby would stay in Allentown. There would be stage engagements for the winter. In October, Johnson listed Mike on the Yonkers reserved list for 1895, seemingly assuring him of at least returning there for the following season if nothing on the big league level opened up.

Had Mike been around for the '95 season, he would not have found Yonkers in the league. They didn't make it to the starting gate.

The Passing

The notices in the Boston newspapers on Monday, November 5, heralded the big show at the Palace for the following evening.

But those who read pages other than the amusements knew that the show was not to be.

Mike had no trouble getting the booking, nor did the Palace have any trouble selling tickets. Never mind that he had played at Allentown and Yonkers a few months earlier; his fame far exceeded his career at this point and few even gave much thought to where he might be playing in '95.

Mike himself had to know that the end of his baseball career was in sight. Yes, he had been reserved by Yonkers for '95, but he wasn't a Yonkers kind of guy, and the life of a showman in the big cities probably held more appeal at this point. Like most players, he probably didn't face his declining skills head on; but he could see that his major league opportunities had passed.

He was now prepared to concentrate on the stage career he had yearned of as a boy in Paterson and had pursued since his arrival in Boston. He had signed up with Mark Murphy's touring company, playing a vaudeville act called "O'Dowd's Neighbors." A week's appearance at the Bijou Theatre in Paterson preceded the booking at the Palace. Critics may have found him lacking in singing or dancing abilities, but he could charm the crowds, recite his poetry, and perhaps exchange in some repartee with the Gaiety Girls. Let Boston know: The King was back to town.

Agnes had remained in Allentown with the baby after the team folded and was still there, a month after the season had ended, while Mike was in Paterson. She must have felt rather alone, with none of their old friends near. And the truth was, Mike was broke.

All of his baseball earnings had been spent at nearly the rate they had come in. Whether losing at the faro table or the racetrack, whether buying himself the finest clothing or a round of whiskey for the boys, he just couldn't handle finances. His future earnings were going to be based on his success on the stage, and with the baseball checks coming to a close, he had better be entertaining and pack the house.

His first show was booked for Monday afternoon, November 5, and he left New York City the night before on the Fall River Line to travel by boat up Long Island Sound to Boston.

But an unexpected autumn snowstorm slowed the journey,

and Mike, whose resistence was not what it had once been, took ill aboard ship in the chilling weather.

One account had him lending his topcoat to a stowaway, ever the champion of the downtrodden. Another had him giving the fellow his best suit of clothes.

The boat arrived in Boston harbor on Sunday night, where Mike was met by a Boston sportswriter, to whom he complained of feeling ill. He was taken to his friend Bill Anderson's Plymouth House on Kneeland Street, where he was put to bed with chills and a fever.

Those looking in on Mike felt that he required medical assistance and another old friend, Dr. George W. Galvin of Emergency Hospital, was summoned at around 2:00 P.M. on Monday. Galvin had been the Beaneaters team physician and was now head of the hospital.

Meanwhile, a second snowstorm was predicted. The first had been so bad that it had knocked out all telephone and telegraph wires. An attempt was made to contact Agnes Kelly in Allentown, but the connection could not be made. Even telegraph service from Boston to New York had to be routed via White River Junction, Vermont, to Springfield, Massachusetts, to Troy, to Albany, and then down the Hudson to New York.

Dr. Galvin arrived to find Mike having difficulty breathing, and considered him to be in serious condition. He did what he could to try and break the fever, departed, and then returned at 4:00 P.M. to find the condition now critical, with pneumonia having set in.

At the Palace Theatre, patrons, many of them friends of Kel's, filled their seats for the Monday matinee performance, unaware that the leading man was too ill to go on. So loyal were his followers that they merely awaited the evening show, only to learn that he would not be appearing then, either.

Meanwhile, it was decided to move Mike to Emergency Hospital on Harrison Avenue, where Boston City Hospital now sits. One report said that as the stretcher was being lifted through the hospital door, Kelly slipped to the floor. "This is my last slide," he was quoted as saying.

He was administered oxygen and was thought to be improving. Penicillin, which might have saved him, was 34 years into the future in the lab of Alexander Fleming. The treatment of pneumonia had not moved far beyond castor oil, ammonia, chloroform, cold water, brandy, and oxygen.

Halfway around the world, another "king" lay dead, with the autocratic Czar Alexander III having succumbed in Russia on October 20, to be succeeded by his son Nicholas II, who would be the last Czar. Now, in American newspapers, King Kelly was moving Alexander off the front pages.

KELLY ILL, headlined the Boston *Post* on Tuesday morning, election day. Paper boys shouted through the streets of Boston, "Famous Baseball King Near Death." "Pneumonia the Cause." "He Now Lies at the Emergency Hospital, This City," "Here With Theatrical Troupe."

Lying on a hospital cot in a private room, Kelly seemed to show improvement. On Wednesday, the day of Alexander's majestic funeral in Russia, he was thought to be recovering. The morning *Post* noted, KELLY IMPROVING, on page two, and stated in a brief dispatch, "Mike Kelly, the well-known ball player, who is at the Emergency Hospital, suffering from pneumonia, was reported as being a little better at an early hour this morning." He slept well Wednesday night.

Galvin's attempts to reach Agnes were fruitless. Ironically, a letter from her arrived at the Palace Theater on Wednesday, telling Mike that she would be leaving Allentown in a day or two to meet up with him in Boston.

Not until Thursday morning, with power restored, could Galvin finally summon her, impressing upon her the urgency of the situation. She would not make it in time.

Mike slept part of the time, was delirious from a high fever at other times, but did not lose consciousness.

His most frequent bedside companions in his last days were Julian B. Hart, the Boston Brotherhood backer who had become a close friend; Denny Sullivan, an ex-ballplayer, who was an Elks Lodge brother; John Graham, another old Elks buddy; Bill Anderson; and little Chippy McGarr, a Brotherhood teammate who was currently the Cleveland third baseman. To them, Mike seemed aware of the seriousness of his illness, but recognized them and spoke briefly with them.

Thursday was a bad day and Mike was sinking. In the afternoon, Father Hickey of St. James' Church was summoned to administer the last rites of the Catholic Church. The abilities of physicians were exhausted. He rallied a little, but then sank into a stupor. Around six o'clock, he said to those in the room, "Well, I guess this is the last trip."

They were his final words. He did not improve from the administration of more oxygen and at 9:55 P.M., on November 8, 1894, Mike Kelly died.

Galvin, Hart and Sullivan were at his bedside. He died in the company of friends, in the city that had embraced him with love.

Agnes arrived by train on Friday afternoon and did not learn of her husband's death until she reported to the Plymouth House, where the Andersons met her. Her first question was "How is Michael?" but the reaction told her that the news was bad. Mrs. Anderson gave her the shocking news. Galvin had not prepared her to expect the worst; the news hit her hard. Her husband, a strapping symbol of American manhood, was but 36 years old, barely one month removed from his career as a professional athlete.

She was at once taken to Jones' Funeral Home on LaGrange Street to see her husband's remains. The Elks Lodge offered to make all the necessary arrangements. Back in Paterson, Mike's brother James was notified and immediately sent a wire requesting that the body be sent home for burial in the Elks plot in Paterson.

But Agnes knew that Mike would want to be buried in his beloved Boston, the city where he had achieved his greatest fame. So many of his friends and baseball companions were there. And so the arrangements were turned over to the Boston Elks Lodge, who owned burial ground in Mt. Hope Cemetery in nearby Mattapan.

The *New York Times* deemed "King Kelly Dies of Pneumonia" to be a page-one story. The *Northern Budget* in Troy noted the passing of their native son, with "The Noted Ball Player Has Made His Last Home Run." The Boston papers all used as large a headline type as was available at the time. KELLY DEAD, said the *Post*. "Baseball King Passed Away Last Night." Said the story,

> Michael J. Kelly, who was the most widely known ball player in the land, died last evening....The most popular of ball players is no more. The idol of the South End

bleaching boards in '87, '88 and '89, and of the Congress street ground patrons in '90, has trod the diamond for the last time, and will never more go to bat.

Wrote the *Globe,*

At 9:55 last night, King Kelly heard the decision of the Great Umpire from which there is no appeal. The famous ball player passed away at that hour at the emergency hospital, with a few of his old friends watching every phase of his last uphill fight in the game where defeat is sure.

In *The Sporting News,* Jake Morse wrote,

I can only repeat what [saloon partner Honest] John Kelly said yesterday: "we will never see his like again." In his day no one approached him in quickness of thought or rapidity of execution. No spectator ever thought ahead of Kelly as is the case with most players, but he often amazed them by the daring character of his plays. The name of no player will live so long after as he has gone as will that of Michael J. Kelly. *Requiescat in pace.*

In Chicago, the *Daily News* sent a reporter to Anson's home for comment. He seemed a bit formal, perhaps even cold.

Why he ought to be just in his prime now. He was only 37 or 38 years old and could have played good ball this very year if he had taken proper care of himself. So convinced was I of that fact that last winter I made him an offer to return to the Chicago club, on condition that he would promise to quit drinking. He knew he couldn't keep such a promise, and so refused to make it.

Anson did not go to the funeral, but sent a wreath. He was ever the soft sentimentalist. Noted memorabilia collector Barry Halper has a letter written by Anson to his daughter, which is signed "Your loving father, A.C. Anson."

Spalding did not not attend either. He sent a telegram which said "Surprised and pained to hear of Mike Kelly's death. Please express my sympathies to his family."

The Chicago *Evening Post* was kinder.

> Everybody in Chicago is sorry to hear that Mike Kelly is dead. No man had more friends than the prince of ball players. The news of his death came as a distant shock today, for it was entirely unexpected....He had been ill for several days, but not even the physicians who attended him believed that he would not recover, for "the king" was a big, strong fellow and of generally robust health. No ordinary disease could carry Kelly off, and in pneumonia he met a powerful antagonist....

> The king was probably the most popular ballplayer that has appeared before the public during the last score of years. He and Captain Anson fairly divided public notice, and perhaps more has been written about Kelly than any other man in the world of sports with the exception of the old champion, John L. Sullivan.

> He had numerous friends in every large city in the country and among them were men of high standing in the industrial and commercial world. From these he borrowed with the same lavishness that he spent. But no man ever said that Kelly did not meet his obligations. He always 'squared up' in a few months.

> Kelly's character was gentle, sympathetic. He never saw suffering of any kind without relieving it to the extent of his power. Wherever he went he left behind him a bright trail of coin, given in charity with real, heartfelt tenderness. Everybody with whom he came in contact felt the force of his generosity. He would borrow $100 from a friend and lend $50 of it to some fellow who would present him with a desperate case. And as Kelly always paid his debts and was seldom paid himself, most of his loans were gifts. That was Kelly's character.

It is told of him that once he went to New Orleans with a crowd of sports from Boston to see a prizefight. He had $50 when he landed in the crescent city. With this $50 he won $800 at the racetrack, lent $500 of it to "friends" lost the rest on the prizefight, got a pass back to Boston from a New Orleans railroad official whom he knew and borrowed $150 from another man he knew to pay his expenses on the way.

Agnes and the Elks funeral committee, headed by Julian Hart, met hourly at the Plymouth House to plan the funeral. It would likely be the biggest one ever held in the city of Boston. The Elks proposed having the service at the lodge hall on Hayward Place, but it was decided to hold a funeral mass on Sunday at St. James' on Harrison Avenue. Until then, the body would lie in state at the lodge.

The body was embalmed at Jones' and moved to the Elks Lodge on Saturday.

"All ball players who wish to attend the funeral are requested to report to Captain William Nash at the Elks Hall at 12:30 p.m.," said a notice in the press.

The London Gaiety Girls Company adopted a resolution on the death of their leading man, and voted to attend the funeral as a body and to wear a badge of mourning for thirty days.

In New York, Honest John Kelly made plans to travel to Boston, as did Jim McCormick, Kel's oldest friend. From Paterson came relatives of Agnes, as well as Mike's brother James, who would be her support.

There was never before a day quite like Sunday, November 11 in the city of Boston. Because it was a church day anyway, it was a day to dress in one's best. On this day however, the destination for everyone seemed to be Hayward Place, where the body could be viewed at the Elks Lodge, and then Harrison Avenue, for the services of St. James. If you were a baseball fan, or just one of the curious, this was an event to behold.

By news estimates, as many as 7,000 people would pay their public respects. As the church, which still stands, held about 1,500, the overflow on the street created quite a sight. For a modern point of view, the shocking death of the young Boston Celtics' captain, Reggie Lewis, in July 1993, drew an estimated

6,000-7,000 onlookers, and was called the largest funeral ever in Boston. If so, it perhaps "broke Kelly's record" after 99 years. But the population of Boston in 1894 was some 100,000 less, the ability to travel to the event far more limited, and there was no way to "catch it on TV tonight" for the lazy.

The body lay in state at the Elks Lodge from nine to noon on Sunday. The casket was covered in broadcloth in the center of the second floor of the Lodge, surrounded by flowers, which provided the beauty and the scent in the room. A large photo of Kel, in his characteristic jaunty baseball pose, leaning on a bat, was atop the casket.

Most floral arrangements had messages from friends far away, with the common message being simply, "Good-bye, Kel." On the lower part of the casket was a huge wreath of roses with a large white chrysanthemum in the center, from Honest John Kelly. A massive ball of white pinks, with seams of purple immortelles was there from Spalding. Anson sent a pillow of roses upon a base of sago palm. Huge displays from the Elks, from the New York Giants, and from playwright Charles Hoyt dominated the base of the bier. A cross of ivy with a crown of roses was signed by Soden, Conant, and Billings.

There was an offering from the Actors' Protective Union, from Charles Byrne of the Brooklyn baseball club, and from A. J. Reach of the Philadelphia Athletics. Another ivy cross with rose crown was displayed from the London Gaiety company. Actor Eddie Foy sent a star and crown. John Graham sent a large floral piece.

A narrow passage surrounded the open casket for those who came to pay respects. Two long and respectfully quiet lines filed up the stairs to view the remains, and then wound down the back staircase. An honor guard stood over the body, which was clothed in a fine suit provided by the captain of the Fall River Line boat. (Kel had apparently, indeed, given his suit to the stowaway.)

The mourning line included not only baseball personages, but women and children, businessmen, and men of the cloth. The *Globe* noted,

> ... was there ever an idol such as Kelly? Will there ever again be such a one in the eye of the boys as "the only Kel?" To have seen the hundreds of little fellows who had

their last look at the favorite and to have heard their simple comments expressed in their own limited vocabulary would be to answer an emphatic no.

At 12:30, a half-hour past schedule, the casket was closed and the line cut off. A quartet sang "Gathering Home," as the pallbearers prepared to move the coffin to the church. They were Frank Selee, Hugh Duffy, Tommy McCarthy, Billy Nash, all of the Boston club, Morgan Murphy, a catcher who had been Kel's teammate in Boston and Cincinnati, and F. L. Donahue from Allentown, plus Denny Sullivan and Charles Kelly from the Elks.

Outside the Lodge, the bier was placed on a horsedrawn hearse for the journey down Washington and Kneeland Streets and onto Harrison Avenue towards St. James. The Elks members, including visiting chapters from Haverhill and Worcester, led the procession. Crowds seven and eight deep lined every inch of the route.

At the church, the crowds were so large that the carriages had difficulty negotiating their way towards the front steps. Women and children, crying, formed a good portion of the crowd, but they were the least able to pile into the building, where every seat and every space in the aisles were jammed. So during the service, without benefit of audio, the huge crowd remained on the sidewalk, just to be there for Kel.

Observant journalists noted the presence at the services of such notables as P. T. Powers, president of the Eastern League, John Chapman, the Buffalo manager, Honest John Kelly, J. B. Billings, Julian Hart, William Merritt of Cincinnati, Mike Sullivan of Cleveland, Con Daily of Brooklyn, George Haddock of Washington, Joseph Sullivan of Philadelphia, Tom Niland of Toledo, manager William Murray of Providence, manager Irwin of Haverhill, Capt. Donovan of Pittsburgh, Joe Kelley of the Baltimore Orioles, Andy Leonard, Tommy Bond, and Harry Schafer, old Boston players, James Sullivan, Herman Long, and Cozy Dolan of the current Boston team and scores of amateur players.

From the theatrical world came Eddie Foy, George Marion, Dan Daly, Samuel Thall, William A. Brady, Frank Buckley, Ike Harris, James Blake, James Russell, Sol Keene, J. W. Kenny,

John Graham, Edward Donnelly, and Miss Maggie Cline herself, along with her sister Miss Lee.

Also spotted were Fire Chief Ryan, Tim Murnane of the *Globe,* Jake Morse and E. F. Stevens of the *Herald,* Dr. Heath of Roxbury, John W. Kelly, the "Slide, Kelly, Slide" composer, Aldermen Bryant and Flood, city officials and bureaucrats, local industrialists, and businessmen.

Murnane could not help but write down the names he felt missing without cause: John Morrill, George Wright, Tommy Burns, Jack Carney, Harry Stovey, Paul Radford, Jack Ryan, Jimmy Bannon, Tommy Tucker and Charley Farrell.

> These are the things that put a man out of the game with me every time. It was in great deal due to what Mike Kelly did for the game that put some of these fellows where they are today, and this is the way they repaid it. Some of these had played with Mike. It wasn't right.

Father Hickey read prayers and conducted a brief service; then the pallbearers placed the casket on the hearse once again for the long, chilly procession southwest down Washington Street and towards Mt. Hope. It was a distance of some seven miles and only those who could follow the horse-drawn hearse by carriage went along. Otherwise, onlookers stood in silence as the King passed. It took about an hour to reach the cemetery.

The Elks plot, about 1,000 feet from the main entrance (lot 1650, grave 21), was snow covered. Nearly all the leaves had left the trees and there was a chill in the air. Dusk would soon begin to settle on this sad day. Kelly would be the 21st brother interred here. The simple grey stones would be uniform, with nothing more than name, date of death and age. In Mike's case, the stone would give him credit for being 37, which he in fact did not quite reach.

An Elks service was held at the site, presided over by exalted ruler W. A. Blossem, and assisted by other brothers. Agnes and Mike's brother James were the only relatives present. Some 5,000 people were said to have made their way to the site.

At the conclusion of the service, Tom Henry played Sullivan's "Lost Chord" on the cornet; the amaranth and a sprig of ivy were thrown into the grave, and the crowd slowly filed out.

And now, what was to become of poor Agnes Kelly? Penniless, with a four-month-old, she was a young widow without a pension.

On the very day of the funeral, her predicament was on people's minds. It was decided to open a public subscription in her behalf, a fund-raiser, so to speak, with A. J. Simmons, New England passenger agent for the Baltimore & Ohio Railroad, to act as treasurer. The committee included Julian Hart, F. L. Donahue, Sol Keene, Bill Anderson, and Dennis Sullivan.

On Monday, the day after the funeral, it was decided to hold a concert at the Hollis Street Theater as a benefit. Some 150 theatrical stars volunteered to perform. Isaac Rich, operator of the theater, offered it for the performance, which would be held on six days' notice, November 18, one week after the funeral.

The funds were slow to arrive. Those who sent money prior to the performance included DeWolf Hopper, of "Casey at the Bat" fame, $25, and Connie Mack, $10, bringing the pre-theater total to $372.

At the show, Manager Seymour of the Tremont Theatre and master of ceremonies Duncan Harrison introduced the acts, which included Miss Maggie Cline, John Mason, George Marion, Miss Rosalind Rissi, Bernard Dyllin, Mackie and Walker, J. W. Kelly, (composer of "Slide, Kelly, Slide"), Dan Daly, and Mr. Emanuel Fiedler of the Symphony Orchestra on the violin.

A total of $1,926 was raised, and Agnes returned to New York, where she and the baby were taken in by Honest John Kelly and his wife. At a National League meeting some days later, the club owners put forth an additional $1,500 for the widow ($125 per team), sending her off into the world with a total of nearly $3,500.

Exactly 90 days after King Kelly died, a baby named George Herman Ruth was born in Baltimore, Maryland. The King would never know of the feats and the fame of the Sultan of Swat. In another time, they might have belonged to him.

Kelly in fact, would never hear of people named Lajoie or Wagner, or Cobb or Mathewson; nor of a concept called the American League.

The legend of Mike Kelly did hold for a time, but eventually, those who knew him well passed away and it seemed that the song would outlive the person. The early pioneers of the game always spoke his praises, always told his tales of daring on the field. Some would rate him the game's best catcher although Buck Ewing usually got that vote and, in truth, Mike may have been an innovator, but he was not a brilliant defensive artist.

Further, while better remembered as a catcher, he played the outfield 758 times and caught only 583 games.

When the Giants' John McGraw purchased Rube Marquard from Indianapolis in 1908, he made certain that the purchase price was $11,000, so that he could garner the added publicity of breaking Kelly's record. Marquard became the "$11,000 Beauty."

A silent movie released in 1927 by M-G-M was called *Slide, Kelly, Slide* and featured Irish Meusel of the Giants, his brother Bob of the Yankees, and the Yanks' Tony Lazzeri as themselves, with William Haines as Jim Kelly. It had nothing to do with Mike.

The original song, "Slide, Kelly, Slide" made its way onto 78 rpm release when discs replaced cylinders and remained a popular American tune into the '20s.

The Boston Beaneaters became the Braves and remained in that city until 1953, when they moved to Milwaukee, departing again in 1966 for Atlanta. In 1994, a hundred years after Kel's death, a rookie outfielder named Mike Kelly, black, made his debut with the team.

The Chicago White Stockings became the Cubs, and their loyal fans today can little relate to the glory that was their club in the 1880s. There are no photos of Kelly in Wrigley Field's inner offices.

In August of 1944, Commissioner Kenesaw Mountain Landis appointed a committee to select early baseball pioneers for inclusion in the Hall of Fame in Cooperstown, which had begun electing members in 1936. The committee included Ed Barrow, Connie Mack, Bob Quinn, Mel Webb, Stephen Clark, and Paul Kerr. They selected ten and made their announcement in New York on April 25, 1945. The ten were Roger Bresnahan, Dan Brouthers, Fred Clarke, Jimmy Collins, Ed Delahanty, Hugh Duffy, Hughie Jennings, Jim O'Rourke, Wilbert Robinson and King Kelly. It was a good year for the Irish. Because it was a war year, there were no induction ceremonies held in Cooperstown, and thus, no need to seek out a descendent who might accept for Mike. The fates of Agnes, and of their child, were undiscoverable.

Although officially enshrined in the Hall of Fame, Mike's fame had all but passed except for the most serious of baseball historians. The last baseball personalities who could say they truly knew him died in the mid-1950s: Hugh Duffy in 1954, Cy Young in 1955, and Connie Mack in 1956. With the end of innocence, both in baseball and in the nation generally, books that exploited Mike's feats (and probably exaggerated them a bit) generally ceased to be written by the late 1960s; readers' interests having shifted to more controversial topics.

Sportswriter Harold Rosenthal, who became a baseball fan in the 1920s, said in the 100th year after Kelly's death, "He had already passed from consciousness by then. I remember George 'Highpockets' Kelly of the Giants, but King Kelly? The Slide, Kelly, Slide guy? No, he'd already been dead a long time. His name never came up."

Ken Burns's PBS special, *Baseball,* devoted several minutes to Mike in 1994, but the 100th anniversary of his passing stirred no interest in the office of the Boston mayor to commemorate the day.

And so what do we make of Michael Joseph Kelly?

He was not without his flaws. Today's standards would make his drinking habits wholly unacceptable; yet if we apply today's standards to his measure, we must also question whether he might have behaved differently. We live in a more health-conscious, politically correct time. The moral teachings he offers in his ghostwritten autobiography seem to show a man concerned with youth getting the right message and living honorable lives. Or at least, with readers seeing that his thinking was upright and his image wholesome.

As a player, he was perhaps not the "greatest" as his fans would have had you believe, but a very good one who was one of the quickest thinkers on the diamond. There were probably a couple of seasons in which he might have won an MVP award had there been one.

Because of the poor equipment and small gloves of the time, it is hard to label him a poor defensive player, but he did rack up a huge error and passed ball total, compared to his contemporaries. His gift seems to be more in innovation, such as the hook slide, the hit and run, the blocking of the plate, the throws from right field to first, the backing up of infielders from the outfield position, the finger signals to the pitcher, signals to infielders on what pitch would be thrown, the stealing of signs, having pitchers and catchers back up infielders, and yes, the advantage taken of but one umpire on the field. He may not have been the first to accomplish any of this, but the attention he attracted to himself popularized many of these strategies. He was even credited with being the first batter for whom "swat" was applied to describe his hitting. Columnist Eugene Field of Chicago said, "Swat on, most admirable paragon, swat on!" in calling Kel's hitting neither "pound nor buffett, knock or swipe or bunt."

Anson, perhaps in a weak moment, called him "as good a batter as anybody and as great a thrower, both from the catcher's position and from the field ... than any other man that could be named."

As a person, he was perhaps best judged as the beloved figure he was. Seemingly without enemies, beloved by fans, teammates, opponents, umpires, actors, and others, he had a gift for friendship most would envy.

His celebrity transcended the playing field, and "The Only Kel" wore it well. More than anything else, he brought the game of baseball into the consciousness of America, expanded the fan base, and perhaps influenced stars of the early 20th century to play the game and seek to achieve his fame.

MICHAEL JOSEPH "KING" KELLY

Born: Dec. 31, 1857, Troy, NY. Died: Nov. 8, 1894, Boston, MA. 5'10" 170 lbs. BR TR.

Year	Team	Lg.	AVG.	G	AB	R	H	2b	3b	HR	RBI	SB	BB	SO	Slg.	PO	A	E	Pct.
1877	Columbus (a)	Int.	.156	23	—	—	—	—	—	—	—	—	—	—	—	—	—	—	.815
1878	Cincinnati	NL	.283	60	237	29	67	7	1	0	27	—	7	7	.321	150	65	43	.833
1879	Cincinnati (b)	NL	.348	77	345	78	120	20	12	2	47	—	8	14	.493	164	139	58	.839
1880	Chicago	NL	.291	84	344	72	100	17	9	1	60	—	12	22	.401	111	68	42	.810
1881	Chicago	NL	.323	82	353	84	114	27*	3	2	55	—	16	14	.433	121	52	33	.840
1882	Chicago	NL	.305	84	377	81	115	37*	4	1	55	—	10	27	.432	133	149	59	.827
1883	Chicago	NL	.255	98	428	92	109	28	10	3	—	—	16	35	.388	183	91	63	.813
1884	Chicago	NL	.354*	108	452	120*	160	28	5	13	—	—	46	24	.524	201	141	86	.799
1885	Chicago	NL	.288	107	438	124*	126	24	7	9	74	—	46	24	.436	259	112	58	.865
1886	Chicago (c)	NL	.388*	118	451	155*	175	32	11	4	79	—	83	33	.534	387	141	59	.899
1887	Boston	NL	.322	116	484	120	156	34	11	8	63	84	55	40	.488	252	163	72	.852
1888	Boston	NL	.318	107	440	85	140	22	11	9	71	56	31	39	.480	395	150	66	.892
1889	Boston (d)	NL	.294	125	507	120	149	41*	5	9	78	68	65	40	.448	211	53	44	.857
1890	Boston (e)	PL	.326	89	340	83	111	18	6	4	66	51	52	22	.450	274	145	55	.884
1891	Cincinnati (f)	AA	.297	82	283	56	84	15	7	1	53	22	51	28	.410	→	→	→	→
1891	Boston (g)	AA	.267	4	15	2	4	0	0	1	4	1	0	2	.467	→	→	→	→
1891	Boston	NL	.231	16	52	7	12	1	0	0	5	6	6	10	.250	351	159	59	.896 (combined)
1892	Boston (h)	NL	.189	78	281	40	53	7	0	2	41	24	39	31	.235	340	101	47	.904
1893	New York (i)	NL	.269	20	67	9	18	1	0	0	15	3	6	5	.284	55	22	10	.885
1894	Allentown (j)	Pa.St.	.305	75	325	82	99	16	3	3	—	—	—	—	.400	573	84	40	.943
	Yonkers	E.L.	.377	15	61	11	23	2	0	0	—	2	—	—	.410	97	17	2	.983
M.L. Totals, 16 years			.308	1455	5894	1357	1813	359	102	69	793**	315**	549	417	.438	3587	1751	854	.862

Post-Season Championships

Year	Team	Lg.	AVG.	G	AB	R	H	2b	3b	HR	RBI	SB	BB	SO	Slg.	PO	A	E	Pct.
1882 vs. Cincinnati							(did not play)												
1885 vs. St. Louis			.346	7	26	9	9	3	1	0	/	/	2	/	.538	18	7	5	.833
1886 vs. St. Louis			.208	6	24	4	5	0	0	1	1	1	2	2	.333	35	12	3	.940
1892 vs. Cleveland			.000	2	8	0	0	0	0	0	0	1	0	2	.000	/	/	0	/
Totals				15	58	13	14	3	1	1	1**	2**	4	4**	.362	53**	19**	8	/

*Led League   **Incomplete

(a) Club disbanded, Sept. 15, 1877. Signed with Cincinnati for 1878.
(b) Released, Sept. 24, 1879. Signed by Chicago, December, 1879.
(c) Sold to Boston for $10,000, February 14, 1887.
(d) Jumped to Players' League.
(e) Signed as free agent with Cincinnati after Players' League folded.
(f) Club disbanded, August, 1891. Released and signed by Boston, A.A., August 17, 1891.
(g) Jumped to Boston, N.L., August 25, 1891.
(h) Released. Signed by New York as free agent, May 25, 1893.
(i) Released. Signed by Allentown, April, 1894.
(j) Club disbanded, Aug. 6, 1894. Contract transferred to Yonkers.

Games Played by Position

Position	Games
OF	758
C	583
SS	90
3B	96
2B	53
1B	25
P	12

Record as Pitcher

	G	W–L
1880	1	0–0
1883	1	0–0
1884	2	0–1
1887	3	1–0
1890	1	1–0
1891	3	0–1
1892	1	0–0

Record as Manager

	W–L	PCT.	POS.
1887	49–43	.533	5
1890	81–48	.628	1
1891	43–57	.430	7
1894	52–29	.642	2

Bibliography

Allen, Lee. *The Cincinnati Reds.* New York: G. P. Putnam's Sons, 1948.

—— *One Hundred Years of Baseball.* New York: Bartholomew House, 1950.

—— *The World Series.* New York: G. P. Putnam's Sons, 1969.

—— *The Hot Stove League.* New York: A. S. Barnes & Co, 1955.

Andreas, A. T. *History of Chicago, Volume 3.* Chicago: A. T. Andreas Co., 1886.

Anson, Adrian. *A Ball Players Career.* Chicago: Era, 1900.

Appel, Martin and Burt Goldblatt. *Baseball's Best: The Hall of Fame Gallery.* New York: McGraw-Hill, 1977.

Astor, Gerald. *The Baseball Hall of Fame 50th Anniversary Book.* New York: Prentice Hall Press, 1988.

Bartlett, Arthur. *Baseball and Mr. Spalding.* New York: Farrar, Straus and Young, 1951.

Benson, Michael. *Ballparks of North America.* Jefferson, NC: McFarland & Co, 1989.

Bergen, Philip. *Old Boston in Early Photographs.* New York: Dover, 1990.

Bjarkman, Peter, ed. *Encyclopedia of Major League Baseball Team Histories: National League.* Westport, CT: Meckler, 1991.

Blake, Mike. *The Minor Leagues.* New York: Wynwood Press, 1991.

Brown, Warren. *The Chicago Cubs.* New York: G. P. Putnam's Sons, 1946.

Cappio, Alfred. *Slide, Kelly, Slide.* Paterson, NJ: Passaic County Historical Society, 1962.

Chadwick, Henry. *The Game of Baseball.* New York: George Munro & Co, 1868.

Charlton, James. *The Baseball Chronology.* New York: Macmillan, 1991.

Danzig, Allison and Joe Reichler. *The History of Baseball.* Englewood Cliffs, NJ: Prentice-Hall, 1959.

Deutsch et al. *Scrapbook History of Baseball.* New York: Bobbs-Merrill, 1975.

DiClerico, James and Barry Pavelec. *The Jersey Game.* New Brunswick, NJ: Rutgers University Press, 1991.

Einstein, Charles, ed. *The Fireside Book of Baseball.* New York: Simon & Schuster, 1956.

Evers, John and Hugh Fullerton. *Touching Second.* Chicago: The Reilly & Britton Co, 1910.

Filichia, Peter. *Professional Baseball Franchises.* New York: Facts on File, 1993.

Frommer, Harvey. *Primitive Baseball.* New York: Macmillan, 1988.

Gershman, Michael. *Diamonds.* Boston: Houghton Mifflin, 1993.

Gilbert, James. *Perfect Cities: Chicago's Utopias of 1893.* Chicago: University of Chicago Press, 1991.

Goldstein, Warren. *Playing for Keeps. A History of Early Baseball.* Ithaca, NY: Cornell University Press, 1989.

Graber, Ralph, ed. *The Baseball Reader.* New York: A. S. Barnes, 1951.

Graham, Frank. *The New York Giants.* New York: G. P. Putnam's Sons, 1952.

Gutman, Dan. *Baseball Babylon.* New York: Penguin Books, 1992.

Hayner, Rutherford. *Troy and Rensselaer County, N.Y.* Troy: Lewis Historical Publishing, 1925.

Henderson, Robert. *Ball, Bat and Bishop.* New York: Rockport Press, 1947.

Herbst, John and Catherine Keene. *Life and Times in Silk City.* Haledon, NJ: American Labor Museum, 1984.

Honig, Donald. *The Cincinnati Reds.* New York: Simon & Schuster, 1992.

—— *The Chicago Cubs.* New York: Prentice Hall, 1991.

Hynd, Noel. *The Giants of the Polo Grounds.* New York: Doubleday, 1988.

Kaese, Harold. *The Boston Braves.* New York: G. P. Putnam's Sons, 1948.

Kelly, Mike. *Play Ball: Stories of the Diamond Field.* Boston: Emery & Hughes, 1888.

Kennedy, Maclean. *The Great Teams of Baseball.* St. Louis: The Sporting News, 1929.

Lanigan, Ernest. *The Baseball Cyclopedia.* New York: The Baseball Magazine Company, 1922.

Lansche, Jerry. *Glory Fades Away.* Dallas: Taylor, 1991.

Leitner, Irving. *Baseball: Diamond in the Rough.* New York: Criterion, 1972.

Levine, Peter. *A.G. Spalding and the Rise of Baseball.* New York: Oxford University Press, 1985.

Lieb, Fred. *The Baseball Story.* New York: G. P. Putnam's Sons, 1950.

Lowenfish, Lee. *The Imperfect Diamond.* Revised Edition. New York: Da Capo Press, 1991.

Lowry, Philip. *Green Cathedrals.* Reading, MA: Addison-Wesley, 1992.

Menke, Frank. *Sports Tales and Anecdotes.* New York: A. S. Barnes, 1953.

Moreland, George. *Balldom.* New York: Balldom Pubishing Co., 1914.

Morse, Jacob. *Sphere and Ash.* Boston: J. F. Spofford & Co., 1888.

Mote, James. *Everything Baseball.* New York: Prentice-Hall, 1989.

Neft, David and Richard Cohen. *The Sports Encyclopedia: Baseball.* New York: St. Martin's Press, 1986.

Okrent, Daniel, and Harris Levine, editors. *The Ultimate Baseball Book*. Boston: Houghton Mifflin, 1979.

Orem, Preston. *Baseball 1845-1881*. Altadena, Ca.: Preston D. Orem, 1961.

Palmer, Harry Clay and J. A. Fynes, Frank Richter, W. I. Harris. *Athletics, Sports in America, England and Australia,* New York: W. A. Houghton, 1889.

Petrone, Gerard. *When Baseball Was Young*. San Diego: Musty Attic Archives, 1994.

Pierce, Bessie Louise. *History of Chicago, Volume 3*. New York: Alfred Knopf, 1957.

Pietrusza, David. *Major Leagues*. Jefferson, NC: McFarland & Co. 1991.

Puff, Richard, ed. *Troy's Baseball Heritage*. Troy, NY: Committee to Preserve Troy's Baseball Heritage, 1992.

Reach. *Official American Association Base Ball Guide*. Annual. Philadelphia: AJ Reach & Co, 1883-1895.

Robertson, William. *The History of Thoroughbred Racing in America*. New York: Bonanza, 1964.

Seymour, Harold. *Baseball: The Early Years*. New York: Oxford University Press, 1960.

Shatzken, Mike, ed. *The Ballplayers*. New York: Arbor House, 1990.

Smith, Robert. *Baseball in the Afternoon*. New York: Simon & Schuster, 1993.

Spalding, A. G. *Base Ball, America's National Game*. New York: American Sports, 1911.

Spalding. *Official Baseball Guide*. Annual. Chicago: A. G. Spalding & Bros, 1878-1895.

Sowell, Mike. *July 2, 1903*. New York: Macmillan. 1992.

Sugar, Bert Randolph. *Rain Delays*. New York: St. Martin's Press, 1990.

Sunday, Billy. *Burning Truths From Billy's Bat: A Graphic Description of the Remarkable Conversion of Rev. Billy Sunday*. Philadelphia: Diamond, 1914.

Tattersall, John. *The Early World Series*. Haverton, PA: John C. Tattersall, 1976.

Thorn, John and Peter Palmer. *Total Baseball.* New York: Warner, 1989.

Voight, David. *Baseball: An Illustrated History.* University Park, PA: Pennsylvania State University Press, 1988.

—— *American Baseball, Volume 1.* Norman, OK: University of Oklahoma Press, 1966.

Ward, John Montgomery. *Base-Ball: How to Become a Player.* Phildelphia: Athletic Publishing, 1888.

Wheeler, Lonnie and John Baskin. *The Cincinnati Game.* Wilmington, OH: Orange Frazier Press, 1988.

Wolff, Rick, ed. *Baseball Encyclopedia,* 9th ed. New York: Macmillan, 1993.

Zoss, Joel and John Bowman. *Diamonds in the Rough.* New York: Macmillan, 1989.

Periodicals

The Sporting News
Sporting Life
Baseball Magazine

Newspapers

Boston *Daily Globe*
Boston *Post*
Chicago *Daily News*
Chicago *Times*
Chicago *Evening Journal*
Chicago *Herald*
Chicago *Tribune*
Chicago *Evening Post*
Hingham (MA) *Journal*
Inter-Ocean (Chicago)
Paterson *Daily Press*
New York *Clipper*
New York Times
Troy (NY) *Northern Budget*
Troy (NY) *Daily Times*

Index

(With few exceptions, names and teams in games are not included in this index.)

Addy, Bob, 22

Anson, Adrian Constantine "Cap," 29, 31-33, 35, 37-38, 42, 47, 51, 54, 59, 61, 66, 69, 76, 78, 84, 98-99, 102, 121, 130, 132-133, 149, 167, 181, 187, 190, 196

Anson on Kelly, 61

Arson-Spalding World Tour (1888-89), 134-135

Atlantics (Brooklyn), 14

Baldwin, Mark, 93, 174

Barnes, Ross, 25, 102

Barnes, Walter, 123

Barnie, Billy, 115

Beals, Tom, 38

Bennett, Charlie, 138-139, 149, 164, 166-167

Bennett Park (Detroit), 139

Billings, J. B. (James), 102-104, 108, 110, 130, 138, 149

Brainard, Asa, 4

Brouthers, Dan, 5, 54, 98, 138-139, 147-148, 156, 163, 165, 194

Brown, Big Bill, 125

Browning, Pete, 177, 179

Buckeley, Morgan, 34

Buckeyes (Columbus, OH), 18, 20

Burdock, Jack, 67, 111, 132

Burn ball, 9-10

Burns, Ken, 195

Burns, Tom, 38, 40, 54, 76

Byrne, Charles, 190

Cartwright, Alexander, 3

Caruthers, Bob, 131

"Casey at the Bat," 128, 193

Caylor, O. P., 26, 30

Chadwick, Henry, 63, 68, 120, 133

Chicago, history of, 36-37

Clarkson, John, 71, 73, 131-132, 139, 141, 149, 164, 166

Cleveland, Grover, 89-90

Cline, Maggie, 136-137, 193

Coleman, Jack, 177

Colts (Chicago), 167

Comiskey, Charles, 15, 78, 83, 165

Conant, William, 102, 110, 130, 138, 149

Congress Street Grounds (Chicago), 74

Congress Street Park (Boston), 150

Connor, Roger, 5, 62, 75, 76, 98, 125

Corcoron, Larry, 38, 40, 54, 59, 68, 73, 165

Crane, Ed "Cannonball," 158

Crane, Sam, 123

Daily, Hugh Ignatius (One Arm), 64

Dalrymple, Abner, 38, 39, 51, 54, 64, 69, 76

Daly, Tom, 101

Dauvray, Helen (Mrs. John Montgomery Ward), 125

Davies, Dummy, 17

Denny, Jerry, 125

Devlin, Jim, 71-72

Dickerson, Buttercup, 52

Doubleday, Abner, 3

Dougan, Mike, 76

Duffy, Hugh, 156, 163, 166-167, 191, 194-195

East End Park (Pendleton, OH), 157

Evers, Johnny, 5, 109, 131

Ewing, Buck, 5, 75-76, 125, 148, 150

Excelsiors (Brooklyn), 4, 14

Fast Day (Patriot's Day), 112, 138

Flint, Frank "Silver," 18, 23, 38, 44, 47, 55, 75-76, 101, 147, 165

Flynn, John "Jocko," 84

Foran, Jim, 16

Foutz, Dave, 18

Foy, Eddie, 167, 190

Fullerton, Hugh, 123

Galvin, Dr. George W., 184-186

Galvin, Jim "Pud," 31, 177

Ganzel, Charlie, 138-139, 149, 164, 166

Gaskin, George J., 137

Gerhardt, Joe, 76

Giants (New York), 5

Gilbert, Uri, 7

Gillespie, Pete, 76

Glasscock, Jack, 101, 103

Gleason, Bill, 158

Goldsmith, Fred, 38, 39, 54, 59, 71, 73

Gore, George, 38, 40, 47, 51, 54-55, 64, 75-76, 79, 98

Gothams (New York), 5

Graham, John, 115-116

Griffith, Clark, 156

Hackensack, NJ, 51

Haggin, James Ben Ali, 52

Hall of Fame Selection Committee, 194

Hanlon, Ned, 147

Hart, James A., 138-139, 143-144

Hart, Julian B., 154, 189, 193

Haymakers (Troy), 4

Haymarket Square Riot, 85

Hedifen, Agnes. *See* Kelly, Agnes Hedifen

Hines, Paul, 132

Hopper, DeWolf, 193

Hornung, Joe, 111

Hoyt, Charles, 190

Hudson, Charles, 178

Hueble, George, 16

Hulbert, William, 31-35, 37, 47, 53-54, 102

Hyde Park, NY, 51, 96, 98, 126, 173

Irwin, Arthur, 164

Johnson, Al, 142, 148, 176, 179, 181
Johnston, Dick, 111

Keefe, Tim, 5, 75-76, 125, 148
Kelly, Agnes Hedifen (Mrs. Mike Kelly), 51, 96, 125-126, 154, 157, 163, 165, 176-179, 181, 183-186, 189, 192-193, 195
Kelly, "Baby," 179
Kelly, Catherine Kylie (Mrs. Michael Kelly, Senior), 2, 7
Kelly, "Honest John," 50, 82, 101, 189-190
Kelly, James, 2, 189, 192
Kelly, John "Kick," 17
Kelly, John W., 136, 192
Kelly, Michael (Senior), 2, 7
Kelly's Killers, 157
Kennedy, Maclean, 45
Kerns, James, 4
Keystones (Paterson, NJ), 17
Kilroy, Matt, 177
Kylie, Catherine. *See* Kelly, Catherine Kylie

Lake Front Park (Chicago), 37, 69, 74
Latham, Arlie, 93
League Park (Cleveland), 168
Lieb, Fred, 123
Long, Herman, 156, 166-167
Lowe, Bobby, 156, 166-167

Mack, Connie, 83, 154, 193, 195

Massachusetts game, 1, 10
McCarthy, Tom, 166-167, 191
McCormick, Jim, 14-18, 20, 21, 51, 68, 73, 75, 99, 130, 147, 189
McGraw, John, 69, 180, 194
McGreevey, Michael T., 122
McKeon, James, 4
McQuaid, John, 143
McVey, Cal, 22, 26-27, 101
Medart, William, 81
Metropolitans (New York), 62
Milligan, Jocko, 177
Montague, Louise, 111
Morrill, John Francis ("Honest John"), 67, 106, 110-112, 121, 132, 138, 141, 149
Morse, Jacob Charles ("Jake"), 130, 187
"Mugwump," 132
Mulvey, Joe, 177
Murnane, Tim, 138, 141
Murphy, Morgan, 191
Mutie, Jim, 74-75
Mutuals (Brooklyn), 15, 18

Nash, Billy, 111, 156, 164, 166, 191
National Agreement, 51
National Association, 4
National Base Ball Club (Washington, DC), 9
National Brotherhood of Professional Base Ball Players, 56, 86, 146-150, 155
National Club (Lansingburgh, NY), 4
Neff, J. Wayne, 21, 30
New York game, 1
Nichols, Kid, 156, 166-167
Nolan, Edward Sylvester, 16, 20, 23, 52

"O'Dowd's Neighbors," 170, 178, 183

One Arm Daily. *See* Daily, Hugh Ignatius

Only Nolan. *See* Edward Sylvester Nolan

Orioles (Baltimore), 42

O'Rourke, Jim, 70, 75-76, 132, 194

Pfeffer, Fred, 54-55, 62-63, 69, 76, 96, 147, 164

Pike, Lipman, 22, 52

Play Ball: Stories of the Ball Field, 129

Players National League, 148

Polo Grounds (New York), 75, 141

Priam Club (Troy, NY), 4

Price, Jim, 123

Prince, Charles, 147, 156, 161

Purcell, William "Blondie," 16, 17, 28, 31, 41, 115

Quest, Joe, 38, 40, 62

Quinn, Joe, 164, 166-167

Racism, 35

Radbourne, Ol' Hoss, 56-57, 64, 70, 111

Reach, A. J., 190

Red Stockings (Cincinnati), 4, 9, 21

Reds (Boston), 150

Reed, Charlie, 126

Reese, George, 127

Reserve clause, 21, 68, 110

Richardson, Danny, 76, 125

Richardson, Hardie, 54, 138-139, 149

Rosenthal, Harold, 195

Rowe, Jack, 54

Rusie, Amos, 164-165

Ryan, John, 51

Ryle, John, 178

St. Lawrence, Billy, 17

Salary comparison to modern players, 105-106

Salvatore, 52-53

Selee, Frank, 156, 164, 191

Sheriden, Jack, 167

Slide, Kelly, Slide (M-G-M), 194

"Slide, Kelly, Slide" (song), 136-137, 165, 193

Small, Frank O., 114

Soden, Arthur, 21, 102, 105, 110, 130, 138, 149

South End Grounds (Boston), 112

Spalding, Albert Goodwill, 31, 34, 35, 54, 63, 73, 84, 87, 91, 99-105, 108, 117, 120, 147, 149-152, 155, 188, 190

Sphere and Ash, 130

Stage debut, 127

Staley, Harry, 166

Stars (Covington, KY), 18

Start, Joe, 14, 56

Stemmeyer, Bill, 111

Stivetts, Happy Jack, 166-167

Stovey, George, 35

Sullivan, Billy, 103-104

Sunday, Billy, 68-69, 76, 87-88, 120

Sutton, Ezra, 67, 70, 102, 111, 132

Tales of the King, 29, 45, 72, 96, 127, 177, 180

Tate, Ed ("Dimples"), 111, 123

Taylor, General Charles H., 121, 143, 145

Thomas, Charles W., 126

Thompson, Sam, 121-122

Thorn, John, 129

Thorner, Justus, 30
Tiernan, Mike, 125
Treado, Dave, 17
Trojans (Troy, NY), 4
Tucker, Tommy, 156, 166-167

Union Association, 64, 68, 73
Union Base Ball Club of Rensselaer County, 4
United States Championship (1885), 78-83

Victorys (Troy, NY), 4
von der Ahe, Chris, 83, 91-92, 94, 131, 157

Walker, Moses Fleetwood, 35
Walling, Dave, 10
Walsh, John, 54

Ward, John Montgomery, 25, 56, 62, 75-76, 86, 125, 146-150, 152, 155, 170, 173
Weise, A. J., 6
Welch, Mickey, 5, 62, 75-76, 95
West Side Park (Chicago), 74
White, Deacon, 26, 54, 132
White, Jim, 23, 41, 102
White, Will, 23, 41
Wilcox, Ella Wheeler, 53
Williamson, Ned, 38, 39, 54, 55, 69, 72, 75-76, 99, 147, 176
Wise, Sam, 67, 111, 121, 138, 177
Wood, George, 177
Wright, George, 56, 58, 112
Wright, Harry, 56, 58, 112

Young, Denton (Cy), 166, 195

About the Author

Marty Appel has won an Emmy Award as executive producer of New York Yankees baseball; a Gold Record for *Yankee Stadium: The Sounds of Fifty Years;* honors from the American Library Association and the Washington Irving Book Awards, and appeared on best-seller lists for his 1978 autobiography with Thurman Munson. He has also collaborated on books with Larry King, Bowie Kuhn, Lee MacPhail, Tom Seaver, and Eric Gregg, and served as public relations director for the Yankees.

He is Director of Public Relations for The Topps Company, Inc., and resides in Larchmont, New York. It is unlikely that had he actually known King Kelly, he would have been able to keep up with him to write this book.

Also by the Author

Baseball's Best: The Hall of Fame Gallery 1977

Thurman Munson: An Autobiography (with Thurman Munson) 1978

Batting Secrets of the Major Leaguers 1981

Tom Seaver's All-Time Baseball Greats (with Tom Seaver) 1984

Hardball: The Education of a Baseball Commissioner (as Editorial Assistant to Bowie Kuhn) 1987

Yesterday's Heroes 1988

The First Book of Baseball 1988

My Nine Innings (as Editorial Assistant to Lee MacPhail) 1989

Working the Plate (with Eric Gregg) 1990

Great Moments in Baseball (with Tom Seaver) 1992

When You're From Brooklyn, Everything Else Is Tokyo (with Larry King) 1992

Slide, Kelly, Slide 1995